Spiritual Mind

Change Your Life NOW and Help Others do the Same

Our Spiritual Mind Directs Our Brain,
Our Brain Directs Our Body!

The Truth About Our Mind – Brain – Body Connection

W. Dennis Parker

with Craig A. Bickmore and Dr. Debbie Crews

Library of Congress 2013

Certified Hypnotherapy Training School

2013

ISBN: 978-0-9893777-0-6

Spiritual Mind Management
Hypnotherapy Behavioral Model

A Generally Accepted Behavioral Model:

We think it
We feel it
We do it

According to Spiritual Mind Management:

We think it
We amplify it in our imagination
We locate memories to justify, validate, and defend it
We feel it
We do it

Our emotions drive our behaviors because we tend to behave the way we feel. Where do these powerful emotions come from?

Each of us has as part of our inner spiritual being an *Intelligence* that guides our thoughts and directs our brains, and then our brain directs our body. It moves from place to place in our spiritual mind. It moves from consciousness which is outward observation, learning and focus, to our subconscious imagination where amplification of any thought, belief, or idea can be enlightened and expanded. Then to searching our memories to justify with validating data the thoughts and beliefs we have already accepted as truth.

The degree to which we amplify a given thought/belief/idea in our imagination plus the frequency with which we recall data from our memories to validate that thought/belief/idea yields the level of emotional content that we feel and call our emotions. The amount of emotions we feel drives the extent of our behaviors.

Table of Contents

Acknowledgements

Many people have assisted us and influenced our lives – too many to mention by name here. To spouses, children, and grandchildren; to parents and other family members; and to church, civic, and other leaders and friends; we say thank you for your love, support, kindness, and friendship over the years.

We also want to acknowledge and thank our many clients who have persisted in doing the internal mental and spiritual work that allows the concepts taught here as Spiritual Mind Management to change their lives. We are especially grateful to those who have shared their experiences here.

We acknowledge some of our early mentors in behavioral change processes and express our admiration and respect for those who have gone before us and set us on our path, such as our first trainer and extraordinary teacher, Virgil Hayes. Virgil is still writing books and being an influence for good. Readers would do well to seek out his books and DVDs and take advantage of all that he offers in the field of behavior modification.

Thanks go to national leaders in the American Council of Hypnotist Examiners, the National Guild of Hypnotists, and the International Medical and Dental Hypnotherapy Association who have directly or indirectly influenced our lives. People such as Gil Boyne, Jon Young, Dr. John Butler, Ormond McGill, Dr. Dwight Damon, Don Mottin, Robert Otto, Dr. Paul Durbin, Norm Caldwell, Betty Finnas, Dr. Jan Tyler, Dr. Anne Spenser, and others have had a powerful influence on the work we do.

We thank our two editors on this project, Carol Cartaino and Cheri Loveless, who have done such a wonderful job of clarifying our thoughts on paper.

Most of all, we want to acknowledge the hand of our Divine Creator in our lives. We are on a journey to understand His ways and purposes, listening for what He would teach us next as long as we are willing to follow His voice of direction in this work.

Dedication

This book is dedicated to all who are seeking to "be renewed in the spirit of their minds" (Ephesians 4:23), even those who do not yet consciously realize that they are striving to do so.

Preface

I am a 36-year-old research scientist working in a university setting, where my research involves understanding the underlying phenomena of migraine and pain disorders. I have always been fascinated with science. The scientific approach appears so rigorous and accurate. However, I have also been drawn to some "not so scientific" approaches to human behavior, including different healing modalities—from the more "conventional" to what is now referred to as "alternative." Even though I have gained knowledge about the science of the body that has helped answer some of my questions, I have also had a feeling that it was simply not enough, and that even the best scientists and doctors stand helpless against some of today's mental and physical ailments.

Personally, I have been dealing with insomnia for the past four years, reluctantly using medications to fall asleep. I hate taking medications, but even though I had already tried the standard psychodynamic therapy, acupuncture, meditation, working out regularly, as well as applying the many other sleeping strategies I had learned, I still couldn't fall asleep. I also sought help from two hypnotherapists, but my issue wasn't resolved.

When I learned about Dennis through the internet, something immediately appealed to me. Information about hypnosis was laid out simply and completely. There were no false promises, just a straight-forward approach from someone who appeared to have a lot of experience. I decided to give it a try.

When I came to Dennis for the first time, I was in an overall good place in my life, besides the sleeping issue. Dennis explained the elements of hypnosis to me and the natural laws of the mind. The information was the most profound I have ever heard. I listened carefully, and although the information was not proven scientifically, it made sense to me.

Afterwards, I found myself on a comfortable chair and was asked to close my eyes and go deeper into relaxation. Dennis then asked me to focus on a feeling that was dominant in my current life. I can't really explain what happened next, but Dennis guided me through an experience I had had at an early age, which I found most interesting.

The following night, I still needed my meds to sleep. But not long after, I remember waking up in the morning quite refreshed after a good night's sleep without needing to take any sleeping pills—the first night in several years I had slept without using them. Still, my scientific mind was questioning whether it was the session that produced this result? Or, maybe it was just the passage of time? Or, maybe all of the therapies up to that point combined?

I had several more hypnotherapy sessions with Dennis. Some of the issues I worked on cleared completely. It's been five months from my first session, and I am still sleeping well without medication. I know one thing for sure. Dennis has something to teach me that I have yet to find with other schools of hypnotherapy.

I have attended Dennis' hypnosis classes and feel that this is the first time a course has exceeded my expectations. I find Dennis to be an incredible teacher with a lot of experience in the hypnotherapy field as well as rich experience with resolving human issues. Unlike other teachers that I have previously talked to, he "walks his talk," and to me that is the sign of a true mentor!

I look forward to continuing to explore the hypnotherapy world and its potential. I continue to challenge and ask many questions. I am aware that the techniques I have learned have yet to be proven scientifically, but I am excited to test the techniques myself, hoping to come up with possible explanations in the future.

I hope that we can find a strong scientific basis for what is happening in these hypnotic processes that help so many people, me included. By so doing, not only will we be able to bridge two seemingly different disciplines, but we could open a door to a better understanding of people in general—enjoying more healing options and making this life journey a wonderful one!

Dan Kaufmann, Ph.D.

Introduction

My name is W. Dennis Parker. In this book I teach new personal problem-solving skills using new forms of self-hypnosis that anyone can learn. These skills will help you discover the root of unwanted behaviors—from eating too much to anger problems to conquering maladaptive behaviors—and they can help you change your life pretty much overnight.

I am not a doctor or a psychologist, what I am is a Certified Clinical Hypnotherapist, a behavioral modification and pain control expert. I don't claim that science has proven the effectiveness of these methods, although some people are working on it. I'm just an old cowboy who married my high school sweetheart and worked successfully managing distribution centers and training sales reps for industrial cleaning supply companies while we raised eleven children. During my late 30's I began to want an end to some issues that had troubled me for many years, and in a sincere search for help, I ended up in the office of a hypnotherapist. I not only found answers, but I began to study hypnotherapy as a tool. I have since spent over twenty five years gaining experience and developing the techniques presented in this book.

My personal story is told in Chapter One. But most of this book is about a means of personal problem solving that I call Spiritual Mind Management. It begins with realizing that we control our brains with our "spirit mind" or "inner Intelligence" rather than just our brains controlling us through a complicated neurological system. We each have this inner Intelligence and can learn to feel it moving freely within our minds. We can learn to recognize where inside our minds this Intelligence is active at any given moment, and we can learn to move this Intelligence intentionally, at our direction.

Because our spiritual minds operate our conscious outward observations in a different place from our imagination and store our memories in a different place from our emotions, we think and feel differently as we move our inner Intelligences from place to place. Knowing how to access these various parts of our minds allows us to change our perceptions of past experiences and to correct our imagined versions of past events. We are then able learn how to both detach and then resolve negative emotions and collapse unwanted feelings that literally no longer exist. In fact, we change unwanted behaviors at beyond the speed of light—we do it at the speed of thought.

As you read this book it will become readily apparent what an incredible force for positive change the techniques will have on you but even more importantly on the lives of those that you love the most; spouses, children, friends and colleagues. Think about how you can apply the principles taught to the betterment of those you know including yourself. The stories are moving and real and they can be replicated in your life and in the lives of others. You are starting on a very fulfilling and enjoyable journey, the more your practice these principles the clearer your thinking will be and your sense of purpose will increase.

We can each learn to be our own best behavioral therapist and coach as we use Spiritual Mind Management techniques, allowing us to overcome self-limiting beliefs, eliminate inappropriate habits, and conquer unwanted emotions and behaviors.

W. Dennis Parker - November 2013

CHAPTER ONE

My Story: Overcoming Personal Problems is how I Became a Hypnotherapist

Learning Hypnotherapy from the Inside-Out

More than twenty years ago, I began earnestly seeking personal improvement. There were a number of things I had always wanted to change and overcome. For one, I wanted to overcome the habit of biting my fingernails. I always bit my nails at emotionally tense times.

I decided to pray about it, and one day, while listening to the radio as I drove to work, I heard an advertisement about people who were stopping smoking or losing weight or overcoming other habits through hypnotherapy. I felt quite strongly that this might be an answer for me as well.

I was surprised by my feelings. I had never been involved with hypnosis before, nor did I have any understanding of what was really involved. I had all the usual prejudices that people have from seeing stage hypnosis, yet this time I felt a strong positive impression and was curious to see if hypnosis could provide the help I was seeking.

My Anger Issue

I was also well aware that I had an anger control issue. It took very little to set me off into a rage—a self-defeating, maladaptive behavior that was certainly not working for me as a commissioned sales rep. Even though I attempted to be enthusiastic and friendly, and to build instant relationships as taught by my sales trainers, my internal demeanor came through far too often. People had better options than to buy from an angry, irritable salesman.

This personality trait, or character flaw, was holding me back from being who I wanted to be. It also kept me from providing more substantially for my wife and eleven young children. This period of my life was one where my dog, Smokey, only with coaxing, would hesitantly befriend me. My children scattered when I appeared and my wonderful wife, bless her soul, tolerated and patiently put up with and unconditionally loved me. She is still a saint, unselfish and always serving, beloved of her family and all who know her—the heart and center of our family and the primary influence in our children's lives. I certainly wasn't being fair to her at this time.

Then one day, I had another of several recent altercations. Someone from a boat trailer shop incorrectly repaired an axle on my boat trailer (from my point of view) and (in my estimation) grossly overcharged me at the same time. The situation became heated and potentially violent. The person I was dealing with went to the back to get something and came back with a knife strapped to his side. I realized that I was so angry I was on the edge of being completely out of control, fully prepared to do whatever harm I could do to another human being.

Somehow I restrained myself, and a couple of days later, while thinking about the incident, I finally asked myself a penetrating question, "Why am I so angry all the time"? (Kind of sounds like a country western song, doesn't it?)

Getting a Cowboy to Try Hypnotherapy

At the time, I was quite involved with horses. My personal identification in life was that of a cowboy, and at home I wore what I had worn most of my life—white T-shirts, Levi's, and cowboy boots. During business hours, I described myself as a cowboy in a suit, someone who put on slacks, a dress shirt, and a jacket just to make a living.

One evening I was working with a mustang that I had adopted from the Bureau of Land Management. Reno, as I called him, was stout, coal black, and gorgeous, yet unusually skittish. My sister, who had heard about the altercation at the trailer shop, came out to the corrals to tell me about a friend of hers who had been helped with similar issues by a hypnotherapist, and she left me the therapist's name and phone number.

Since I had already been considering hypnosis, I put the number in my shirt pocket. But I struggled with the idea of actually making the call. I grew up in the 50's and 60's, part of a generation whose fathers, for the most part, had been in the military and believed "Big boys don't cry" and macho dudes don't show their emotions! It was the razor-strap and "spare the rod, spoil the child" era of childrearing,

I had a macho image of myself that could never allow for taking ridicule or chiding from my brothers or buddies about being in therapy. I didn't want to have to explain to anyone that I was going to a therapist. Then a week or two later, I had another altercation with someone on the freeway. I knew I had to get some help, and I made the call.

My Therapy Session

Arriving for my session, I felt like someone I had seen on television going to their first Alcoholics Anonymous meeting: "Hi. My name is, and I am an alcoholic." Even though it was just me and the hypnotherapist, it was difficult for me to open up and explain what my problems were and what I wanted to accomplish.

But in so many words it finally came out: "I am Dennis, and I am a fingernail biting anger-a-holic." I explained that I hadn't always been so, but in recent years it seemed to be growing worse. I was at the point where I felt something bad was going to happen if I didn't get things under control. I gave her some examples of the problem, including the boat incident.

She began to explain hypnosis and hypnotherapy. Most interesting and exciting to me was the concept that every conversation, every touch, every smell, every sensory perception, and every thought we have had, from birth until now, is archived in the subconscious mind and can be made available through hypnosis or trance. She described, in some detail, what she called "the theory of the mind"—how we inductively generate our own behaviors and deductively can learn to challenge and change them. She was the first person to explain to me that our thoughts generate our emotions and our emotions generate our behaviors, as we tend to behave the way we feel. She told me that she and I were going to explore my subconscious mind and thought processes to discover what *predominant thoughts or behavioral scripts,* as she called them, were driving the emotional content of my behaviors.

She also described what I would experience in trance, including what she wanted me to do at certain points to reduce emotions and clear up inappropriate thinking. I was skeptical, but intrigued, and I decided to continue with the session.

She began her induction ritual, and I passed into hypnosis or trance. As with most people, it was not what I expected at all. I thought I would be in some out-of-consciousness or unconscious state, maybe like when you're knocked out. But I was fully aware of everything going on around me while I was becoming more internally focused.

The more she talked the deeper into trance I went. She had me go back in an age regression to the time I first started biting my fingernails or was aware that I was biting my fingernails. She wanted me to understand where that habit came from and how it developed. With that knowledge, I would better understand what I needed to do to correct it and to handle similar *sensitizing* situations differently in the future.

The Initial Incident

My mind regressed back to an experience when I was six years old. As clear as if it were happening that day, I saw myself as a young boy in my grandmother's living room with my grandmother, my mother, and two of my aunts. They were having a heated argument in which I became emotionally involved. The situation was extremely conflicting for me. I saw myself standing over in the corner of the room listening to all of the bickering and fighting, biting my fingernails.

I realized right then that biting my nails, just as the hypnotherapist had pointed out to me, had become an emotional release or *abreaction.* I had undertaken biting my nails as an emotional release in conflict situations—a reaction to the emotions of the conflict, the same way other people tap their feet or twiddle their fingers.

In trance, I could tell the hypnotherapist the exact words of the argument. The entire conversation was clear and present to me. The feelings and emotions that I experienced were just as real to me thirty-one years later as they were when I actually experienced the conflict. I actually relived the entire situation and circumstance.

Then the hypnotherapist took me through a desensitizing process, and we discussed this experience in detail and at some length. I came to understand the false beliefs or *scripting* that I had incorporated into my belief system because of my youthful misinterpretation of the circumstances and the things said in the argument.

As the therapist talked me through the conflicts I was experiencing in my mind, I finally understood why I had begun biting my fingernails, why this problem had plagued me all these years, and why I still resorted to it in times of conflict: it was a learned means of emotional venting. This understanding gave me the power of choice. I could choose to react differently in similar circumstances in the future.

This personal knowledge of me, from what was now a conscious memory; shed new light on the incident. I began to develop a different interpretation of the original circumstances and argument from my current perspective as an adult, replacing what I had thought and understood as a child. This new understanding of the original experience became a source of power to me. As my original understanding was altered, so were my emotions and my behavior. The nervous tension I had carried for years in my fingers began to dissipate.

The Source of my Greatest Anxiety

As I sat in the chair, I could sense that I was still feeling uneasy and was moving nervously, but I didn't know why. The therapist, who had also picked up on my body language, prompted me to go back in my mind to the time of my greatest anxiety. The idea was to discover what my subconscious would reveal as she asked searching questions. She guided me to recollect the time of my greatest emotional upheaval: What was bothering me the most? What one thing was binding me down in my mind and spirit? (This was the moment when I came to understand the term *dis-ease* as an uneasiness of mind and spirit that eventually manifests itself in the body.)

In my mind's eye, I could see my sister Sherry's face. Sherry had been killed in a car-train accident twenty-one years earlier when I was sixteen and she was eighteen. She had been driving my car to a church social one snowy, breezy December evening. She crossed a train track at an unmarked crossing and didn't see the oncoming train. She was hit broadside, and the car burst into pieces. It was snowing heavily that night, which is why she took my car. I had just put on new snow tires. I believe the side windows must have been steamed over or covered with blowing snow, and there were no flashing lights or warning signs of any kind, so she drove across the tracks into the oncoming train.

I saw Sherry's face in my mind, and the hypnotherapist asked me what I was seeing. I was imagining the wreck and the impact of the train hitting the car and my sister. I didn't understand what was happening to me in my mind to imagine such things. The hypnotherapist asked me to tell her about my sister, so I related the above scenario of the accident. She prompted me to recall other details, times, or instances where I had experienced deep anxiety over this situation.

My mind went back again, and I could see myself standing in our family room. It was some two or three months after Sherry had been killed. I was alone with my mother, and we were discussing the accident. I told her that it had made me reflect upon my own life. I had stopped smoking, which I occasionally indulged in, and I had also stopped drinking the occasional beer with my friends and other inappropriate teenage experimentation.

I let my mother know that I was trying to improve my life and get my life back in order because I had come to realize just how short life could be. I said that I knew better than to do wrong things. In hypnosis, I could hear our lengthy conversation word for word, just as before, and I could hear my mother's exact words again in my mind. She was deep in thought, and then she looked at me reflectively and said, "Maybe the reason Sherry had to go was because of you."

The therapist said that she thought I was blaming myself for Sherry's death. "You feel responsible for her being killed," she said.

"I don't think so," I replied. That didn't make much sense to me.

She said, "No, I think that is it. Your mind has brought that incident back to you. You went back to the source of your greatest anxiety." She handed me a large pillow and asked me to take my right hand and hit the pillow. She told me that as I hit it, I was to say out loud, "I am not responsible for Sherry's death."

I began to laugh, to release the emotional pressure of having to hit a pillow in front of somebody else. I was not feeling any emotion or any real anxiety over Sherry's death at that moment. I now know that I had learned to stuff these feelings down, primarily with the defense mechanisms of amnesia and denial. I didn't want to believe that the therapist was right.

She then became more insistent and said, "Hit the pillow, Dennis, and say, 'I am not responsible for Sherry's death.'" I told her I didn't want to do it. Her tone became even more demanding as she said, "Hit the pillow, Dennis, and say it."

I kind of chuckled at the next thought that came through my mind, which was that I was paying real money for this, so I ought to go ahead and try what she said. After all, it had brought back the memory of why I bite my fingernails. So I raised my arm, made a fist, and hit the pillow lightly while I said, "I am not responsible for Sherry's death." "Do it again," she insisted.

As my hand came up to hit the pillow the second time, something inside of me snapped. All of a sudden I felt this huge emotional volcano grow and then erupt inside of me. I was no longer able to contain the enormous rage of hurt and anger. My emotional content, pent up for years, just came bursting out all over.

I started beating and punching the pillow with both hands, and then I broke down in tears and cried and cried, a natural and healthy emotional venting action that I had not done for many years. Now I was shouting, "I am not responsible for Sherry's death! I am not responsible for Sherry's death! I am not responsible for Sherry's death!" I said it over and over again, all the while beating on the pillow. I felt like I was going insane, like I was losing control or had lost it.

Resolution

I continued to do this until I had another experience that I never expected. As I was having this tremendous emotional release, hitting the pillow and yelling and venting, releasing emotions I had carried around inside of me for years, everything suddenly became clear.

I realized I had been angry with my mother for thinking that I could be the cause of Sherry's death. I was angry with God for having taken my sister. I was angry that I had not been able to do something more than just loan her my car. I should have been there. I would have seen the train.

I did believe it; that somehow Sherry's death was my fault. What a tremendous personal revelation and insight into my life. These thoughts had been building in my imagination and compounding their emotional content inside of me, becoming amplified in my subconscious imagination.

Then the hypnotherapist said, "Now tell yourself the truth. Say 'I am NOT responsible for Sherry's death.' Say it over and over again." I did so and began to feel an enormous weight—something pressing on my spirit that I had never recognized or understood—simply lift off from me.

Freedom from Misconception

For me it seemed normal to feel weighed down and heavy in spirit. I was not really aware that there was any other way to feel. My personality was mostly sober, and these feelings were so familiar to me that I had learned to be comfortable being uncomfortable. As the emotional content was released, I stopped crying, and was again emotionally in control and feeling relieved.

The therapist asked me how I felt. I told her that I felt as if great amounts of darkness had left my soul. She said, "What do you feel now? I was then feeling the Spirit of the Lord stronger than I had ever felt it before. It felt like I was filled with love, light, and truth. I knew that I had gained an understanding of a process, of one way to heal mind, body, and soul mentally, emotionally, physically, and spiritually.

I was also feeling comforted. Peace and serenity flowed through me of a magnitude I had never before experienced. My spirit and body seemed as though someone had taken a hundred-pound sack of potatoes off my left shoulder and another hundred pounds off my right shoulder. I had become so accustomed to carrying this mental and emotional weight around that I had never even recognized it was there. My entire spirit and being felt lighter and free. Even my body seemed to move more freely.

When I recognized and embraced the truth, the darkness or weight or negative emotional content, whatever you prefer to call it, had left me; it had no more power over me. I now believe that the darkness of this world loses its power instantly when we finally accept truth in place of the lies, misinterpretations, misunderstandings, and deceptions that we have within us. The truth really does have power to make us free, to set us free.

The hypnotherapist then brought me to a lighter state of trance and suggested that I would remember everything that I had been through. I have clear recollections of it to this day. It has been over twenty-three years since my first session. I can still see clearly how I had developed false beliefs and believed lies.

My hypnotherapist talked me through certain necessary concepts and steps that helped me to reframe my thinking with obvious truths about the accident. I like to call it a reconstruction of the experience. I wasn't driving the car. I was not in charge of the weather. It was not my fault that Sherry did not see the train. In fact, I was the one who loaned her a car with new snow tires so she would be safe. I am not in control, God is. He was very much aware of his daughter that night, and He is still in charge of things like this, not me.

I now understood the truth, and I had corrected my thinking errors. I overcame some false beliefs that I had taken on in a moment of emotional weakness. I had taken on these false beliefs when my mother inadvertently made a statement while trying to figure out why she had to lose a daughter.

The hypnotherapist explained that this is a common way that "inappropriate predominant thoughts" become part of our belief system. However, the therapist made it clear that my mother was not to blame. She had not intentionally tried to hurt me, but was just voicing her thoughts out loud. She had no way of knowing the effect it would have on me for all those years.

Hypnotherapy as a Path to Healing

It was vividly clear to me that I had just experienced an amazing way to clear the incorrect thoughts from someone's mind that help develop their inappropriate feelings and beliefs. It was an effective way to remove the effects of those thoughts from the subconscious—the fear, guilt, anger, and other negative emotions from my past that were harbored in my mind and spirit. I could never have overcome the thoughts that were making me angry and unhappy, that were weighing me down with a false sense of responsibility for my sister's death, unless I knew that I was carrying them in the first place. I had no conscious recognition of the root of so many problems in my life until this hypnotherapy session.

It was now obvious to me why hypnosis was the answer to my prayers. It was also obvious to me why the adversary would want others to believe these processes are evil in nature and not to be studied or understood. Evil influences do attempt to use our natural trance abilities against us, and the devil promotes the idea that these abilities are evil, because he doesn't want people to understand that this is one of the best ways to clear up the lies and deceptions in our lives.

Now that I had this understanding and knowledge, I knew I needed to pursue it further. I desired the same cleansing benefits for my family and for others around me. I began to study the materials given to me and bought books suggested by the hypnotherapist. Over the next several weeks, I went back to her and did a number of sessions. I cleared up all kinds of issues in my life, like conflicts with my parents from my teenage years. I had several other powerful emotional releases that freed additional trauma from my body.

My life was changing rapidly for the better. I was enjoying life more than I had ever before. My personality changed completely once all of the anger, rage, and hostility were gone. My sales career took off and my health improved. The hypnotherapist I worked with taught me how to self-hypnotize and to reprogram myself with positive affirmations or new predominant thoughts in any area of weakness that I identified. I began to look for other areas of false beliefs. I learned that while in trance, which might be described as when the conscious or logical thinking mind is set aside, I could call up subconscious answers or truths.

It was not always easy, without further training in self-hypnosis, to move from consciousness to the desired trance levels. Nor was it easy to formulate questions to ask myself. But I reviewed the questions of my life consciously, questions for which I earnestly sought answers and understanding. I would pray about my questions, asking for divine assistance, and then hypnotize myself. Once I was in a trance state, my mind could pull up answers to my questions, and I gained wisdom and understanding about myself that I never before thought possible.

I believe that what I was learning to do is pondering and meditation as taught in the scriptures. "Ponder the path of thy feet, and let all thy ways be established."(OT | Proverbs 4:26) For me hypnosis skills are pondering skills, and hypnotherapy is meditation. "My mouth shall speak of wisdom; and the meditation of my heart shall be of understanding."(OT | Psalms 49:3) I was gaining wisdom and understanding of life and the lessons to be learned from my life's experiences.

With this newfound freedom and peace of mind, every relationship in my life improved. My sales skyrocketed, and within a few months I was asked to be the sales manager. Several months later, I was asked to be the general manager for the company where I worked. Life was improving all around me with the positive changes that I had learned to make in my predominant thought processes.

Some call this "The Secret" or "The Law of Attraction," whereby we attract into our lives the people, places, circumstances, and things that harmonize with our most important predominant thoughts. We mentally put our thoughts out into the universe and begin to realize that thoughts are things of substance, and like attracts like, and kind attracts kind. This is also in accord with the law of the harvest, in that we reap what we sow. In fact, this is consistent with everything else we see all around us in nature.

Becoming a Hypnotherapist

Some six or seven weeks after my first session, I was out working with my horses in the evening when my brother, who was living next door, came over. He told me he wanted to know who I was—he didn't know me anymore. "What do you mean?" I asked. He said that he'd been watching me for the past several weeks and that there was something different about me. For instance, he had noticed a marked difference in the way I treated animals and my family. My overall demeanor was friendlier and happier.

His observations and statements took me back because the changes I had been making did not seem to me to be that perceptible to others. He asked, "What are you doing that is making you so different?" I thought about it for a moment and then told him that I had been going to a hypnotherapist. As I knew would be the case, he began laughing and making fun of me. I told him that I didn't really care what he thought, because of the difference hypnotherapy or meditation was making in my life.

When he saw that I was serious, he asked me exactly what I had been doing. I told him that I was about finished with the chores and animals, and that if he really wanted to know I'd be happy to visit with him in the house. When we went in and sat down, I explained to him about hypnotherapy and my sessions. I explained how every thought, every word, every action, every conversation, even every sensory perception that we have experienced from birth is still in our subconscious mind and can be accessed through trance. I explained that we can come to understand those things that are binding us down, holding us back, and keeping us from being all we know we want to be, that all of these things can be addressed, dealt with, and changed with trance, meditation, or hypnotherapy, which were now all synonymous terms to me.

He then said that there were things that had been bothering him and asked if I would help him. I told him that we could give it a try. I had him sit comfortably in an overstuffed chair, as I had done, and simply started doing the same things that I had become so familiar with in the sessions I had been through. He immediately went into trance and regressed back to an issue that had been bothering him, and through the same processes that I had learned, he was able to clear it up. An hour or so later he walked out of the house feeling better about himself and his life. His demeanor and nature also changed somewhat.

The next day at work, he was talking to his best friend and said, "You'll never guess what my brother did for me last night," and he related the experience. His best friend then asked if I would spend some time with him. My brother called me and we set up a time. I worked with his friend and got the same transforming results. His friend then told someone else and they came over. Then they told someone else, and that person came over.

This started a pattern for about a year and a half where I practiced doing hypnosis and hypnotherapy with a number of people, all with beneficial effects. It seemed that I had an intuitive knack for it, thanks to the therapy and experiences that I had been through myself. I understood the processes personally and was able to duplicate them with others, and I never charged a dime for my time. Those I helped were all friends or friends of close friends, and everyone felt as though they had benefited from the experience. And I enjoyed it. There was a satisfaction in helping someone else discover and overcome limiting beliefs in their lives and eliminate unwanted behaviors.

Then one night, when I was putting some sales proposals together at the dining room table while my wife was clearing off the table and finishing the dinner dishes with some of the children, the phone rang. My wife answered it and started to laugh as she put her hand over the receiver. "Dennis," she said, "There is a man on the phone who wants to know if Dr. Parker is home."

When I answered the phone, I told him that he must have the wrong number as there was no doctor here. He then inquired, "Are you the Dennis Parker who worked with—last week from the Seattle area while they were visiting in Utah?" I explained that I had spent some time with them as a friend, as I had known the man since high school. The voice on the phone continued, "I have visited with—and he told me what you did and that he feels better than he has felt in many years. Whatever you did for him I want you to do for me."

He explained that he had been seeing a counselor for the past eighteen years. I told him that I was not qualified to work with him and that what I had done, I did as a favor for some friends. He persisted and told me that money was not an object for him, that he would be willing to fly to Utah, put himself up in a hotel, stay as long as I thought he needed to, and do as many sessions as it took for him to receive similar results.

I then explained to him more clearly that I was not a therapist and that he need not buy a ticket as I would not be seeing him. He asked me what I thought he should do. I told him he should go out and find a local competently trained Certified Clinical Hypnotherapist. I wished him the best of luck in his search and expressed hope that it would turn out well for him.

With the phone back in place on the wall, my wife and I then discussed in all earnestness what I had been doing. We decided that if I were going to continue to attempt to help others and continue to study the processes myself, that I needed to receive further training. I contacted the hypnotherapist who had worked with me and asked what it took to become a Certified Clinical Hypnotherapist. She explained to me what school she had attended and where to find information on the courses. I enrolled the very next day.

I spent the next year attending classes—ten hours a day on Saturdays for most of the year, as well as doing the homework assignments and reading the books and manuals that were required to accomplish the courses. In 1991, I was certified as a Clinical Hypnotherapist by The American Council of Hypnotist Examiners (A.C.H.E.). I have attended many conferences and workshops since, keeping up with my continuing education and recertifying requirements. I have been a presenter at A.C.H.E. International Hypnotherapy annual conferences, and since 2003, I have been a Board Approved Examiner, Instructor, and Approved School Operator.

Hypnosis and hypnotherapy or pondering and meditation have greatly changed and enriched my life. It was no coincidence in my life that I was directed to Marilyn and hypnotherapy. It has been my privilege now for many years to assist hundreds of career associates and hypnotherapy clients in overcoming their self-limiting beliefs, eliminating inappropriate habits, and conquering maladaptive behaviors as I teach these personal problem solving skills. It is rewarding to be part of the change processes and progress of others, to assist them in going from being a victim of their life's experiences to being a thriving survivor. After reading the above, if you should feel a desire to move ahead in your own life, and if you have positive feelings about learning these processes, I would suggest that for you too, reading this story might not be a coincidence.

Hypnotherapy processes and techniques develop conscious awareness of choice and free people to choose new courses of action as determined by them. They are given positive input and suggestions by the therapist in an effort to strengthen their decisions. This process helps the individual to deeply internalize their new decisions, which when acted upon, become their new behaviors.

Hypnotherapy is the re-decision-making process, choosing anew.

CHAPTER TWO

The Inner Intelligence that is Your Spiritual Mind

It was 1991 and the last day of my clinical hypnotherapy training course at Hypnotism Training Center of Utah—just a week away from the certification. Our instructor, Virgil Hayes, asked us to put our pencils down and place our hands comfortably on our laps, then to sit up straight and place our feet firmly upon the floor. We already knew this drill from the many times we had done it before. We were about to experience another group "hypnotic induction."

My mind was now mostly calm and clear, thanks to weeks of individual and group hypnotherapy training. We had observed and participated in hundreds of hours of hypnotherapy sessions, both individually and as a group. Each session added much to my education as I listened to Virgil's questions and directives to the group and experienced personal answers.

Freedom from Our Own Issues

Virgil was of the opinion that in order to be good hypnotherapists we needed to have our personal issues cleared up first. We would then avoid being triggered emotionally during a session with a client, and we would understand what to do when a client experienced "automatic emotional venting" (referred to in hypnotherapy as an abreaction) during a session, as we would already have been through the same or similar circumstances ourselves or have observed others go through them.

Thus, our minds were becoming free of childhood issues. Many altercations or misunderstandings with classmates, friends, parents, grandparents, and other authority figures had been dealt with. In the language of hypnotherapy, such incidents had been desensitized, reconstructed, or reframed by altering the perceptions we each held of our memories. Now, as a group, our minds were clear of most of our negative early experiences, including major traumas of life such as abuse.

This class experience of becoming clear-minded had been a gradual process—hour upon hour, precept upon precept—fashioned from the combined experiences of each of our lives. By learning from each other's personal life experiences, we each had increased in wisdom and understanding for individual problem solving.

When I first started the training classes, my personal assessment of myself was a person with a severe attention deficit. My mind raced from subject to subject and experience to experience. I had so many voices, so many thoughts, and so much "mind chatter," as I now call it, that multiple memories constantly bombarded my mind and distracted me.

These thoughts or voices felt familiar and seemed normal to me. There were thoughts recalling situations in grade school where I had felt rejected—experiences where, in my mind, I wasn't quite good enough to win something or smart enough to get the right answer. Constant thoughts and feelings of inadequacy, fear, and guilt ("it must have been my fault") filled the minds of most every member of the class as we worked our way through such personal experiences.

I found it fascinating to observe Virgil as he worked with different individuals. We discovered that every class member was experiencing thoughts and feelings that were creating a negative barrier in some aspect of their lives. These negative thought scripts that individuals were fixated on were binding them down, holding them back, and keeping them from being all they wanted to be.

Once I understood the basic process of challenging negative thoughts and replacing them with more appropriate decisions, I found myself doing so over and over again, especially while I was asleep. Dreams would come and go, and issues would be resolved while I slept. Almost everyone in the class reported the same phenomenon. While awake, your mind now being open to these concepts, you continue to *"think through your thought processes."*

Observing and participating as each individual in the group went through a similar process actually strengthened the confidence of the group. We rose together in our individual strengths as we witnessed continual changes for the better in ourselves and in one another week after week. We came to realize that it was normal to have negative and inhibiting experiences and feelings—part of life's regimen or curriculum, if you will. Everyone on this earth needs to learn how to overcome the world's buffetings, and during our schooling in hypnotherapy, our training increased our capacity to do so with mental, emotional, and physical skills, processes, and procedures.

Our Final Class Session

Virgil began by explaining to us once more that our minds have a conscious area that processes analytical and logical thinking and also observes and learns new information. All of the thoughts that pass through our minds are evaluated in this area. They are accepted or rejected based on analytical and logical thinking weighed against our accepted prior learning and established beliefs.

During our hypnotherapy coursework, we had also studied and come to understand *the critical factor*, the division barrier that is the storage area of our belief systems. It exists somewhere between consciousness and our subconscious functions of imagination, memory, and emotion where it filters out unacceptable thoughts as well as thoughts not believed to be right, true, and correct for us.

Virgil started the induction by directing us to focus closely on his hand. As he moved it, we were to observe the length of each finger and how far it was from his thumb, and so forth. We were to focus intently on the creases of his hand, so that we were learning and observing outwardly, in conscious focus only. Learning to be conscious at our own will and choice was his main objective.

Then we were prompted to observe and become aware of the fact that while in total outward conscious focus—this mental state of total singularity of focus—we had virtually no imagination, no memories, and no emotional content. We were disconnected from the subconscious functions of imagination, memory, and emotion. It was amazing to experience such an awareness of our mental capacity to compartmentalize both conscious and subconscious functions.

Virgil then explained that a part of us exists inside of our minds that he named "I am of self." This separate part of our being, our intellect or Intelligence or whatever else you might choose to call it, is us. It thinks, reasons, decides, and moves within the mind, connecting to one part of the mind or another at any given moment in time. I have come to refer to this phenomenon of experiencing the movement of our Intelligence as "having a free mind."

Next, Virgil had us observe again that while we were in this conscious focus, observing the fingers and wrinkles on his hand, our Intelligence was fixed in consciousness. Since it had no connection to imagination, memories, or emotions, we could experience one aspect of temporary *hypnotic amnesia*. In order to demonstrate this, he asked us to recall our address and at the same time continue to focus intently on his hand.

When we tried to do as he asked, we found that we had no memories—no names, no addresses, no recollections of any kind. He asked us next to let go of this fixation and find our addresses, observing the movement within our minds of our newly found Intelligence.

We realized that to find our addresses, we had to think. Within our minds we could literally feel the movement as our Intelligences left the place of total consciousness to enter a place where we could recall facts. As our Intelligence went back to where our memories are located, somewhere toward the middle back of our heads, our addresses just seemed to pop into our minds, and we all were then able to verbalize them.

It was startling to me to feel this movement in my mind and head. It was also extremely delightful. I remember grinning from ear to ear, not able to resist commenting, "Cool!!!" I looked around the room of thirty-plus people and found everyone smiling with pleasure.

Moving Around Within Our Minds

Then Virgil asked us to look at his hand again and to become aware of the movement. I felt part of my mind literally move from back in memory (in the back of my head) forward to conscious focus (somewhere in the front of my forehead). One person there described it as being the area of the "third eye." We discovered that we were able to meditate in this deep trance with our mental processes focused to such a degree that we could fixate on individual thoughts and individual emotions, isolating one thought from another and one emotion from another.

Next, Virgil had us experience where our imaginations were located in our spiritual minds by pretending and imagining that, with our eyes closed, we each could see a rose. We were to imagine this rose as the most beautiful rose we had ever seen, felt, or smelled. He asked us to touch the stem, being aware of the prickly thorns. We even put our imaginary roses to our noses and could literally smell the fragrance. Virgil then had us place our index fingers on our heads to show where we were in our minds while imagining a rose. We had kept our eyes continually closed to that point, and now he had us open them. Every one of us had our index finger somewhere towards the front of our heads above the forehead.

We also learned where our emotions are experienced inside of our spiritual minds' compartmentalization. For this, Virgil had us remember a very happy time in our lives, when we were experiencing a favorite birthday, Christmas celebration, or some other time with family or other loved ones on a most joyous occasion. When my Intelligence went back into that emotion, I vividly felt the joy and happiness that was stored there. I learned that those feelings are always there; we just are not always connected to them.

Finally, Virgil had us quickly open our eyes again to look at his hand, and as we did so, the movement in our minds was so delightful it caused many of us to laugh out loud. My Intelligence went back to conscious observation again and became completely disconnected from those joyous feelings.

Developing these concepts within me as I experimented with this physical movement of my Intelligence was a continually surprising and enjoyable experience. Becoming aware of its movement from function to function, allowing me to view issues from different viewpoints inside my own mind yet under my own mental control, was nothing short of amazing! My mind was clear, clean, and calmer than ever before. To that point in my life, I had never experienced such a wonderful sense of peace.

Bringing Spiritual Mind Management Skills to Others

On that last day of Virgil's instruction, we knew where we were in our own minds at any given moment. We even knew, from our prior instruction, what trance state we were in and that we were intentionally choosing to move our Intelligences within our minds for our own goal achievement. In addition, we were learning at an amplified rate, experiencing and practicing the many mental skills we had been developing. On that day, we were free to think as we chose to think.

It was wonderful to be able to move around in my mental functions at will and also to understand the positive effects of being able to do so. Below are some thoughts that I wrote out after my first experiences of recognizing what I call my Intelligence.

My Intelligence is:

- Clarity of being
- A feeling of well-being
- Completeness within myself
- Strength of inner choice and freedom
- A sense of unity
- Oneness of self
- Independence of being—I am strong, purposeful, loving, caring, and powerful as I am empowering others

In this state of being:

- I am honest with myself. No more excuses.
- I am free to choose my response to each situation and stimulus.
- I choose to be of service to those who choose to be of service to others.

According to Virgil, the ability to purposefully move our Intelligences in and out of various parts of our minds represents conscious choice, conscious awareness, and conscious decision-making. I learned from working within myself and with clients over the years that, in the state we call a *free mind*, each of us has the power to see things from different points of view, this allows us to see what a potential decision looks like using various parts of the imagination; to see which memories surface to justify, validate, and defend a particular thought or belief. Few people know or experience this "secret" of the mind because of the effort and energy it first takes to clear one's mind of the darkness and negativity caused by past accepted, predominant thinking errors. These are predominant thought scripts that the Intelligence is stuck on, and are what we call *fixations*. Yet everyone has the capacity to experience a free mind should they desire it and be willing to do their personal work of weeding the garden of their mind of thinking errors and negative predominant thought fixations.

My experience in class that day back in 1991 rewarded a personal spiritual and mental quest I had taken on. But beyond that, it helped me to understand and appreciate the great gifts of agency, freedom and the power of choice that our Creator has given to each of us. It increased my desire to bring an awareness of these gifts to others. Since then, I have felt the need to speak out about the existence of the spiritual mind and to assist others who want to experience this freedom and peace of mind for themselves.

For the past twenty-five years, I have worked hard to develop ways to introduce others to the conscious awareness of their power to choose and to utilize their personal agency in the best possible way. During those years, my understanding of how to use my knowledge of the spiritual mind for personal improvement and positive change has increased many times. The Spiritual Mind Management techniques and processes you will read about in this book grew from the basics provided by Virgil Hayes and go beyond anything currently taught in hypnotherapy. You will be amazed at the personal progress you can make in your understanding of yourself and the changes you can more easily make as you practice doing your own Spiritual Mind Management.

Eventually my desires led me to establish the Certified Hypnotherapy Training School in Farmington, Utah. There my associates and I empower others with our advanced Spiritual Mind Management techniques. Basically, we teach our students and clients to "think about the way they think."

We believe the world needs tens of thousands of hypnotherapists who understand these principles and can teach and assist others in overcoming the negative, dark side of life's experiences. All people ought to be able to utilize what I believe is a God-given gift of using natural hypnotic trance for goal-directed, productive, and positive purposes and for understanding their true potential. We have developed these concepts into new protocols of hypnotherapy. In this book, we will teach them to you.

The Purpose of this Book

Our purpose in writing this book is threefold. First, we introduce Spiritual Mind Management techniques and skills. We begin by describing the areas that make up the spiritual mind as well as what an individual with a free mind experiences when moving from one part of the mind to another. We also discuss the mental skills someone can develop after becoming liberated from fixations on past problems. This is the state of mind that allows an individual to be in better control of their thoughts and emotions than they have ever imagined. Those who achieve such a state of mind find greater self-empowerment, better self-control, and improved self-confidence.

Second, we explore the role of trance or hypnosis in helping people obtain a free mind. We do so in hopes of assisting the reader to understand the many benefits and blessings that come from hypnosis and hypnotherapy. Because of exposure to Hollywood-type myths on renditions of hypnosis, the general public struggles to understand the natural ability we each have to enter into various trance states of our own free will, creating personal control of our own mind.

In this book, we handle questions that are usually left unanswered. We let people know there is no mystery at all to hypnosis. In a similar vein, we define the trance levels or states of mind that most people can readily identify or experience, and we attempt to explain these trance abilities clearly enough that our readers will understand how to put them to use.

We each have capacities, gifts, and talents associated with trance that we may have misunderstood or just not been aware of before. We promise that you will be thankful you took the time to learn about them.

Third, we give some detail on the nitty-gritty of the personal problem-solving skills of hypnotherapy. We explain exactly how we help people become clear and free minded, and how we resolve past traumatizing events and experiences that still hold people back. Every one of us has experienced events that inhibit us from being who we want to be and whom we feel in our hearts we're meant to be. We may sense that we have great things to accomplish, yet we are held back. Many people will discover that such issues can be successfully addressed with hypnotherapy.

Let's get started and introduce Spiritual Mind Management for personal problem-solving and behavior modification.

CHAPTER THREE

Becoming Familiar with Your Spiritual Mind

In our science-based world, most people are used to discussing functions of the body as if all of our thoughts and actions originate in the brain and are carried out by its physical mechanisms. I don't pretend to be familiar with or to understand current scientific theories about how the brain works or what part of the body specific areas of the brain might control. This book isn't based on those theories.

Instead, I know that I can move my hand and make my fingers wiggle. I don't know which or how many neurological impulses coming from my brain allow me to do that. I just know that I can make myself do it—that when I want or need to do so, I can move my hand and wiggle my fingers. Similarly, my co-authors and I may not be able to explain the physical processes behind the results we get, but we do know how to get those results. We can only explain it by the way we go about it.

Over the past 25 years, I have taken the concepts I was taught in personal sessions and hypnotherapy school and I have developed them further, both in my own mind and by working with clients. I carefully observed additional patterns of the inner movements of the mind and taught myself to use these patterns to accomplish hypnotherapy in new ways. I came to understand what I refer to as amplification of the imagination and its effect on the emotions. These additional concepts are what I want to explain to you in this book, along with much of my original learning.

In other words, our system of hypnotherapy is based on observation and results. It grew out of what we have experienced with our many clients over the course of two decades. We understand that, in the future, others will assimilate some of the concepts and ideas presented here who will be able to teach and explain them far better scientifically than we can now. This book is simply a first attempt at communicating what we have observed, learned, and applied during a great many hypnotherapy sessions. We believe it is results that count, and our clients have shown both results in overcoming self-limiting beliefs and limiting behaviors, eliminating inappropriate habits, and conquered their maladaptive behaviors, utilizing these personal problem solving techniques. Then they enjoy the benefits of being in control of themselves. There is peace of mind and happiness that comes from knowing how to be in charge of you. You can know how to productively use agency and choice take personal responsibility and accountability as you do your mind management and are in control of you yourself!

Your Inner Intelligence and the Compartments of Your Spiritual Mind

Most people I have worked with over the years seem to agree that we are dual beings—that we have a body and what many people refer to as a spirit. Some people have felt the presence of a third part of themselves, sometimes referred to as the "spirit of the mind" or the "inner mind." This is the inner Intelligence that Virgil had his students experience on the last day of my hypnotherapy coursework.

I'm proposing that this inner Intelligence is a reality and that it guides both our spirits and our physical brain. This Intelligence is a part of you and me that can actually move from place to place inside of our minds. It can shift from being conscious of the present physical reality to visualizing things in imagination, then switch to perfect recall of any memory. It can also lock onto old emotions. It is more readily identifiable by people who have a mind free of fixation—that is, not caught up in thoughts of the past that still upset them emotionally, binding them to certain imaginings, memories, or emotions in the subconscious.

Each of us can come to know where our Intelligences are in our own minds at any given moment. We can also come to understand how to use our Intelligences to direct ourselves in ways that give us greater understanding of our power of choice, of our personal accountability and responsibility, and of our natural, God-given ability to choose what is right, true, and correct for us. These processes enrich our lives. They empower us with greater self-control, self-confidence, and self-awareness. We can both obtain this self-understanding and maintain it through daily Spiritual Mind Management.

In the following chapters you will learn that you have the power and ability to move your Intelligence so that you can consider different points of view—right within your own mind. You can actually see, hear, and feel what is within the different compartments of your spiritual mind. For instance, you can choose to view a particular event from a conscious outward focus, or you can review that same event from your imagination or from the perspective of your memories or your emotions. In this way, you can learn to do critical and analytical thinking more clearly than ever before by visualizing things more distinctly in both positive and negative directions, enhancing your understanding of an issue or an experience.

It is this force within our spiritual minds, our Intelligences, that actually operates our brains, then our brains operate our bodies—not the reverse. With proper direction from our Intelligences to our brains, some people learn to mentally control bodily functions.

Whether we are aware of it or not, we each have a natural or inherent mental capacity to alter blood flow, saliva flow, and pain level during dentistry procedures, to detach or disassociate from pain as intense as child birth, or to desensitize from the misery allergens cause. Most of us have simply never been taught how.

I want to teach you to recognize how your Intelligence operates as it moves inside of your mind. This will give you greater control of your own mind, increasing self- control, and it will improve your recall of memories, helping you to detach from the negative emotional content of past events. You will learn to control your emotions by disconnecting from the thoughts that are generating those emotions, leaving you with better peace of mind. You can also learn how to disconnect intentionally your Intelligence from your imagination, your memories, and your emotional content whenever you choose to, then to reconnect when you want to.

These mental skills will reveal the importance of personal responsibility and accountability for your actions and deeds.

Freeing the Mind First

Some people are able to experience an awareness of their Intelligence initially. However, most of us have layers of mental barriers that we call fixations. A fixation occurs when the Intelligence is "captured" or fixated in one area of the mind. Examples of this will be given in upcoming chapters.

In our experience, it generally takes several sessions of hypnotherapy to clear up these barriers or predominant thought patterns of past experiences before most people are able to begin moving with awareness from place to place in their minds. We call this process becoming clear and free-minded. With the protocols and programs that we use with clients who avail themselves of our hypnotherapy services, most can learn to accomplish their goals in 4 to 6 weeks of participating in a 1½ to 2-hour hypnotherapy session each week, including some reinforcing work in between sessions.

Our goal is to work with people until we get them to a state I call free-minded. Once their minds are clear from all the past experiences that have been binding them down and holding them back, they usually can start to sense the movement of their Intelligences inside their own minds. At that point, they are able to do the Spiritual Mind Management processes described here. They can control their own minds in the ways described in this book.

A Guide to the Spiritual Mind

Your mind functions in useful patterns. Once you understand these patterns, you can start to figure out your true thoughts and feelings. Spiritual Mind Management is based on using this compartmentalization of your mind to your advantage. It includes the following: a place where we each make conscious outward observations and learn new things *(consciousness),* a place where we visualize where we "see" imagery *(imagination),* a place where we store past experiences and learning *(memory),* and a place where we generate emotions according to the amount of imaginary amplification being applied to the experiences stored in our memories *(emotions).*

The chart on the following page specifies where the spiritual mind's compartments are located and identifies where the Intelligence moves for which process of the mind.

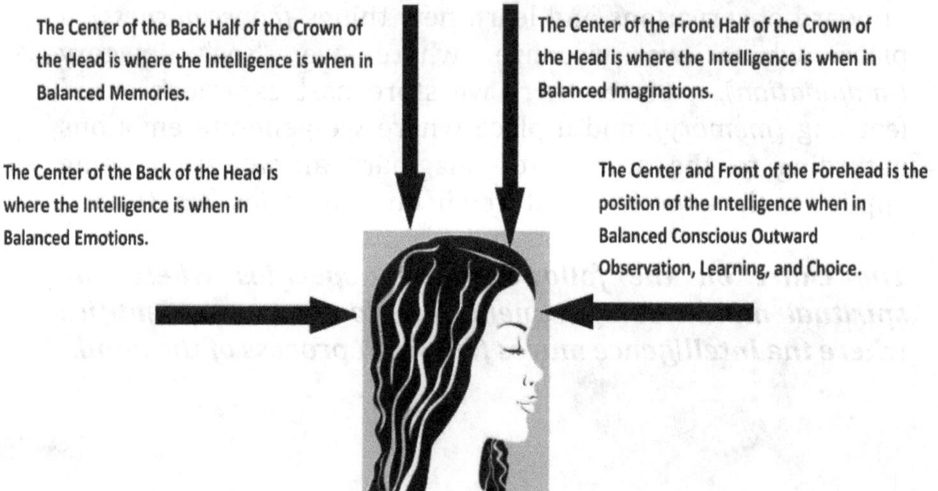
This Chart Explains the Functions of the "Spirit of our Mind, our Intelligence" and the Identification of where the "Intelligence" becomes fixated or moves to, for various processes of the mind! Learn new viewpoints inside your own mind, giving personal mind control, through the power of conscious choice! Overcome self-defeating, self-limiting beliefs, eliminate inappropriate habits, and conquer maladaptive behaviors!
ENJOY A FREE MIND!
The Center of the Back Half of the Crown of the Head is where the Intelligence is when in Balanced Memories.
The Center of the Front Half of the Crown of the Head is where the Intelligence is when in Balanced Imaginations.
The Center of the Back of the Head is where the Intelligence is when in Balanced Emotions.
The Center and Front of the Forehead is the position of the Intelligence when in Balanced Conscious Outward Observation, Learning, and Choice.

The center and front of the forehead is the position of the Intelligence when in balanced *conscious outward observation, learning, and choice.*

The center of the front half of the crown of the head is where the Intelligence is when it is in balanced *imagination*.

The center of the back half of the crown of the head is where the Intelligence is when it is in balanced *memories.*

The center of the back of the head is where the Intelligence is when it is in balanced *emotions.*

In a free mind, the Intelligence can move from conscious outward observation and learning, to imagination, to memories, and/or to emotions—from place to place from moment to moment at our direction.

When the Intelligence is in the conscious part of the mind, towards the front and center of the forehead, we are in *consciousness.* When in consciousness—outward focus, observation, and learning—we are not in our subconscious; we are *not* connected to our imagination, memories, or emotions. It is as though they do not exist. If the Intelligence moves or travels back through what is called *the critical factor or belief system filter* (to be explained later) into the subconscious mind, we then again experience our imagination, memories, and emotions. When the intelligence passes through the critical faculty into the subconscious, you are now in trance, or an altered state of consciousness.

See the chart on the following page.

When your Intelligence is in Consciousness - outward observation, learning, and focus, you are not in your subconscious functions of imagination, memories, or emotions. It is as though they do not exist.

"A double-minded man is unstable in all his ways." (James 1:8) - "...be renewed in the spirit of your mind." (Ephesians 4:23)

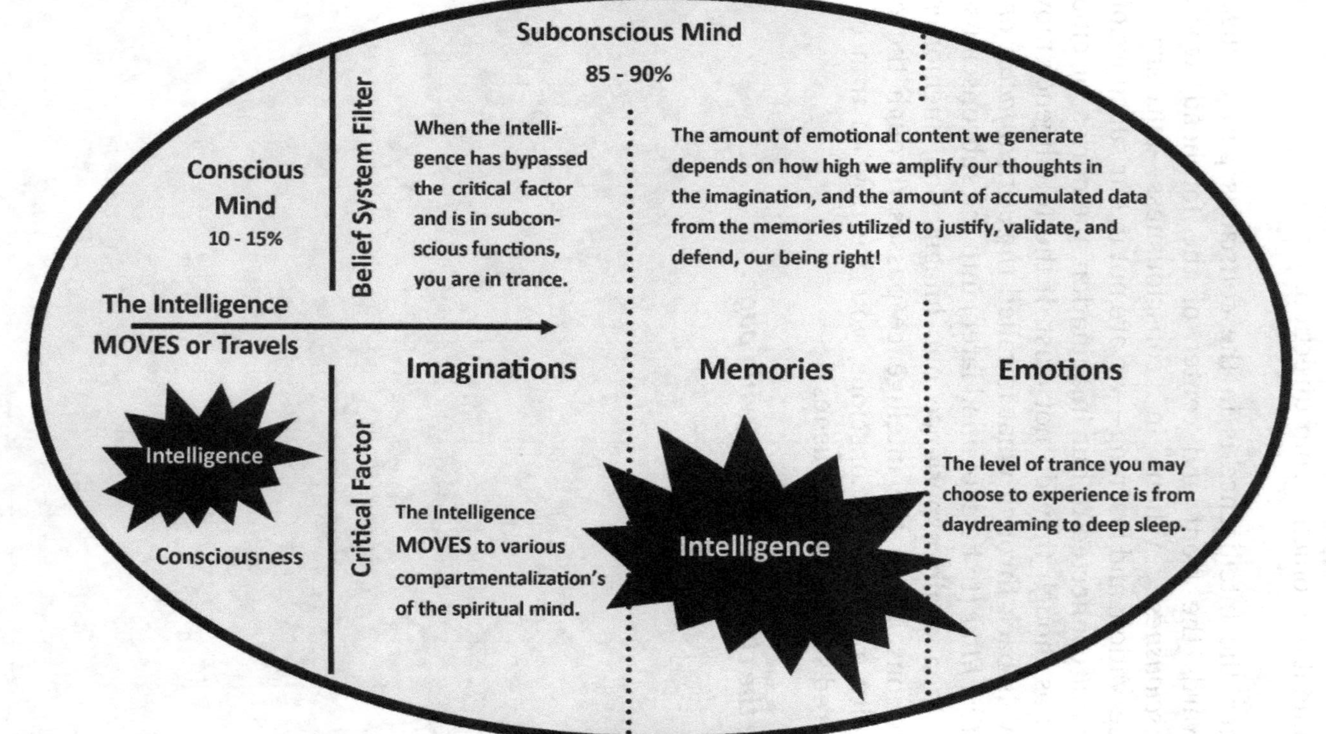

Subconscious Mind
85 - 90%
Conscious Mind
10 - 15%
Belief System Filter
When the Intelligence has bypassed the critical factor and is in subconscious functions, you are in trance.
The amount of emotional content we generate depends on how high we amplify our thoughts in the imagination, and the amount of accumulated data from the memories utilized to justify, validate, and defend, our being right!
The Intelligence
MOVES or Travels
Imaginations
Memories
Emotions
Intelligence
Consciousness
Critical Factor
The Intelligence MOVES to various compartmentalization's of the spiritual mind.
Intelligence
The level of trance you may choose to experience is from daydreaming to deep sleep.

Certified Hypnotherapy Training School - http://certifiedhypnotherapytrainingschool.com/ -

Clients Describe the Inner Mind

The following are excerpts from some of my therapy sessions with clients, in which they describe their experience of the movement of the inner mind.

Speaker 1, an eleven-year-old boy whose parents brought him to address some fears

Dennis: If you were to say the best things you have learned from all the stuff that we have done what would they be? What's the best part of all of this for you?

Speaker 1: The cool part is that you have something moving around in the top of your head—it feels different.

Dennis: Okay, now that you've been able to play around with that for a while, I'm going to ask you to practice moving your Intelligence around. I want you to look within and lock on to that feeling right there, that movement in your head, and go find your address. Put your finger on your head where you can find your address. Okay, describe that feeling as best as you can. What would you say it is?

Speaker 1: It's smooth inside. It doesn't feel sharp or anything; it's soft and not hard.

Dennis: Good description, anything else?

Speaker 1: It's kind of like the water in this water bottle when I turn it sideways.

Dennis: So it's kind of like water moving through your head?

Speaker 1: Yeah.

Dennis: And you like that?

Speaker 1: It feels good!

Dennis: I know you practice moving around in your head quite a bit now.

Speaker 1: Now that I know about it, sometimes you can actually feel it

Dennis: Yeah, and that's what this is about and that's what you're going to help other people do—become aware of that movement and how it works. You'll help some other kids because they need to learn the same skills you've been learning to help them overcome their fears. Most kids have fears of spiders and snakes...

Speaker 1: Things that crawl around...

Dennis: Yeah, and aliens. All that stuff that you've been dealing with.

Speaker 1: Yeah, and stuff like taking tests at school, when you don't have enough time.

Dennis: Exactly, all those things you've been going through. Is there anything else you want to talk about today, or you feel like that was it?

Speaker 1: No, I'm good.

Dennis: Nothing else you want to talk about? You have to be going? Good job. Give me a high five.

Speaker 2, a ten-year-old boy whose mother brought him in to eat a more balanced diet

Dennis: Now I want you to bring your Intelligence right back here, and feel it move up, and tell me when you feel it.

Speaker 2: I feel it.

Dennis: Describe that feeling for me right there, now that you're moving around in your head. What does it feel like to move around inside your head?

Speaker 2: It feels like it's going from one place to another.

Dennis: And what does it look like to you inside your head?

Speaker 2: It looks like there is a road that keeps going on to reach different places.

Dennis: Yeah, and what does the feeling look like itself? Give me your thoughts.

Speaker 2: Maybe a car.

Dennis: You can feel that moving around like it's a car driving around on a road inside your head?

Speaker 2: Uh-huh.

Dennis: So you feel that movement kind of the way you move around when you're in a car?

Speaker 2: Uh-huh.

Dennis: Okay, excellent description.

Speaker 3, an adult client

Dennis: Close your eyes. See my hand more clearly now inside your mind than you do with your eyes open. As you do that, take your index finger, and put it on your head. Exactly where is it that you're actually seeing my hand right now?

Speaker 3: It felt like back here, but it kind of feels like here.

Dennis: Kind of both, huh?

Speaker 3: Yeah.

Dennis: Okay, I want you to bring your awareness right here. Tell me when you have it there.

Speaker 3: Okay.

Dennis: You got it there? Did you feel that movement inside your head?

Speaker 3: Yeah.

Dennis: What did that feel like?

Speaker 3: Felt like a wave.

Dennis: Excellent job. Okay. Look at my hand. Now that you know what that wave feels like, lock onto that wave. Take your index finger and feel that wave in your mind, the place where it actually goes to now, again. I want you to look around the room, and now that you're out of that kind of fog, mist, or dullness as people describe being in the back of their heads, how do things look different, brighter, and newer?

Speaker 3: It looks completely different. In fact there's parts of the room I don't even remember having any memory of.

Dennis: And you spent a lot of time in this room?

Speaker 3: A couple of hours, at least. Wow, that's crazy.

Dennis: How would you describe this conscious observation state right now?

Speaker 3: Just one of greater detail, greater clarity. By clarity, I mean sharper. I don't know how to describe it. It's hard to put a finger on it, but it doesn't look the same.

Dennis: Good job, you've just broken some major fixations. You're now freer in your mind, and your spirit is clearer, freer. I see that in your eyes. There's clarity in your eyes right now. It's really incredible.

Speaker 3: Cool! Thank you!

Speaker 4, another client

Dennis: Okay, look at my hand so intently that you have no name, no address, and no phone number; got it? Pay really close attention to where you go inside your head. You can close your eyes and focus when you do this if you want. Feel that movement inside your head. Tell me where you go to find your phone number. Put your index finger on your head where you find it.

Speaker 4: Here

Dennis: Excellent job. Did you feel that movement back there?

Speaker 4: Uh-huh.

Dennis: What did that movement feel like?

Speaker 4: Like I was just going there.

Dennis: How would you describe it, like you were just going there?

Speaker 4: Traveling?

Dennis: Like you're traveling? So you're traveling inside your own head?

Speaker 4: Yeah.

Dennis: Everybody describes that a little differently. Some will say, "Well, it's like I just slid on back there." Others say, "It's like there is a marble that's rolling around back there." How would you describe it?

Speaker 4: Maybe more like a jet of white light going back.

Dennis: Okay, good.

Here are some further excerpts from sessions with clients, commenting on the effectiveness of Mind Management for them; how it has helped them deal better with various troublesome situations in their lives.

Client/Speaker 5

Dennis: The Mind Management stuff that we went over last time, how has it been working for you?

Speaker 5: Good.

Dennis: So it's been about a week since we did that last session?

Speaker 5: Uh-huh.

Dennis: And tell me, when you say good, what have you noticed in the way you are able to control your emotions and your imagination? Give me an example of what good means.

Speaker 5: Well, there have been events and comments made in the last week that would generally have really, really, bothered me. But what I have learned made it so much easier for me to process these things, and respond, without having any emotion, negative or positive. I just kind of flipped the thoughts out of my mind, rather than dwelling on them, as I would have before.

Dennis: That's pretty cool, huh?

Speaker 5: Yeah, it was exciting. [Chuckles]

Client/Speaker 6

Dennis: How far in the number of sessions were you, before you started to notice changes in yourself?

Speaker 6: My second session. After my first one, I went home, and my mom was like, "Okay, tell me everything. Tell me everything about it." I was like, "Well, I don't really know how to explain it. It's kind of interesting. I will have to see what happens next time." And then the second session, we went into a few more experiences and got a few other things cleared. I came out afterward and the sun was brighter outside, like my emotions were brighter. I was really happy. I was able to communicate with my mom like, "Well, this is what happened and this is how I feel," and I was able to talk to her about things that she might not have known affected me, but they did, and I explained it. So when I do these hypnotherapy processes it affects our whole family.

Client/Speaker 7

Speaker 7: I've hated my father basically my whole life, and the first time I did a session, I thought I'd gotten over that, but then there were times when I got confused about how to feel about it. So the second time I met with you, I got to the point where I don't necessarily like him, but the pain is mostly gone. I can understand it and move forward. And that's pretty life-changing—to sit down and after hating someone and not understanding it for thirty years, to get over it in a couple of hours. It's amazing.

I mean, I have a relationship with him now. I don't have any intention of becoming close, because I don't know that I want that. I'd like it if he was a different person, but I can recognize that it's not something that's going to happen with the type of person he is. But he's around me, and that's a constant stimulus to me. I have to do a lot of my Mind Management stuff to not let myself slip back into anger and frustration. So there's some of it there still, but it's just like a dog that keeps biting your heels. You want to chase it away, but you don't hate it. You get used to it, and understand the situation. This whole thing is pretty powerful. That's why I'm here.

Client/Speaker 8

Dennis: So, the Mind Management stuff that we've been through...

Speaker 8: It's hard, really hard. I didn't realize it before this, but 90% of the time I'm off thinking about something else or imagining another negative scenario.

Dennis: Now when you say hard, you mean, it's hard because you have to stop and think about it and do the work?

Speaker 8: Yeah, I have to challenge the thoughts that are coming to my mind, second to second, what I'm thinking, and change my future expectations, question whether or not someone's judging me, or that person's motivations. I have to stop and remember that I don't actually know their intentions. I don't know that whatever outcome I'm thinking about is going to turn out bad, and I didn't realize that I spend so much time doing this. I get stuck. It's a struggle to stay positive, I guess.

Dennis: You can be fixated into that thought pattern.

Speaker 8: Yeah, for sure.

Client/Speaker 9

Dennis: You're spending more and more time out of the back of your head and focused on and looking at the life around you. How would you describe that, brighter? People call it clearer. What does that do for you when you get out of the back of your head and know you're consciously focused outward now?

Speaker 9: Well for me, it feels more like I'm using both hemispheres of my brain, which is different for me and nice. And being able to do that, I can think more clearly, and instead of seeing things as flat, I'm seeing them in three dimensions. Then too, I have a positive sense of not doubting myself. I think I feel reassurance there, and confidence—I'm not doubting what I'm seeing and I'm seeing more than a flat surface.

Dennis: When you say confidence, do you feel this has actually increased your self-confidence?

Speaker 9: Uh-huh.

Dennis: And your judgment, decisions?

Speaker 9: Right, before, even though I was looking at something, I was like, "Am I seeing this correctly? Do I really understand what I'm seeing?" Even with my eyesight now, I am seeing well.

Wendy's Story

My name is Wendy and I am thirty-eight, married with two children. I worked with Dennis twenty years ago when I was a senior in high school. I was having some problems with my emotions then, especially understanding why I was sad so much of the time. So he took me through the process of Mind Management, and as I learned about consciousness, imagination, memory, and emotion, he taught me how to move through each section of my mind. As I did so I was able to understand why I was feeling the way I was. In the years since, I've noticed that when I have a situation that I don't understand, or I'm reacting in a way that seems contrary to how I feel I should, I go into my memory and find out why, and I've been able to pull out past situations that explain why I've been reacting the way I have. Then I am able to handle it—let it go and move forward.

For all of these years, I've been able to move within my mind in ways that have been very positive. I've found that I can create emotions within myself that are positive or negative. I also find that when I choose to experience the emotional aspect of myself, it helps me when I need to grieve or be happy. But then I can also pull out of that when I need to be logical. I find that if I need to understand things, it is easier for me to find the knowledge I need when I move my Intelligence forward to consciousness, to the middle of my forehead, where I am in the logical analytical state. Here is where I can best figure out and resolve problems.

If I didn't have the ability to do this, I think I would be lost, and I wouldn't be able to understand and help my children or help others. I think as we understand ourselves, we are able to reach out and help others a lot more effectively.

CHAPTER FOUR

My Understanding of the Mind/Brain/Body Connection

I received an early morning call one Saturday from a client who felt he had received wonderful benefits from our hypnotherapy sessions. He said he wanted me to visit with someone—a good friend of his who was having some difficulty. An hour later, he picked me up and we drove towards the mountains and into the upper bench areas of a very classy neighborhood. The home looked like a grand hotel or a mansion in a Hollywood movie, with a gated entrance and a long, winding driveway. I asked who this friend was and was told that he was a financial investor.

My friend rang the doorbell; the owner of the house answered the door. My client introduced me by saying, "This is Dennis, my friend the hypnotist." The gentleman of the house was an older man who immediately stated that no one was going to hypnotize him. He displayed all of the normal misinformed notions about hypnosis as he made it clear that no one was going to be allowed to control his mind. He was obviously completely unaware of our actual intention in coming.

I then said to the gentleman, "Your friend here is concerned about you, and he drove me all the way up here. Would you mind telling me what it is that you are worried about or are having difficulty with?" I had already observed that he had a tic in his right hand—the thumb and forefinger would jerk upward once a minute or so.

My client said, "Is there something you could do to help him with his hand?" The gentleman looked at him with disgust and asked, "How in the world is a hypnotist going to help me with my hand?" I explained that hypnosis or trance can help us gain access to our subconscious, where most of our problem thoughts are located. I said that I would not hypnotize him in the way he may have seen done in stage shows. But if he was willing to simply concentrate and focus on his thoughts for a moment, like he does when he daydreams, there might be something that we could do for him.

He looked at me with curiosity as I explained that we sometimes have a mental *script* or phrase stuck or fixated in our belief system, words that get repeated over and over again in our subconscious mind. These thought scripts may generate specific electrical frequency content in the brain that we identify as emotions. The brain is an electrical center that runs everything in the body through a myriad of frequencies sent to the various parts of the body. I told him I believed that thoughts have specific frequencies that seem to correlate with particular parts of the body. In his case, certain thoughts of his mind, generating electrical energy in the brain, identified as emotions were dumping off as a maladaptive electrical energetic frequency into his hand causing his had to spasm or jerk each and every time he experienced the thought script.

I went on, "It's just like when we wake up in the morning and have a song repeating over and over in our mind that we find ourselves singing for half of the morning." I had never known what to call this experience other than useless "mind chatter." Now it is referred to as an *earworm*.

I continued explaining that if he were to focus and concentrate deeply, just close his eyes for a moment, he might be able to connect the dots between the thoughts that I believed were generating what we call a *physical abreaction*—in this case the repeated involuntary jerking motion of his forefinger and thumb. The abreaction could be the release of electrical energy in the brain every time he thought the repeating phrase. That *predominant thought* needs to be changed and shut off permanently from nervous system, I said, adding that I didn't know why he had a particular thought dumping into his fingers, but he could probably find out.

Out of pure curiosity, as we still stood in the entrance of his home, he closed his eyes and started to focus, looking for a thought that came whenever his hand jerked. In just a moment his hand jerked, and his head involuntarily turned to the side as he felt a faint understanding and acknowledgment that a specific thought was indeed connected to the jerking motion.

A little while later his hand jerked again, and this time his head turned further around, a *secondary abreaction* connected to his recognition that there was such a thought. The third time his hand jerked, he opened his eyes, looked at me, and said confidently, "I never should have signed that check. I never should have signed that check. I just never should have signed that check!"

I asked him if he would mind sharing the story so I would understand what was going on. He then described how six months earlier a group of investors had come to his house and talked him into investing in a project. He wrote a substantial check, in the millions of dollars, and within ninety days, he had been swindled out of the money.

I asked him if this was when his hand began to have the tic. He acknowledged that it was. He said that he had signed the check because of the social pressure coming from people he thought were his friends. He was extremely disappointed in both himself and them.

At that point I turned from my role as a hypnotist to my role as a hypnotherapist. As a hypnotherapist, I challenge thinking errors, to help shut down the incorrect thoughts that generate the electrical content that is being dumped into the body. I did so by looking him straight in the eye and saying, "But you did sign the check, didn't you?" I asked him what it really meant to him to have lost that money. "Are you going to lose this mansion? Are you not going to be able to eat next week? What does losing that money really mean to you?" He answered that he would not lose his home or starve, as he had plenty of money left. But it hurt his feelings that people whom he respected, loved, and trusted would take advantage of him in such a way. I acknowledged that anyone would feel the same way he did about the situation. But I continued to challenge him to take responsibility for his action, to acknowledge that he was still okay, and to admit that even at his age we all can learn lessons about people and about discernment. He acknowledged that there were still things for him to learn and grow from in life.

As he changed his thought processes towards accountability and responsibility, recognizing the lessons learned from this experience, he replaced the negative script and his hand relaxed to normal.

How Negative Emotions Produce Illness

There is a conversation that I have had with many about whether it is our thoughts that cause chemical imbalances in the brain or the chemical imbalance that generates thoughts. Again, I am not a doctor or scientist, but from personal observation I have developed an opinion on this "which comes first, the chicken or the egg" question. I have come to believe that our accepted primary or predominant thoughts generate the chemical releases in the brain, as the emotional energy is created. Then the released chemicals generate frequency sensations that are stimulations interpreted as secondary or sub-thoughts giving supportive structure to the accepted predominant thought beliefs.

Most of us have long heard, "Don't worry so much! You'll get an ulcer." The thoughts we associate with worrying are often those we have magnified in our imaginations, then justified and validated with data from our memories, and in turn amplified through our emotions. This unhelpful electrical emotional frequency that is generated as worry then knocks the stomach off its normal frequencies and may cause it to secrete excess acid. The excess acid burns holes in the lining of the stomach, and now we have ulcers. I know that in some cases it is stated that stomach ulcers are created by a particular bacteria or virus. In those cases it may be that the worry maladaptive frequencies are enough to keep the stomach in an immune compromised state and thus the organic pathology has opportunity to grow and flourish.

It makes sense to me that emotional content in the brain is energy that acts somewhat like electricity. It also makes sense to me that when we hold a predominant behavior-producing belief, especially one we think about regularly, the electrical content it generates may be dumped into the body via the central nervous system. It's as if every thought has a frequency, but certain thoughts generate frequencies that are *maladaptive* (unsuitable, inadequate, or faulty) in the body.

Every organ, every gland, every muscle group, and so forth provide a potential dumping ground for particular maladaptive emotional frequencies, even as they are receiving a normal range of frequencies meant to operate that part of the body. For example, some researchers believe that anger often dumps into the liver and can cause the liver to malfunction, leading to digestive problems such as irritable bowel syndrome.

It's long been accepted that love and hate dump into the heart, and that depression and other emotions may also affect its functioning. Think about it: When we are in love, the heart tends to beat firm and strong, delivering increased oxygen levels throughout the body which energize our entire being. Hate generates the opposite effect.

I believe that thoughts are matter that has energetic frequencies and every part of the body—organs, glands, muscle groups—run on different frequencies emitted from the brain. Healthy, positive thoughts emit healthy frequencies and stimulate the brain and body in healthy processes.

Maladaptive thoughts generate inadequate or faulty frequencies that are also released from the brain, but interfere with normal, healthy frequencies and so cause long-term chronic dysfunction and eventual disease.

*This **dis-ease** in the mind eventually becomes disease in the body. We have come to identify these unsuitable or maladaptive frequencies as emotions with names like fear and hate.*

Thus, the concept of producing maladaptive frequencies may account for psychosomatically induced illness or the process of *dis-ease* in the mind that eventually manifests itself as *disease* in the body. Whenever someone successfully challenges and releases worrisome, hateful, vengeful, angry, anxious thoughts through hypnotherapy and replaces them with positive future expectations, or when someone challenges anger and replaces it with peace and love, the brain can begin to send out natural healthy frequencies again to the parts of the body that were negatively affected before. Once back into healthy frequencies, these body systems begin to heal naturally. Many hypnotherapists have observed that the side effects of successful hypnotherapy (in the way that we teach it and do it) include increased mental, emotional, spiritual, and physical health.

In fact, long-term or chronic pain not associated with an acute injury or illness, and which doctors have a difficult time diagnosing, is usually called stress induced illness or pain. The root cause can be often discovered in pain-control hypnotherapy sessions. It results from emotional content being dumped into a part of the body that causes an organ or a muscle group to spasm or tightens up, nerves to twist, and so forth. The pain actually comes from the continual release of maladaptive electrical energy into that part of the body and the pain is created by emotional content. The following headache story from a student illustrates these points.

The headache

It was during the afternoon class of the second week of hypnotherapist training that I had developed an extreme headache. It must have been obvious that I was in pain, because Dennis looked at me and asked me what was wrong. I told him that I thought my head was about to burst. He asked me if I knew of any organic pathology or reason why I was having this headache. I answered no, that I did not know of any reason I should be having it, other than I had been being triggered emotionally by the subjects of the day.

He explained that if it were psychosomatic induced pain that we could possibly clear it quite quickly and that if it was not emotionally induced and did not clear, then I should go be checked by my regular medical practitioners. He then asked if I would like some help with the headache pain. I said that I would appreciate it if there were something that could be done. He walked over to me, placed one hand on my head, and began to rotate my head in a counterclockwise fashion. He later explained to me that he did this as a misdirection to get my conscious mind out of the way so that my critical factor would be open where it would take in the intended suggestions.

As he was rotating my head, he made a number of positive suggestions and affirmations to me and asked me to lock onto them and make a choice to believe them or not. This lasted for maybe a minute or two. Then he asked me on the pain scale from 1 to 10 where my headache pain was just a minute before he started rotating my head. I told him that it was at an 8. He asked me where it was now and I told him that it was about a three or four.

Then he explained that there were still several more negative thoughts that were painful thoughts to me about me. This time he had me lock onto the feelings of the pain itself. He had me go deeper into trance and asked me to hear and understand the voice that the pain represented. What was the pain saying to me about me in negative ways? I was able to identify these thoughts and tell him one by one what they were. Each time he had me restate the negative self-defeating, self-incriminating, negative thoughts, with what he called the opposite truth for me. As I restated those thoughts, telling myself the opposite idea in positive ways, my pain levels continue to decrease. We did this for a few more minutes until we had cleared all of my negative thinking.

My headache was completely gone and I was experiencing zero pain. It was a surprising experience for me to learn that our own negative, self-incriminating, self-defeating thoughts are painful to us in our spirits and are manifested to us as pain in our minds and bodies. When we learn to challenge and change them to new more appropriate thoughts that are the actual truth for us, the truth sets us free. I was immediately free of the painful headache and the entire process only took a few minutes.

We can successfully challenge and change self-incriminating and self-defeating thoughts. However, if we allow them to once again be part of our thinking they can regenerate the previous painful conditions. Psychosomatically induced disease is caused by the release of maladaptive emotional content. This is the mind/brain/ body connection as I understand it.

Client Comments on her Experience with Dis-ease

A middle aged wife and mother of four children reports: I came to Dennis because it was suggested to me from a nurse practitioner that works in the same clinic as Dennis. I was having panic attacks and she felt it would help. I had seen his flyers in the office and read about hypnotherapy on the internet. I was curious about it but also nervous. I had gone to a stage show and been what is often referred to as hypnotized, but I knew this was something totally different.

I have a history of trauma which causes major anxiety. I was very nervous about going to Dennis because I was afraid of not being in control and feeling out of control is a major anxiety issue for me. So I went to Dennis because of panic attacks due to an eating disorder, past trauma panic attacks, and premenopausal.

When I came to the first visit I was very scared. Dennis talked with me and explained things and made sure I was okay with everything. I brought my husband for support. Dennis put us both at ease and was very open and honest and very comforting. I felt safe and supported.

Each visit was a time for me to work through things I hadn't been able to fully work through in the past. I have done lots of traditional talk therapy and other forms of therapy. The hypnotherapy helped me to fully work through some issues I never worked through. Each time I came in the office I felt I could be totally honest with Dennis. If I wasn't comfortable with something, I could tell him. He never pushed me, which was very important to me. Also he took time to explain the process so I knew what was going on. I felt as though I was in the process of this healing work. It wasn't something that was done to me, or done to "fix me", which was an issue for me with other therapies.

I learned to stay in the present. (Conscious) I use the tools I learned in hypnotherapy (Spiritual Mind Management) and I feel like I am on the path of healing and happiness, which is not something I have ever felt in the past.

Using Hypnotherapy to Heal the Body

This mind-body connection is one of the major reasons why working through past negative experiences is so important. As hypnotherapists, we can often alleviate painful thoughts, which in turn can improve health by alleviating physical pains. We teach people how to *desensitize* the thoughts that are causing the pain in the first place. That is how to make certain thoughts less sensitive by altering their perception of the memory and adjusting the amount of imagination they have applied to the event. In this way improved health, both mental and physical, is the natural result of doing behavioral change work that helps people recognize unnecessary negative thinking and accept more appropriate positive thinking in its place.

Much related information can be found online from searches for the mind-body connection or psychosomatic illness. One common example of successful hypnotherapy sessions that result in better physical health is the reduction of migraine headaches. People who come in for assistance with migraine headaches are usually thinking in terms of pain-control training, similar to training expectant mothers in painless birthing techniques. Thus, the main concern of the medical community about using hypnotherapy for pain control is that it might mask symptoms that are important for medical treatment. For instance, a doctor might worry that removing or relieving pain when someone has something like a brain tumor would simply delay a proper medical diagnosis.

However, no client I have ever worked with has come to see me before first seeking medical treatment for migraine headaches. Such clients show up at my door because they have been everywhere else and no one has yet come up with an answer as to why they are experiencing debilitating headaches. Since the normal course of allopathic treatment is to medicate (and not much else), the suffering person is still searching for answers and decides one day to try hypnotherapy.

I would also like to add that I have never seen anyone who has been taught to use hypnotherapy for pain control develop the ability to stay pain free for more than a short period of time in the wake of an ongoing organic pathology (like a virus or bacteria) or an acute injury. As a hypnotherapist, I am always cautious in chronic pain situations. I ask the client to inform their doctors that they will be working with a hypnotherapist for behavioral modification. Sometimes I ask the client to obtain a prescription from their attending physician and to have the doctor call me if they have any questions or concerns; it depends on who referred them to me.

One of my associates or I will then proceed to do the hypnotherapy work of discovering what painful thoughts are in the person's subconscious. We know how to desensitize the painful thoughts stemming from events or experiences; we can also help the person shut down the specific thought that is being amplified through the imagination, thereby stopping the emotional content or electrical energy that is causing the pain. When this is accomplished successfully for those who do not have a clear medical reason for the pain, the mind relaxes and shuts off the pain-causing maladaptive frequencies, and the pain dissipates. This is our normal course of action for helping people to eliminate migraines that were caused unbeknownst to themselves by their emotions.

A recent client experience

I have suffered from migraines since my early 20s. About seven years ago they got so bad I had a migraine almost daily for over a year. I had all of the tests done, MRI, heart bubble study, CT scans etc.; but nothing showed why I was having such bad migraines. I have been on all of the different prophylactic medications for migraines, as well as acute medications for when they hit. All of the medicines I have taken have had bad side effects, some that I am still dealing with after stopping the medication years ago and none of them took away my migraines. I have had to just learn to live with them and occasionally I've been so sick I've had to go into the ER for stronger medication. But even those medications don't get rid of my migraines; they just help me sleep so it's duller when I wake up.

Then I started my hypnotherapy with Dennis. I knew to expect migraines because every time I talked about past emotional problems, it magnified my migraines by at least 10. The second time with Dennis, I just mentioned my migraine so he had me work on that first. He got rid of my migraine that day, which in itself was amazing. But I haven't had one *since*, which is even more amazing! I haven't gone this long not only without a headache, but without a migraine. If this were the only benefit to hypnotherapy, it would have been enough, but it's only a small part of the benefits! I would recommend this to anyone experiencing pain, emotional problems, anxiety, low self-esteem... basically, you name it, and you can learn to control it!

Hypnotherapy to me has been instead of me letting the world control my decisions and reactions to things, I have now learned that I have control over my entire life! - Megan

We address other long-term chronic pain successfully in the same way, pain that has no known or diagnosed attachment to any acute or chronic medical condition. Much of our success comes from teaching client's self-hypnosis skills that help them learn to relax and sleep soundly, change their eating habits, and exercise regularly—all of which improve overall health.

Thirty-two Years of Misery

My coauthor, Craig, relates his personal experience with this entire process: One autumn, when I was in fifth grade, a young girl in my class whom I had known for several years would occasionally pass out and go into a convulsion. This was quite alarming for a young person to see, especially since I didn't know or understand that she had epilepsy. Over a period of years, I saw her struggle with this several times.

One day she had another seizure and I was affected differently than before. A feeling of panic and despair came over me. I felt sick to my stomach, and I had to make a dash for the bathroom because of instant diarrhea. Not being in control of the situation in general and then having to deal with an urgent restroom problem was all very upsetting.

I have learned since that this was a *sensitizing event* for me. There are three different kinds of sensitizing events: 1) initial events, where a thought pattern is first established; 2) symptom-producing events, where a behavior pattern emerges; and 3) symptom-intensifying events, which compound the behavioral effect. Seeing her seizure was the symptom-producing event (2) for me.

In those days, if you were feeling sick at school you could go and tell the teacher, who would either call your parents to come and get you or you could walk home. It just so happened that my folks were out of town, and so I walked home and lay down on my bed to recover. Our next-door-neighbor, Mrs. Jorgensen, came over and gave me a bottle of Pepto-Bismol and told me it would make me feel better and help with the diarrhea. Apparently the school had called her and asked if she would check on me. In my small rural town, things just worked that way.

Unfortunately, Pepto-Bismol would come to be a staple in my life for the next twenty years. The diarrhea continued to occur, infrequently, for the next couple of years. Then, in seventh grade, it became a near daily occurrence, especially right after lunch or dinner. My folks finally took me to the family doctor to see what could be done, and he prescribed some pills that helped, but were not the cure-all I had hoped for.

It was highly inconvenient, as a junior high kid, to have the most pressing thought every afternoon at school being, "When will the diarrhea problem appear next, and how fast and discreetly can I make it to a bathroom?" I became far too familiar with the location of just about every restroom facility in my small town. Often sweat would bead up on my forehead because of pain, nausea, and the feelings of pressure in my abdomen, not to mention how anxious I was not to have an accident in class.

I made it through those very difficult years without letting my friends know about the problem. But when I was in high school, in addition to the pills I would take, I had to be careful of what I ate as well. I would often not eat when traveling with the track team or choir because I had to spend several hours on a school bus. Many times I would just plain suffer until we arrived at our destination. Being on the track team was great; however not being able to eat for hours before a race did not exactly add to my strength and endurance.

When I began to date, I didn't often take my dates out for dinner. Most people thought it was because I was cheap, but the main piece of the equation was that my system was too unpredictable, and I didn't want to take the chance. I will say that I was pretty good at slipping away quickly if I needed to, without drawing attention to myself. It's amazing how adaptable we are to circumstances that come about if we have enough determination to do something we absolutely have to. By now it should be clear that the difficulties I was having with my intestinal tract were trying, to say the least. In those days, no one thought about my condition as anything other than chronic diarrhea; we now call it Irritable Bowel Syndrome. It plagues about 45 million people in the U.S. and is caused by several factors, including stress.

Throughout a two-year mission for my church, marriage, and then children, my hope was that this highly inconvenient situation would fade into the sunset and I would have peace. This was not the case, however. In fact, things got worse. Not only did the diarrhea continue, but a new situation developed where, when I didn't have diarrhea, I had the opposite situation. The constipation caused hemorrhoids and rectal fissures that would bleed and be so painful that nothing could mask or even take the edge off the discomfort and pain.

By now I had learned that certain foods were time bombs in my system, such as all the good stuff: cake, ice cream, chocolate, cheese products, candy bars, pizza, and other rich foods. In fact, my wife would often say, when we finished a meal and I needed to excuse myself, "You can't possibly have to go; things don't work that fast!" All I could say was that they did for me!

How Hypnotherapy Ended the Pain

After about fifteen years, I could no longer stand the pain, and after several months working with a noted colorectal surgeon to see if my body could mend these physical problems on its own, I finally scheduled surgery. To explain the time frame, I was forty-two years old when I scheduled the surgery and this condition started when I was ten.

Three days before I would enter the hospital, my wife and I were near my closest friend's home. I called Dennis Parker and said, "Do you have a few minutes to see if there is anything in my belief system that is causing this condition?" I did not want to repeat the experience of the last thirty-two years since all the surgery was going to accomplish was to repair damage that had been done to my body for over three decades.

Dennis and I had worked through lots of concerns and issues over the years, but it had never occurred to me to work on this one even though I had had hypnotherapy courses and knew the power of what the mind could do. As I write this chapter, eleven additional years later, I remember vividly the two hours Dennis and I spent routing through the process to find the root cause for my three-decade-long problem. We did a lot of laughing as I went through the emotional releases of the different layers. In fact, there was so much laughter that he and I were literally crying tears from the funny things I was saying and describing as I regressed back to the age of four where we finally found the root of my dilemma.

The beginning was simple but impactful. My initial sensitizing event was a discussion I had with my mom about taking a nap. I was protesting that I didn't need chairs put by the side of my bed in case I would roll off. In those days, most people didn't have bed rails to put between the mattresses, so my mom would take two dining room chairs and put them next to the bed. Using all the abilities I had as a four-year-old, I tried to convince her I didn't need the chairs. But she would not relent.

For some reason this made a deep impression on me — it was clear to me that I would not roll off. Having her put those chairs there was such a seemingly tiny thing; however it would have a huge effect on my life starting from age ten for the next thirty-two years. It boiled down to the fact that I felt I was not in control of the situation.

Once we understood what the cause of my thirty-two-year-old problem was, we were able to use the process that we have come to know so well to find the erroneous belief I needed to desensitize and correct it so that it would not cause me any more grief. And that is exactly how it happened.

As soon as I could eat regular food following the colorectal surgery, I did not have any symptoms of irritable bowel any more. I had averaged at least two to three episodes of diarrhea every week for the past three decades, and now it was gone. I was able to eat without concern; ice cream, cake, chocolate, cheese, pizza, and even the richest foods did not bother me at all. I hardly knew how to act because I could pay greater attention to other things without a constant feeling of anxiety.

When I sleep now, I'm always on the edge of the bed and I stay there all night long. I like it there. I think I could sleep on the edge of a cliff and never roll off!

I share this experience to illustrate the kind of negative things that can be conquered once we correct our belief systems. If this had not happened to me, I don't know that I would have believed it myself. The connection between the mental and the physical is amazing, and this experience brought home the power that the mind has over the body in a whole new way to me. If something so trivial could have such a long-lasting effect, what else is going on in my head that is holding me back or causing me to not be the best I can be? I can't help but wonder.

Hay fever as told by Dennis

As a young boy and into my adult life, I had suffered with hay fever for many years. We had always had animals, some cattle and horses. I had done chores from as early as I can remember, throwing hay and other feed into their troughs was a daily experience. When we would go out into the fields in the summer and haul the hay out of the field and stack it into the barn, it was always dusty, and made me extremely miserable. I had all the symptoms, the cough, the itchy watery eyes, the painful sinuses, the drippy runny nose, the continual sneezing, and so forth.

While in hypnotherapy training I learned that we can detach from allergens, desensitizing ourselves from symptom producing substances such as hay and hay fever. So with what I had learned about how to access the subconscious, I went into deep self-hypnosis searching for my stories in my mind, my personal truths if you will, about hay fever.

I went back in my mind to a time of about the age of six years old. I was in my grandmother's living room in Clearfield, Utah. Several of my aunts and uncles there were with my mother and other family members. My uncle Bud was sitting in the corner sneezing and coughing and exhibiting all of the symptoms and signs of hay fever. It was the first time that I had heard of such a thing and yet as I observed him, he was getting a lot of attention from everyone in the room. Poor Bud they would say, he has such a hard time this time of year. Poor Bud hay fever just causes him so much misery.

I realized somehow I had associated myself with my uncle Bud and had taken on the same symptoms through association. As I went through the desensitizing, disassociation processes, it took me several attempts throughout a couple of years to be able to control the symptoms. As the symptoms would start to develop I would have to stop and find a quiet place. Then take the time to challenge and change my personal behavioral producing inappropriate beliefs. It actually took me a couple of seasons of working through this desensitization process until I can now say that I have been free of hay fever for the past fifteen years.

I have also worked with clients who have been able to shut down other allergic causing symptoms such as spider bites, bedbug bites, rashes, and other such physical symptoms and ailments.

Hay fever as told by Craig

As Dennis shared his story about hay fever, I had to share mine as well. I had hay fever since the time I was about twelve years old. It was at age thirty two that I did the same kind of search as Dennis did to see what prompted my allergies. Over the years, I took several medications to calm the symptoms so that I would not look like a glazed donut every time I ground wheat for my wife to make bread, mowed the lawn or got out in the yard.

I went back to the time that I was twelve years old hauling hay at a church farm and remembered how heavy the bails where and that the hay would get into my eyes and nose and just stuffed everything up. I hated the hay and what it did to me, however it did gave me an excuse not to have to haul hay anymore. That was convenient, but it had a long term impact on me, think back to the glazed donut scenario. Now it is gone. As I worked through the false belief that it was ok to hate hay and not do the work, my allergies cleared up and very seldom do they ever return. Just to test the staying power of the new belief, I would often take a big sniff from the freshly ground wheat flour my wife would use for the bread. I didn't sneeze.

Boils (as told by a student)

When I started the hypnotherapy class with Dennis I knew that I would have a few things to clear up. Little did I know that I would be clearing nearly my entire forty six years of life. I had been breaking out with boils on my entire head and neck. I could not figure out what was causing this. I had talked to my doctor about it and he did not have any answers for me. During one of my sessions with Dennis the emotion of hate and anger surfaced and I was able to vent it out. I instantly felt the results of removing anger. I felt lighter, brighter and the boils stopped surfacing. I also looked like I had just had Botox. The lines between my eyes and the lines around my mouth softened. It was an amazing feeling.

I also was listening to the white cd's series during the night. I was falling asleep so fast that I didn't know what the cd's said. I could feel a lot of physical, emotional and spiritual changes happening. I felt a little overwhelmed with how fast things were shifting. One night I turned the weight loss cd on and was able to listen to the words before I fell asleep. I realized why I felt such a change. The next morning I weighed myself to see if my body had responded to melting off sixteen ounces a day. I had lost five and half pounds in four days. That is the first time I have lost weight without trying.

The mind/brain/body connection is a powerful one!

CHAPTER FIVE

The "Mystery" of Hypnosis and Trance

Before I can go any further in teaching you about your inner Intelligence, I need to introduce you to the benefits of using hypnosis and hypnotherapy. Both are an important means of allowing individuals to feel and control the movement of their Intelligences within their minds.

For centuries this subject was remarkably misunderstood, even shrouded in fear and narrow thinking akin to keeping people on shore waving to those few who understood that the earth is really round or that heavier-than-air objects can fly. But stereotypes of the past are just that—stereotypes, based in fiction, not reality.

The truth about the non-mystery of hypnosis is that it is not just one state of mind. Hypnosis is a general term used to describe our natural ability as humans to enter a number of trance states that we commonly experience. We describe these states of mind in everyday language, calling them by such names as "daydreaming" or "deep sleep." We naturally go through hypnotic states as easily as we slip into and out of daydreaming or go from consciousness to deep sleep. In fact most of us naturally go in and out of trance all day long as our minds shift into various levels of concentration and focus, both internal and external. The Intelligence moves fluidly through various states of awareness, concentration, or trance.

Hypnosis Helps People Change Habits

The general public is finally beginning to have an awareness of some of the benefits of the proper use of hypnosis and hypnotherapy. It is becoming more common, for example, to see hypnosis portrayed positively for its effectiveness in overcoming unhealthy habits like overeating and smoking, eliminate fears and phobias, and develop confidence and self-esteem.

In spite of the reputation of hypnosis (and by implication, hypnotherapy) as a way to control the minds of others, both are the opposite: they are gifts that can help us bring ourselves and others into the state of having a clear and free mind. As Virgil Hayes stated over and over again, "Powerful people empower others, and weak people create dependencies."

One of my favorite success stories is a gentleman who came into one of our group therapy programs who was seventy-three years old and had smoked for fifty-seven years. He said that he had been everywhere and done everything to try to stop. He had chewed gum, used all of the patches, and more. It required several hypnotherapy sessions, but this man is now a nonsmoker and is excited to have the prospect of his health improving. He continues to listen to our recordings as an ongoing strengthening program.

Another is the story of an airline pilot who was having difficulty sleeping in the many changing hotel environments he was constantly subjected to in the course of his travels. He is now able to sleep well and enjoy a peaceful rest no matter where he is.

Hypnotherapy is a very effective tool in other personal journeys as well. What would it be worth to correct self-limiting beliefs, bad habits or problem behaviors like the following in your life and in the lives of your family members and friends?

- "My parents don't love me."
- "It must be my fault."
- "I am not as smart as others."

- "If only I had been better."
- "I am not good enough to… "
- "I am unworthy because… "
- "I'll just sleep a little longer."/"I wish I could sleep."
- "I should exercise, but I'm just too busy."
- "I'll get started on that important project tomorrow."
- "I'm sorry I missed the deadline. I just couldn't help it."

Self-limiting beliefs like these are generally developed in childhood. They are taken into our belief systems before we have the ability to think critically. Unfortunately, they are easily amplified in our imaginations, generating a great number and variety of self-defeating behaviors. But hypnotherapy can help you gain the upper hand.

My colleagues and I routinely see our clients resolving past issues and establishing new, positive behaviors. We have witnessed hundreds of people using our hypnotherapy techniques for:

- Stress management and relaxation
- Sleep problems
- Pain control, including painless childbirth
- Unresolved grief over the death of a loved one
- Memory improvement, including help finding lost items

- Improved study habits and overcoming test-taking anxiety
- Anger management
- Improved self-confidence
- Overcoming bed wetting and thumb sucking
- Increased self-control and self-discipline
- Enhanced sales performance, sports performance and public speaking
- Overcoming fears and phobias, such as flying, heights, or insects

In addition, we have seen people conquer maladaptive habits and halt repeated inappropriate choices that cause harm to themselves and others, such as:

- Smoking
- Weight management problems (over or under-eating)
- Gambling
- Fixation with video games and electronic gaming
- Constant seeking of sensory stimulation, such as pornography
- Excessive TV watching

Hypnosis throughout History

Hypnosis has been used throughout history by healers from witch doctors to priests. According to *The Complete Guide to Hypnosis* by Leslie M. LeCron, the oldest reference to it found so far is in the Egyptian Evers Papyrus of three thousand years ago. The ancient Greeks had sleep temples where patients came to be healed and were put into hypnosis. Most primitive peoples have used hypnosis and do so still at the present time.

Continuing the next few paragraphs with the *"Complete guide to Hypnosis"*, the modern history of hypnosis appears to have begun in the 1780's with a physician named Franz Anton Mesmer, who was practicing in Vienna. One day he watched a street magician perform an act with lodestones or magnets. The magician declared that he could make a spectator do his bidding by touching him with one of these magnets, and he proceeded to put on a demonstration that proved it to be true. His secret was the power of suggestion, of course. Mesmer, however, believed the magnets actually had power of their own. From this belief he developed his theory of magnetism, claiming that good health depends on the direction of magnetic flow, which could easily be reversed.

At one time, three thousand patients a day begged to see Mesmer. In order to accommodate them all, he had to change his technique. Initially he would place a tub in the middle of a large room from which protruded a number of so-called "magnetic rods." People sat in the tub holding onto these rods, believing that the magnetic flow in their bodies would be corrected and thus cure them. Again, the power of suggestion was at work.

Since it became impossible to accommodate all of the prospective patients in such tubs, Mesmer would go into the yard, touch a tree with his so-called magnetic rod, and declare the tree to be magnetized. People only had to touch the magnetized tree to be miraculously cured of their ills. He became the vogue of French nobility and the upper class, and his practice became very profitable.

However, Benjamin Franklin, then the U.S. Ambassador to France, was put on a committee appointed to investigate Mesmer. Franklin watched a demonstration of his techniques and pronounced this verdict: "If these people get well at all, they seem to do so by their own imagination." Thereafter, mesmerism suffered a decided drop in popularity.

Still, patients in an obvious hypnotic state had been observed, and many doctors studied mesmerism in secret, one of these being an English physician named James Braid. By accident, a patient of Braid's entered the first stage of mesmerism while staring at a fixed light as he waited for an eye examination to begin. In 1841, to avoid the contempt in which mesmerism was held, Braid coined the term hypnotism, derived from the Greek word for sleep. Braid's observation of our natural trance abilities revealing sleeplike qualities was responsible for his choice of this term for induced trance phenomena. He published a paper on achieving hypnotism through fixation that was eventually published in 165 languages and dialects.

In the 1840s, another British surgeon, James Esdaile, who worked in an Indian prison hospital, saw a demonstration of mesmerism while in England on vacation. He witnessed a patient anesthetized by hypnosis, and when he returned to India he began to use the methods he had seen demonstrated. Esdaile performed over three thousand operations with hypnosis as his sole anesthetic agent, over three hundred of these being major surgeries. One observer told of witnessing Esdaile remove a cancerous eye from a patient while the other eye looked on unblinking.

Like others interested in this subject, Esdaile was persecuted by his colleagues. He was forced to leave the hospital in India and return to England, where the British Medical Association tried him for charlatanism. During the trial, one of the physicians claimed that Esdaile was sacrilegious because God meant for man to feel pain and Esdaile was preventing that with hypnosis. Hypnosis continued to go through periods of high popularity and times when interest waned. By 1955 the British Medical Association reported that hypnosis was a valuable tool in medical treatment. In 1958, the American Medical Association followed suit. Although advocates of hypnosis are no longer persecuted, few courses on it are offered in traditional schools. Those interested in it usually have to seek out training on their own.

Hypnosis and Hypnotherapy Today

Hypnosis is still the name commonly used today to describe a state of trance, although some people prefer other names (such as autogenic conditioning, a name for hypnosis used in sports conditioning) to avoid using a word with negative connotations. The idea of hypnosis as "mind control" is still strong and keeps many people from trying it.

Many uninformed people feel uneasy with the idea of being hypnotized. For example, questions about hypnosis that I am often asked by those considering hypnotherapy include:

- Will I lose control?
- Will I do or say anything against my will?
- Will I remember everything about the session?
- Is it the hypnotist who makes me change?

People seem to think of hypnosis as having an independent power all of its own. Meanwhile, movies contribute to the misunderstanding by portraying negative or incorrect impressions of its supposed powers. The idea of mind control is perpetuated by stage hypnotists who attempt to create an illusion that the subjects are "now in my power."

Should the truth be known, people on stage who seem to do things they would not normally do are choosing their actions. Perhaps they have personal reasons for wanting to participate in the show; maybe they like attention or have always wanted to be onstage; or maybe they simply wish to experience what it's like to be hypnotized. More often than not, the people who accept an offer to come up and participate in a stage show are natural somnambulates (sleepwalkers) who are highly suggestible and walk around unawares in a chronic state of trance.

The fact is that no one will say or do anything in hypnosis that they would consider a violation of their morals or their core conscious beliefs. They in fact make a decision to do whatever they do. When hypnotized, you will not do or say anything that you normally would not do, say, or even think about naturally in your daily routines of life. Yes, you can lie in hypnosis or trance; it is not truth serum or some other Hollywood super power.

If I were to make an improper suggestion while you were in trance, you would likely do one of two things: reject the suggestion through what we call an abreaction, such as laughter or a jerking motion of your body (whereby the mind releases the rejected suggestion, the electrical emotional content release), or simply come out of trance.

When clients who are apprehensive about hypnosis come to me for a consultation to see if they might benefit from it, I explain the different trance states (described below) and assure them that I will assist them through the processes of hypnotherapy so that they will learn to control their own feelings. I explain that the only mind control involved is the improved control of their own minds that they will develop.

When it is properly understood, going into trance is a choice that can give each of us better internal control. All hypnosis is self-hypnosis. It can both lessen influences from the past or from outside sources and promote personal freedom through an increased conscious awareness of choice. The biggest danger in being in trance or hypnosis is being there unaware that you are doing so, and leaving yourself in a state of hyper suggestible vulnerability, or unawareness of dangers around you.

In fact, some potential clients are surprised to learn that they still have to personally make the changes they are hoping for. They are disappointed that hypnosis is not mind control. They are looking for the "magic pill," the quick easy fix. They want a "fast food" variety of mental, emotional, and spiritual sustenance that may provide plenty of calories, yet still lacks the truly nourishing substance that satisfies what their hearts hunger for.

These people must come to understand that their issues are in their minds and so they are ultimately the only ones who can change things. To make changes using hypnosis, they will need to work with the positive affirmations that are right for them, take time to listen to the appropriate recordings we make available, and follow the directions of the therapeutic prompts on our White Series CDs. Hypnotherapy is to work with a qualified hypnotherapist who assists you in finding, challenging, and changing thinking errors at a deep level.

The processes of hypnotism that we teach are ways to intentionally use certain states of mind that you and I enter every day without awareness or thinking about it. Recognizing and learning to utilize the natural ability to enter different kinds of trance is the easiest and fastest way to make desired changes and achieve goals. Individuals undergoing hypnotherapy must still make important changes in their own thoughts and beliefs as they work through the processes we teach. As with other things, inconsistency of effort and lack of diligent follow-through inhibit achieving desired results.

The Geometric Gradient: Making Changes Fast and Faster

You may have heard the term "paradigm shift"—when a change in belief or point of view radically alters the way you view your life and the world around you. Consider what we are suggesting: The axiom that it takes twenty-one days to develop a new behavior is more about the method of implementation than the speed at which change can really occur?

The hypnotherapy principles we teach in our trainings, seminars and at Certified Hypnotherapy Training School are the easiest and fastest ways to make positive personal change. Personal improvement is self-directed and has the potential to be accomplished at amazing speed. Rapid and permanent behavior modification is easier to achieve than you may have previously thought or imagined. How it works is surprisingly simple. My coauthor Craig recalls how he encountered one concept that has proven to be a game changer in describing what we do and how effective hypnotherapy can be.

> Twenty-five years ago in a graduate level class in finance, I learned the principle of a geometric gradient. In its simplest form, this can be described as a line graphed in such a way that it rises upwards at a gradual incline, then suddenly explodes in a way not unlike a rocket pulling away from the earth's atmosphere—first going hundreds of miles per hour, then tens of thousands of miles per hour once the restrictions of gravity have been overcome.
>
> If we could overcome the human gravity that restricts us in our subconscious minds, it makes sense that we could go from hundreds of miles an hour to a level exceeding tens of thousands of miles per hour, or as I like to think, going *past light speed* in changing our beliefs. After all, a geometric gradient occurs in nature, so why not allow it to occur in each one of us? Today we call this concept "going viral," something

that only had reference years ago to the spread of a dread disease.

Information is indeed powerful, so if the possibility of human beings achieving geometric gains does exist, how do we make the gravitational separation that will move us beyond our present sphere? In the next few chapters, you will see that we are working to get you to the point of having to determine for yourself if you have enough courage to learn something new and different from what much of the world sees as true. If you don't have the courage, kindly give this book to someone who you think is ready to jump on to a boat, plane, or rocket ship in order to achieve geometric outcomes.

The ability to become our own best behavioral therapist may seem lofty, but keep reading to broaden your point of view. What you will learn if you are open-minded is a natural process that can have such an astonishing effect upon you that it may seem unbelievable.

Read on, indeed! What do you have to lose except a few bad habits or a non- productive belief or two?

The Goal of Hypnotherapy

Hypnotherapy is the process of inducing varying levels of natural trance states and utilizing them for therapeutic behavior modification and change. It assumes that thoughts generate feelings and that strong emotions can be developed from those thoughts and feelings as people amplify them in their imagination. In other words, feelings generate behaviors since most of us tend to behave the way we feel. We act out our most predominant thoughts and our most predominant beliefs because they create our strongest feelings. We also develop habits or routine responses to our predominant thoughts and feelings. So our behaviors automatically manifest our most predominant thoughts, beliefs, and feelings as we naturally act them out.

Our goal at Certified Hypnotherapy Training School is to help individuals eradicate their harmful predominant thoughts and to establish new, more appropriate ones through the use of common, natural states of hyper suggestibility known as hypnosis. We teach people to establish new, positive, goal-achieving thoughts and beliefs by helping them to induce a suggestible state of mind and to employ "the power of suggestion."

Basically, we help develop new habits—new automatic behaviors—by establishing new predominant thoughts in place of formerly accepted undesirable mental programming. Most people become excited about this process when they begin to understand that they can change anything they want to in their behaviors by learning to program their "mental computer" for success. We aim to make this process of change a welcome and ongoing lifestyle where individuals seek continuous improvement and success in life.

Common areas of success include the following:

Pain control

One of the deeper trance states, where the mind desensitizes from pain, is now commonly called the Esdaile state after Dr. James Esdaile. This induced state is utilized today by many medical facilities for pain control. For example, painless childbirth programs based on hypnosis are standard in many hospitals and clinics across the country, allowing mother and child to experience faster recovery from the birthing process with less residual anesthetic for their bodies to overcome afterward. Hypnosis to control pain also has become a common practice in many dental offices throughout the country.

Two of our recently graduated students wanted to test our training and their ability to use hypnosis for pain control. One worked with the other in preconditioning, and then they went to the dentist together. They were excited to relate that the person having the dental work done had three fillings installed free of pain and discomfort without anesthetic.

Young people

As the father of eleven children who has seen them all through their teenage years, I have a keen interest in youth. Some of my most rewarding sessions are with young people facing behavioral issues—from bedwetting and thumb sucking to difficulty focusing on schoolwork and trouble memorizing, or test taking. Some children have difficulty focusing on their lessons in school or being quiet and sitting still. It is a pleasure to see the excitement these young people exhibit as they make their desired changes and improvements. Many parents and educators take our certifying courses just to work with such situations both in their families and professions.

Help with business

I have been a distribution center manager, sales manager, and sales trainer for many years with a national distribution company. With hypnotherapy and self-hypnosis training, I have helped people to overcome the many fears that come with sales, such as fear of public speaking or doing public demonstrations. I have helped people learn to pick up that fifty-pound telephone, excited to prospect for sales, make new friends, and grow their business and personal income. I have also assisted many to overcome fear of rejection, fear of failure, fear of the unknown, even—believe it or not—fear of being successful.

Advertisers make use of our Natural Trance States

Our natural trance abilities have been used for centuries to establish thoughts and beliefs in the minds of people. And like most things in life, these suggested beliefs could be meant for good or ill, depending upon the intent of the person making the suggestions and the content of the suggestions themselves.

People can be stimulated through suggestion to release and enhance the natural healing capabilities and properties of both the mind and body. On the other hand, people with evil intentions can attempt to use our natural trance ability to promote ill will.

Much advertising today takes advantage of our ability to go instantaneously into trance and become hyper suggestible. Incantation in the form of advertising jingles is used to implant thoughts, ideas, and beliefs in our minds. Radio and TV advertisers use catchy, suggestive phrases (a form of what we call affirmations) to encourage, influence, and persuade us to buy their products or services. In particular, music enhances our natural inclination to go into trance, increasing our susceptibility to suggestions. Television advertisements combine music, affirmation scripts, and visuals with the intent to put us into trance.

Most of us have noticed a consistent bombardment of advertising spots whenever a new product launch begins on radio or television. Advertisers know that we need to hear the name of the new product and picture ourselves using it in our imagination several times to get us to accept a mental association whereby we internalize the message, memorize it, and then have a desire to own or use the item. We may often accept their suggestions unaware of the processes being used on us.

It has long been known that this type of advertising works. Consider some of the jingles you have in your head, which have been there for many years. Have you ever "deserved a break today" and gone to a particular fast food restaurant to have it?

All People Experience Trance Daily

Hypnosis, then, describes perfectly natural processes of our mind. In fact, everyone experiences multiple trance levels every day during the normal routines of life. We each constantly go in and out of trance or hypnosis, experiencing different altered states of mind on a daily basis. Think of the various trance levels you go through as you go in and out of deep sleep, for instance. We also have the ability to program our minds by simply repeating several times in a row a particular action that we want to happen regularly. Think of the last time you had to arise early for an early morning meeting. You may have said to yourself, "I must be up by six o'clock, or I'll be late. I've got to be up by six o'clock." Then you set your alarm to ring at 6:00 a.m.

What often happens when you go through this mental programming? Even though you may not have thought about what you were doing, you have likely found yourself waking up just before the alarm goes off. Your subconscious mind did what you programmed it to do. You automatically awoke on time because this is something you directed your subconscious mind to perform. Our subconscious mind does for us what we have established as our most predominant thoughts.

A recognizable and light level of hypnosis is the state of mind commonly called daydreaming, also known as waking hypnosis. An example of this would be when you begin to think about the events of the day while driving down the freeway, focusing inwardly to the point that you drive right past your exit, unaware. Or have you ever been on a lengthy road trip, pulled up in front of your garage door, and suddenly realized you are home? You can't even remember the past hour or so of the trip. This is commonly referred to as "highway hypnosis" or "white-line hypnosis." You have simply shifted from an external-only conscious focus, to a dual state of external and internal focus. In this state of mind, you have the ability to perform both functions—consciously drive the car, yet internally are focused on other thoughts, at one and the same time.

Perhaps the most obvious signs of trance are a deep and profound physical relaxation and a lack of awareness of time.

You have likely been in trance while concentrating on reading a book or watching a movie, or when you are highly focused on a project. When the book ends and you direct your thoughts towards an external focus, you become aware of time again. You might exclaim, "I can't believe it's been two hours already—it seemed like just minutes!" Or you may have experienced the opposite, when in reality something has only lasted a short period of time, but it seemed like hours.

A deeper state of trance or hypnosis may be experienced while watching television. When another member of the family announces that dinner is ready, the person watching TV may not blink an eye or acknowledge the announcement. In this case, both the conscious part of the mind and the subconscious mind has been brought into greater concentration or singularity of focus.

Hypnotherapy utilizes this intense mental focus to further enhance our hyper suggestibility for goal-directed changes in our thoughts and beliefs, which then change our behaviors. In this way, it allows an individual to consider problems and eventually to challenge the root cause of behaviors in a clear, focused, and precise manner. Other examples of our natural abilities to develop singularity of focus, trance, or hypnosis would be when someone is speaking on the telephone in a noisy area, and they block out all other sounds, focusing on only the voice that's coming through the phone. We do this routinely while on our cell phones in busy, noisy places.

We also have the natural ability to block out unwanted sensory perceptions and focus solely on what it is we choose to hear. Even with many conversations going on in a crowded room, we can pick out what to listen to and ignore everything else. Or, we decide to listen to several conversations at once, taking them all in. This is sometimes referred to as selective hearing.

Our minds also have the ability to adjust to other sensory input, such as smell. When we initially encounter foul odors, such as when I clean my horse areas on Saturday mornings, for the first few moments, I smell everything. Yet, in a relatively short time, I smell nothing. I do this automatically, without consciously thinking about it.

I have often wondered how people could live by a very odorous dairy, factory, or processing plant. Then I realized that, just as I desensitize from the smell of my horses, people living by such things have not smelled those odors in years. Their minds have simply tuned out the sensory perception, perceiving it to be unnecessary to continually stimulate their senses in this manner.

This particular ability of our minds to adjust our sensory perceptions is also utilized in hypnotherapy to help people desensitize themselves from allergy-causing substances. By this means you can learn to control, or eliminate altogether, ailments such as hay fever.

We can and may learn to desensitize ourselves intentionally to things that have formerly sensitized us in unpleasant ways. This is the basis for pain control— intentionally desensitizing and detaching. You naturally experience this desensitizing state when you sit too long in a chair and, upon standing up, find that your legs have "gone to sleep," or become numb. You may not have noticed the tingling feelings that had been there for some time. But coming back to a more conscious focus and sensitivity to your body, you become aware that you have been blocking out those uncomfortable tingling feelings in order to stay focused on something else.

The Seven Observable States of Mental Awareness: Consciousness, Five Trance States, and Sleep

Some people are afraid of trance simply because they have never studied it. They have an understandable fear of the unknown and have not yet learned the ways in which they can use hypnosis for accomplishing worthwhile projects, behavioral changes, and healing. Towards this end, trance can give you access to every thought, feeling, emotion, every sensory perception—touch, taste, scent, and sound—you have experienced from birth until now.

Hypnosis is best defined and understood as states of deep mental and physical relaxation that increase suggestibility. Another way to say it is that hypnosis is a sleeplike state, a state of enhanced concentration. In these states, suggestions more easily bypass the conscious mind and the critical factor filter and go directly to the subconscious mind to establish new, selective thinking. We can utilize these states of hyper suggestibility for our own goal-directed purposes. Hypnotherapy is the intentional use of our natural decision making processes.

There are experts who acknowledge thirty-three trance states and some who have claimed to have identified even more using modern technology. For our purposes, I will explain seven observable states of mind: consciousness, deep sleep, and five other levels of hypnosis in between.

Each trance state has different characteristics and is a different experience. Also, each trance state has different beneficial therapeutic effects when used appropriately in hypnotherapy and so is referred to by a different name. I will do my best to explain each of the states of trance and how to recognize them based on the personal experience and observations of our clients.

Keep in mind that our natural trance abilities have been called by different names over time. Also, attempts to describe trance often fail, as each person's experience is somewhat different, and two people in the same room full of people being hypnotized together may describe completely different trance experiences, since they are in different trance states.

The observable states of mind are described in the following 7 illustrations:

Observable Trance State 1: INTENTIONAL CONSCIOUSNESS or WAKING SUGGESTION	
We observe the outside world, learn from it, and freely exercise agency and choice.	
Mental Focus	Outward conscious observation; analytical, logical, and critical thinking and evaluation.
Physical Signs	Wide awake, fully alert, and focused outwardly. Eyes clear and bright, looking around, paying attention to detail.
Benefits	• Life is generally happier, and more enjoyable; a feeling of increased self-confidence • Greater clarity—more detail, greater sharpness, and brighter colorsMore peace • Self-empowerment • Greater self-control The state of agency and choice

Observable Trance State 2: WAKING HYPNOSIS or DAYDREAMING	
We are in a familiar dual state, functioning both consciously and subconsciously with the primary focus in the subconscious.	
Mental Focus	Internally focused while gaze is fixated and focused on something externally – on a movie, a scene out of the window, etc.
Physical Signs	Relaxation, sag in jaw and shoulders, tearing of the eyes, dryness in mouth, an urge to swallow
Benefits	• A highly imaginative state where we become the hero or heroine in the book or movie • Dreaming about what we want to accomplish or achieve, producing new goals • A great state for doing affirmations • *We often experience this state while driving: we might experience "white-line hypnosis" where we focus on the lines going by. Our minds gets tired of processing stimulation, so we simply slip into the back of our mind, still seeing the lines, but actually experiencing a state of trance, the same way a student spaces out in a classroom. We may end up driving right past our exit in the freeway. People often do this when watching a movie or reading.*

Observable Trance State 3: HYPNOIDAL TRANCE	
We experience this in the morning when we first wake up. Our mind becomes conscious, but body is still asleep and hasn't moved. We are mentally awake and often wonder if we have overslept or what time it is.	
Mental Focus	Mind awake, mental awareness, but body still asleep
Physical Signs	Body asleep, muscles totally relaxed with feeling of total lethargy; may experience a single body jerk or other physical abreaction
Benefits	• A state of natural meditation and personal reflection • Experiencing inspiration, thoughts of personal improvement, and a sense of direction • Best state for affirmations, autosuggestions, and intrapersonal communication because in the internally focused nature of this state it is easier to discern one's subconscious thoughts • Best state for prayer and inspiration in the early morning

Observable Trance State 4: CATALEPSY	
This state is preferred for hypnotherapy and new decision-making processes because the person has conscious and subconscious functions at one and the same time.	
Mental Focus	Ability to analyze things and think and speak logically, as well as access subconscious imagination, memories, and emotions
Physical Signs	Robot- or Frankenstein-like movements, slowed breathing, balance between extensor and flexor muscles: ability to hold arm out or up for long periods of time without tiredness or awareness; perhaps. muscle rigidity such as hands or arms
Benefits	• State preferred for Mind Management hypnotherapy behavior modification • Access to conscious/subconscious functions at the same time • Can bring conscious/subconscious into alignment and eliminate double-mindedness • Good state for doing behavior rehearsal • Individual can consciously rehearse reacting to old stimuli in new and different ways and sense any subconscious emotional content still active despite behavioral rehearsals to date

Observable Trance State 5: SOMNAMBULISM	
Somnambulism is the act and practice of somnambulating or sleepwalking—walking around in a chronic trance with the Intelligence locked into the imagination.	
Some individuals have been in somnambulism since childhood due to experiences that fixated them in this level. They are functioning in a chronic state of being hypnotized or in trance. In this state, there is limited filter capability (critical factor filtering) to block out negative thoughts and suggestions, making the person vulnerable to suggestions and the direction of others. We have ways to identify such people, and we de-hypnotize them.	
Mental Focus	In a state of high suggestibility; critical faculty or belief system filter is not fully functioning; may rely on others to make choices for them; generally feel others' opinions are of more value than their own
Physical Signs	Lethargy or complete muscle relaxation; eyes roll up
Benefits	• Highly suggestible state • Highly creative and imaginative state • Architects, musicians, artists, designers, and writers are often in this state • Analgesia is achieved in this state for pain control

Observable Trance State 6: ESDAILE STATE	
This state was named after Dr. James Esdaile, who pioneered pain control through hypnosis in India in the 1800s. This state of sensory desensitization is widely used today as pain control during child birthing, for dentistry, and in pain clinics.	
Mental Focus	Deep trance and internal focus, producing temporary amnesia and a resistance to following suggestions from others; can hear and understand what is going on around them, but chooses not to respond, may state later they did not respond because this state is so pleasant and peaceful that any distraction is annoying; want to be left alone to enjoy it.
Physical Signs	Person becomes robot-like and oblivious to pain
Benefits	• Desensitization from troublesome sensory perceptions • Natural anesthesia and amnesia for pain control— painless medical and dental procedures

Observable Trance State 7: SLEEP	
The state just before sleep. We go through all of the states described above as we go into and out of sleep, a process so gentle and natural we are not consciously aware of it. We do occasionally have the experience of feeling as if we are falling as we "fall asleep." When this happens, part of us is moving and creating this sensation. We identify that part as our spiritual mind, our Intelligence, or the spirit of our mind.	
Mental Focus	Conscious mind becomes dormant; subconscious mind dreams away accumulated emotional content
Physical Signs	Eyes closed, deep muscle relaxation, deep and rhythmic breathing
Benefits	Overall health and well-being enhanced by deep prolonged rest up to 7–9 hours per night • Health and weight loss also enhanced as the body goes through cleansing cycles and make repairs needed to stay healthy • Reduction of stress to body and mind achieved; benefits are many: improved heart functioning, reduction in mental dis-ease which leads to disease. • With proper and adequate sleep, one is more alert, with improved memory

On the following page, is a summary comparison with other descriptions of these same natural phenomena that we are calling hypnosis, trance, or states of pondering and meditation.

When the intelligence has bypassed the critical factor and is in subconscious functions, you are in a degree or level of trance. The level of trance you may choose to experience can range from daydreaming to deep sleep. Some people (natural somnambulists) need to be de-hypnotized to bring them back to consciousness. We de-hypnotize as many people as we hypnotize, teaching them how to come to consciousness at will, and how to live in the current moment of time. They learn to enjoy living in the present, here and now! It is always an amazing experience for the client and us as hypnotherapists to have someone become fully conscious and view life anew.

Hypnosis - Trance

Consciousness and the Observable Hypnotic Trance States or Levels

Name of Hypnosis or Trance State — Signs and Characteristics	Hypnotherapy	Waking or Sleep State	Brain Wave Activity
Consciousness or Waking Suggestion - outward conscious observation; analytical, logical, and critical thinking and evaluation. Fully alert.	Positive Self-Talk	**Normal waking**	**Beta**
Waking Hypnosis - Internal focus – faraway look – glittery/glazed eyes – body slouched dryness in the mouth – urge to swallow	Affirmations	**Daydreaming**	**(15-30 cycles per second)**
Hypnoidal - mind awake, mental awareness, but body is still asleep – muscles relaxed – lethargy – abreactions: jerk or hypnotic mask (whites of eyes turn red, skin is flushed)	Auto-Suggestions	**Meditation**	**Alpha**
Catalepsy - robot-like movements or immobile limbs – dynamic balance of extensor and flexor muscles – eyes move from side to side—rapid eye movement – easy access to subconscious functions of imagination, memories, and imagination - good communication between conscious and subconscious minds	Age Regressions Gestalts	**Hypnogogic** - of relating to, or occurring in the period of drowsiness immediately preceding sleep	**(9-14 cycles per second)** **Theta**
Somnambulism - A somnambulant is a sleepwalker – eyes roll up under eyelids - focus inward – highly imaginative and creative state – may achieve analgesia – in this state we are vulnerable to suggestion	Guided Imagery Stories - Scripts	**Sleepwalking**	**(4-8 cycles per second)**
Esdaile state - Natural anesthesia – amnesia – robot like movements of limbs or immobile limbs – dynamic balance of extensor and flexor muscles – a person in this state is unlikely to follow suggestions due to the deep internal focus and imaginative nature of this state	Pain Control - Dentistry Painless Child Birthing	**Hypnotic Coma**	**Delta** **(0.5 - 6 cycles per second)**
Sleep—conscious mind becomes dormant; subconscious mind dreams away accumulated emotional content - eyes closed, muscle relaxation, deep breathing	Restoration, Repair, Detox, Rejuvenation of Mind and Body	**Normal Sleep**	

Certified Hypnotherapy Training School - 722 West Shepard Lane—Farmington, Utah 84025 - Phone: 801-628-0693 —

Two Stories of Somnambulistic Trance

There are times when our natural trance abilities are used as self defense mechanisms against the pains and sorrows of this life. The following two stories are personal experiences of this type of phenomena:

I had accomplished several hypnotherapy sessions with a gentleman and his wife. He was impressed with the differences it was making in both their lives, and he told me he wanted me to attempt to help his mother. She was in a nursing home and had been for some time. He stated that she had had some periods of coherence in the past, but that he had not been able to have a real conversation with her for some time. He asked if I would join him for a visit with his mother to see if something could be done to allow him to have another conversation with her.

I explained that I had no idea what we might be able to do, but agreed to the visit. We arranged a meeting at my office, and I arrived early so I could observe her in the car, getting out of the car, and responding to the external environment outside of the nursing home. I observed that she was consciously looking around, observing the new surroundings, and paying attention to what her son was requesting and his introduction of me.

I gave her a chair, and when she sat down, she immediately closed her eyes and "checked out," so to speak. I observed her eyes rolling up to the top of her head underneath her eyelids, and she immediately became lethargic. These are the two primary physiological signs of somnambulistic trance.

I explained to her that I wanted her to stay consciously focused with me, and that her son was here and wanted to have a conversation with her. Having observed numerous clients in this state of trance, I knew that she could hear me and was fully aware of what was going on around her, including my request. I also knew and understood that she was off visualizing and imagining some other experiences in her head that were more important to her than being consciously focused in the current moment in time. She was using this highly imaginative state to avoid reality and consciousness.

I spoke to her again, and she continued to ignore me. At that point I took my hand and slapped the big metal filing cabinet that was next to where she was seated. The loud boom caused her to immediately come out of this somnambulist state, and she indignantly demanded, "Why did you do that?" I explained to her that her son was here and that he wanted to have a conversation with her.

She stated that she did not want to have a conversation with him. Then she immediately closed her eyes and went back into somnambulist trance. She was obviously using somnambulism as the state of amnesia and denial for whatever else was bothering her.

I slapped the filing cabinet again, making another loud boom. She immediately came out of trance and again asked me, "Why do you keep doing that?"

I then asked her, "Why do you keep going into the back of your mind? What is it that you are avoiding feeling in daily reality?"

She then told me that she was tired of living because life was just too painful. She explained that her husband had passed away some time ago, and that she just wanted to go and be with him. She told me that her daughter was going through a terribly devastating divorce and that her family seemed to be torn apart. She just did not want to have to deal with the painful reality of her loss and her daughter's loss.

Then she closed her eyes and immediately dropped back into somnambulist trance. I slapped the filing cabinet again. (This is what I believe is accomplished in shock therapy, when it brings the preservation of self-defense mechanisms back into play. It brought her Intelligence forward into outward conscious observation, once more allowing her to be consciously coherent.)

She came back out of trance, and once again I asked her, "Where do you go in your mind when you're not here with me?" She said, "I go back into my childhood memories of playing in the yard with my brothers and sisters and being around my parents. I go back in my mind and review all of the wholesome, fun times I enjoyed as a child."

I told her again that her son was there, that he wanted to speak with her, and that I was not going to quit pounding on the filing cabinet until she visited with him for at least a few moments. She rather indignantly said, "All right. Where is he?" I called for him to come out from where he was standing just out of sight.

They visited alone for some 15 to 18 minutes, as I recall. He was able to ask her all of his questions and learn what he wanted to know about his family situation. At the end of their visit, she closed her eyes and went back into somnambulist trance once more. She refused to come out again, proving that it was her choice.

He then led her to the car and took her back to the nursing home. Sometime later, he stated that that was the last time he held a coherent conscious conversation with her. She lived a few more months in the nursing home, and then passed away.

I later had a similar experience with my own grandmother. She had been in a nursing home for many years, and my wife and I would go visit her occasionally on Sunday afternoons. We couldn't have a conversation with her because she would just sit in the wheelchair and, whenever we were around, she would simply say, "Ruff, ruff, ruff." We honestly thought she had lost her mind and that she thought she was a dog or something.

Then one particular Sunday, we decided to take all the children with us to see Grandma. She was 93 at the time and her health seemed to be failing. We wanted all the children to at least know who she was and have one memory of meeting her. At the time, we had 10 children under the age of 11, so it was quite a production for us to go anywhere as a family, much less herd all the kids into grandma's room.

I was holding our latest arrival in my arms, our third girl who was about three months old. Grandma looked up from her wheelchair, and saw the baby in my arms. She asked in a somewhat pleading, but pleasant and polite voice, "May I hold the baby?" It was the first time I had heard her say anything in years other than, "Ruff, ruff, ruff." I looked down at her and into her eyes, and wondered if Grandma was fully conscious.

I said, "Certainly," and I put the baby on her lap, standing close enough to keep a hand on the baby to prevent her from falling. Grandma started to cry, and over and over again said, "What a beautiful child! What a beautiful child!"

Then she noticed our 2 ½-year-old toddler who was also standing by her, take off running down the hallway. She said, "You'd better go get her before she gets away!" It was then I realized that grandma was in fact fully conscious. I had to ask, "Grandma, why is it that all you ever say when we come to see you and ask you how you are doing, is, 'ruff, ruff, ruff?'"

She answered, "Life is just rough, rough, rough." I finally understood what she had really been communicating! Grandma had been in this nursing home for nearly 20 years, and it had been rough, rough, rough.

We continued to visit with her for some time. When we started to leave, she closed her eyes, and I watched them roll up to the top of her head under her eyelids. She went limp, loose, and lethargic, slouching into her wheelchair once again. We were so grateful that we had been given an opportunity to spend some time with her consciously. She passed away a short time after that, so it was the last time we saw her alive.

Understanding these true principles of trance and how our minds work, has blessed my life with many rich experiences. I count these two among the most meaningful.

CHAPTER SIX

How Unwanted Behaviors Evolve
by Craig A. Bickmore

How often have you gotten an annoying little sliver of metal or wood in your finger—a piece so small that it's hardly noticeable? It bleeds a bit and what small pain was associated with the wound is soon gone, so you force a little more blood out to make sure all the germs are out, and then go back to whatever you are doing without a second thought. A day or two later, that innocent sliver that you believed had been removed has now festered and your finger has become sore and painful.

The solution is a little more complicated now and involves a procedure with some alcohol, a sharp needle, and a bullet to bite on. (The bullet is just for effect, for those of us who have watched our share of John Wayne movies). After probing for the source of the problem, which by now has become imbedded even deeper in the tissue, you finally pull it out with a sigh of relief. The swelling goes down, and the normal healing process of the body goes into action.

Similar things happen to the body all the time. Whether small or large, once the natural healing processes take over, the body has a great way of mending itself if the pathway is clear for it to do so. This is as true for mental and emotional anguish as it is for physical scrapes and breaks.

The Iceberg

Over thirty years ago, I was introduced to a concept known as "The Iceberg" by a gentleman I learned to highly respect. He was a clinical psychologist, and he had practiced for more than thirty years at the time I met him. He focused on helping people achieve goals that they did not believe they could reach. He said that if people could just get positive thoughts into their subconscious minds, where the real driving force of who they are actually resides, amazing things would happen.

Over the course of several months, a group of us met in his office to picture and imagine our goals and aspirations, as we relaxed, in an effort to get those positive messages into our subconscious minds. We carried index cards that listed our goals in our shirt pockets and looked at them several times a day, picturing them as if they had already come true. These goals were always written as positive statements, in the present tense.

His theory was that our minds are like an iceberg, with the 10% of its mass that floats above the waterline representing the conscious mind and the 90% below the surface being the subconscious mind. He told us that slowly, over time, even drop by drop, if we could program that incredible part of our mind below the surface with positive characteristics and beliefs, the mind could achieve anything it believed it would. The problem was making the sort of impact that would really take hold, since this process involved a long-term, continual effort.

Over the past twenty years, I have come to believe that his theory was correct in his explanation of the 10%/90% composition of the conscious and subconscious mind. However, I have also come to believe that, under the right circumstances, it is not necessary to wait months or years for our affirmations to slowly penetrate down to the subconscious level. In fact, change is possible at lightning speed.

Uprooting False Beliefs

Some seventeen years ago, I visited my friend in his home and shared with him some of the material I had been exposed to, including outcomes I had experienced since taking a series of courses in hypnotherapy. He was not only interested in what I had to say, but he said that in all of his years of practice he had not seen as dramatic results as I was explaining.

Back in his clinic, where we learned to relax and picture our goals in vivid colors, as it were, none of us knew or realized that, in order for those goals to take hold rapidly, old prohibiting beliefs had to be uprooted first. Only then could the new *"correct"* beliefs be successfully planted in their place. Like creating an outstanding garden, the ground must first be free of weeds, and then treated with proper fertilizer, enough water, and TLC in order to produce a great harvest. The fruit does not grow until all steps of the law of the harvest have been fulfilled.

Most people know and understand that farming and gardening just works that way. However, when they encounter a concept they are not so sure about, they conjure up all kinds of doubt, fear, apprehension, and other negative emotions to impede or block their own progress, even in areas where they have potential for geometric growth. This is not an indictment of humanity, but a reality of human nature.

We fear what we don't know and some of us are very good at making pretty darn sure that we will never know. We will rarely make the effort to discover new things especially if they seem uncomfortable to us. This hesitancy to learn may very well be costing us some incredible opportunities now and in the future. But if we actually want to learn what we don't know, we have to learn what subconscious beliefs are limiting us in the first place. The question then becomes, "how do we go about figuring that out?" What is the process by which we can uncover those areas in our lives that need to be corrected, even though they are hidden from our view?

I found the answer in hypnotherapy classes where I learned that the process of relaxation opens the door to the subconscious. There we can understand the events of the past and turn them into blueprints for the future. In the subconscious, we can locate "slivers" from the past in the form of misinterpretations of our experiences that caused inappropriate false beliefs and nonproductive thoughts. These kinds of thoughts, if allowed to stay in our subconscious mind, continually fester and create problems until they are dealt with and removed.

My High School Track Career

When I was a twelve, I was enthralled with the Olympics of 1972. They were staged in Munich, Germany, and will always be remembered because of the terrorist attacks that tragically killed many on the Israeli Olympic team.

This was the Olympics in which swimmer Mark Spitz won seven gold medals, setting seven world records in the process. This same year, Jim Ryan, the first high school athlete to run the mile in under four minutes, lost to Kip Keino of Kenya when he tripped and fell during the finals of the mile run. Frank Shorter won the marathon, which popularized that distance in the US, and Dave Wottle won the 800 meters wearing his signature ball cap that inspired thousands of young runners to wear the same.

Determined to be an Olympic runner myself, I started to train a little and made it onto my high school track team. (Anyone who wanted to run and was skinny made the team.) I had the great fortune to run with some outstanding teammates who gained national prominence, so I had a lot of motivation to do well because the stage for winning was well established amongst my peers. Our track team also had the great fortune of training with runners from a small college in the same town, giving us an extra level of experienced runners to push us.

Ours was a team that would become state champs and ride the much-heralded fire truck down Main Street in celebration of the title. But I was not on that bright red truck. Instead, I watched the parade from the sidewalk.

The track season started off with a race in Arizona in which I ran the mile in under 5 minutes and won. Whenever our competitors were average, I knew that I had to win because I was in better shape. It was just expected. So in the bigger races, I always ran a mile in under five minutes or faced getting chided by my teammates and especially my college friends.

An interesting pattern developed that I didn't see until later—a pattern of incredible underperformance. My race times were nearly always between 4:50 and 4:57 for the mile, but my running buddies mostly ran mile times nearly half a minute faster. They would often say to me, "Bickmore, what is your problem? You train like an animal in practice, but you are a head case at the meets." The mile is four times around the track, and my first two laps usually indicated a 4:30 minute pace. But during the third lap, I just was not able to get my wind, and I would start to fade.

Thoughts have consequences, and for years I have wished that I could go back in time to my youthful body with a corrected mindset and belief. I would have been a force to reckon with. In the qualifying regional meet for state, I was in seventh place at the end of the second lap. The top four would qualify for state. But going to the back stretch coming out of the fifth turn, as the front of the pack was starting to pull away, I vividly remember telling myself: "I can catch these guys and qualify for state." Then came a second thought, the game changer: "No, you can't!" Physically, I had all the skills to be an accomplished runner, but something far more powerful was preventing my success, something that my subconscious mind knew while consciously I had not a clue.

Self-defeating Beliefs: "I can't win."

The course work I began shortly after turning thirty was quite different from any of the MBA material I studied at Utah State University. It was about how the mind works and the reasons why we do the things we do. It was not psychology or psychiatry, but about the practical application of our God-given, innate human ability *to access our conscious and subconscious minds at the same time,* to make adjustments and corrections to beliefs that inhibit growth and progress. This powerful series of instructions have changed my life and those of my family forever.

Let me share why the body was willing and the mind was not as I labored around the track in that final region high school track meet. Inside our subconscious minds is a reservoir of beliefs, whether positive or negative, real or imagined. Once a belief is stored in that reservoir, it starts to impact who and what we are as well as how we function. If a particular belief is not correct, it really matters. We will support and defend our beliefs, even at the cost of losing a race.

If the subconscious mind is almost ten times that of the conscious mind in scope, function, and ability, think about attempting to exert enough willpower to overcome a wrong belief. It would be a long shot at best. If willpower is a conscious function of thought, and belief is a subconscious function with similar energy (including the force of inertia), it would be like throwing willpower on the tracks to stop a diesel locomotive fully loaded with cargo running downhill. At track meets back in high school, my subconscious mind simply overran my conscious mind because, unknown to me consciously, I had developed the belief that "I can't win."

To find out why I never achieved my goal of being a great runner even though I had the talent, I applied hypnotherapy. First I allowed my mind and body to relax to the point of, say, watching a good movie sitting in a comfortable chair. Then Dennis and I went on a "search and find" mission in my subconscious mind. At this level of trance (relaxation), I had conscious and subconscious functions at the same time, but because everything I had done or even thought was stored in the subconscious, I needed to find the place in my own super computer where the program (belief) had developed an error in the code.

Discovering how to challenge beliefs that are self-defeating, not to mention those that are just plain wrong, is worth much more than the cost of this book or a college education in my opinion. In trance (relaxation), a person's heart, mind, and spirit have a sense of what is right and correct, if we allow those feelings to surface. When the thought, "I can't win," came to my consciousness, Dennis was able to skillfully challenge this very wrong belief. It was remarkable what happen next, almost simultaneously my lung capacity opened up and I breathed in more air than I ever had before. It was as if I was sucking the curtains off the wall, and I began yelling out, "I can win! I can win! I can win!" How interesting that the physiology changed as soon as the belief was corrected—what a mind/body combination!

Apparently, the mind will defend and validate a wrong belief to the point of shutting the body down to prove it. If I had only known at age sixteen what I discovered at age thirty, I might have had a very successful high school track career, maybe even a college scholarship—or what about the Olympics? If the mind can deter a capable athlete, imagine what it could do if it were channeled in a positive manner. Could our accomplishments explode in geometric fashion to break all kinds of records? In sports, I think most successes are accomplished by getting the mind right. I had just been given a taste of how to achieve that kind of thinking power.

Dennis Explains: Experiences Generate Thoughts

Most of us have had experiences in life that we become very emotional about when they come to mind. We are still hurt, angry, resentful, anxious, or sad, and so forth, even though the experience may have taken place many, many years ago. In hypnotherapy, we call these *sensitizing events,* and our reactions to them are often responsible for the behaviors we struggle most to overcome.

In other words, behaviors are part of a process; they don't just happen. They start with a stimulus that initiated strong emotional feelings, probably from one of four sources:

1. Our conscious mind or outward observation and learning. The Conscious mind generates thought as we observe and learn. You might remember the first time you started to drive a vehicle and had to learn to brake just right or to drive a vehicle with a clutch. Dennis was eight years old, and could barely see over the top of the dashboard standing up, when his dad put him in the driver's seat of a hay-hauling truck. His father showed him how to push in the clutch, put the vehicle in low gear, and then said, "Let it out real slow, and don't spill the hay load." That was his first driver training as a little kid, driving a truck through a hayfield. And so he learned. The first time he let that clutch out, he felt a jerk. The next time, he let it out slower. We figure things like this out because we're able to observe. We watch and learn, because we do what we do outwardly. We make conscious observations with our conscious mind.

2. The environment. This of course means our surroundings, including climate, geography, weather, landscape, buildings and other structures, etc. We get up in the morning, for example, and see that it's raining outside, and so we dress for rain. We change our leather shoes to our neoprene-soled shoes, get our umbrellas out of the closet—those kinds of things. We make certain behavioral changes at a conscious analytical level for the stimulus of rain.

3. Our peers. Peers can mean just about any other human being, as well as radio, TV, and other media that we pay attention to regularly.

4. Our central nervous systems. Dennis uses the following story to illustrate how the central nervous system generates thoughts:

> I was helping my dad build a barn. I thought I was big stuff because the other people who were helping Dad were sawing and cutting boards, and my job was to stack the unused pieces of boards in the woodpile. Since we were building the barn out of used wood, those pieces had a lot of old nails in them. My job was to take the boards over to the woodpile and pull all the old nails out.
>
> I was in my gym shoes, and when I stepped on this one board, I felt pressure on the bottom of my foot. I had never felt that before, but I just kept walking. A nail pushed right through the bottom of my foot and came up through the top of my gym shoe. I had literally nailed that board to the bottom of my foot. Being only five or six years old, I started crying. "Dad, look at this," I yelled. I held up my foot and there was this board hanging off the bottom of it.
>
> My dad has had John Wayne as his hero his entire life. He's always watched John Wayne movies, and he has a John Wayne room in his house that is almost a shrine with shelves of John Wayne videos and books, and pictures of John Wayne. One included the famous picture of Wayne on a Pinto horse going up the trail. And so he picked up my foot and grabbed that board as if he were pulling an arrow out of some early pioneer, and ripped the nail out of my foot. "Now, quit crying!" he demanded, "And go see your mom and have her fix your foot."
>
> You know what you did back in those days, right? You squeezed some blood out to cleanse the wound a bit and then soaked it in Epsom salts. That was the cure of the

day. So I had this hole in my foot, and it took all week to get better. The next Saturday, we worked on the barn again. As I walked around working on the barn, I felt that same pressure on the bottom of my foot again. Only now I had experience, right?

In hypnotherapy school we learned that in about a thirtieth of a second we can process these types of thoughts. The central nervous system in your brain reacts and says, "Hey! There is another nail down here!" We process warnings and thoughts like this so quickly, we don't even realize they're thoughts because we don't recognize or acknowledge them at the conscious level. I immediately reacted by picking up my foot and not continuing to put pressure onto the board with a nail in it. We learn from our central nervous system experiences.

One advantage of utilizing hypnosis or trance is that it slows the thought processes down and gives us access to such subconscious thoughts so we can discern them with awareness. If we don't discern what our thoughts are, we might go through life repeating the same old mistakes, the same old patterns forever, all because we have never actually slowed our minds down to find out what it is we're thinking and why we're doing what we're doing.

Accepted Thoughts Enter the Subconscious

All of us experience these four areas of stimulus that generate thoughts. And because our conscious minds are analytical and logical, consciousness is where we do our critical thinking—where we first assess the thoughts that come into our minds. When a stimulus generates thoughts, we analyze; we begin to make conscious evaluations, choices, and decisions.

So how do some or any of those conscious thoughts become problematic and even hidden from our own view? That has to do with the critical factor. The critical factor is the area in our minds that divides the conscious mind from the subconscious mind. It contains our belief systems and acts as a belief system filter to the subconscious. As we analyze thoughts and make choices in our conscious minds, we choose to accept some thoughts and reject others.

When a thought is accepted as being true and/or right for us, we allow it to pass through our critical factor/belief system filters into our subconscious minds. There it begins to stimulate the subconscious functions of imagination, memory, and emotion. If we reject a thought as untrue or not right, it hits the critical factor like a trampoline. We just "bounce" it back out—meaning we do not let it go through to the subconscious functions of imagination, memory, and emotion.

As long as we keep a particular thought in the conscious part of our minds, it doesn't generate behavior. Consciousness is where we maintain personal self-control; it is the seat of power in the mind. However, a thought that passes through the critical factor and into the subconscious part of the mind can be amplified many times within our imagination. We can take any experience, no matter how small, and magnify it to the point that it's a problem. Now that it is in our imagination, it can be bolstered by selectively chosen memories, and our emotions become involved. We soon begin behaving the way we feel.

Behavior from Sensitizing Events

Some experiences can have a particularly strong effect on us, even when they don't appear traumatic. We call these *sensitizing events.* They generate thoughts that pass quickly through the critical factor/belief system filter and are accepted within us as being true. Such events continue to produce emotional content and behavior even when the event that triggered them took place decades earlier.

In hypnotherapy, we call thoughts that produce behavior *predominant thoughts* or *predominant beliefs.* An individual may have a number of conflicting thoughts/beliefs on a single subject, but the one that actually produces behavior is the predominant thought or pattern at that particular moment.

These behavior-producing thoughts may in fact be misinterpretations of an event experienced as a child, a misrepresentation of oneself to oneself, or a misunderstanding of the intent of an experience. For instance, the outright acceptance of a lie can generate emotional content that, in turn, generates behaviors. Our memories, imagination, and emotions can work for or against us, depending on which set of thought beliefs is the predominant behavior-producing belief.

In other words, long after an initial sensitizing event occurs, we may still be carrying the original stimulus with us in the form of buried memories and thoughts that continue to generate emotional content. Because these memories include unresolved experiences, we also carry ongoing imaginary amplifications of those memories and predominant thoughts. The unresolved memories or sensitizing emotions affect our actions because, again, we tend to behave the way we feel.

For example, one of the most common ills of humanity is the thought, "I'm not good enough." Among the hundreds or even thousands of possible self-limiting beliefs and doubts, we have each had some experiences where we felt like we were just not good enough. If you were to accept this as a predominant belief and then amplify it in your imagination, what kind of emotions and then behaviors do you think it would generate?

Such beliefs can become fixated in our minds, and they will stay there until we appropriately challenge and change them, no matter what age we were when they were first developed. At some point, we have to go back to when the behavior was first developed and start there to move forward towards permanent change.

Someone who amplifies the thought, "I'm not good enough" thousands of times could reach a state of total incapacitation and sink into despair and hopelessness. This same pattern can be followed with any self-defeating or self-limiting belief.

The chart on the following page gives insight into how amplification works:

The Imagination can amplify any thought generating stronger emotions.

This chart shows the effect of the amplification in the imagination of an accepted predominant belief system behavior producing thought, and its effect on the emotions. Behaviors are produced from our emotions. As the imaginary amplification increases, so does the intensity of the emotional content.

The emotional content is released and collapsed, as the imagination is desensitized, and the perceptions of the memories are altered.

Example: "I am not good enough……"

Amplification Amount		The clients self-description of the emotion
Some Amplification	←————→	Some discomfort or uneasiness when attempting new things
Additional Amplification	←————→	Anxious about new things or fears of the unknown - inadequacy
More Amplification	←————→	Stressed about any new experience - reluctance - hesitation
Greater Amplification	←————→	Discouraged, despondent, unwilling to try things, rebellious, contentious
Greatest Amplification	←————→	Despair, hopelessness, feeling use less, stuck, or incapacitated

Certified Hypnotherapy Training School - http://certifiedhypnotherapytraining.com/ -

The good news is that in the upcoming chapters, we start to teach you how to adjust, control, or even shut down your imagination when you want or need to. We teach you how to take control of the imagination so that no matter what level you amplify something to, you will be able to turn it down, down, and down. The very fact that you have already learned how to turn it up to those extremes tells you that you also have the power to turn it down.

As we teach you how to do this, and you start to turn down your imagination concerning a particular event, what if you were to turn it all the way down? What if you finally clicked the dial, so to speak, and just turned it off? Then what you have done is collapsed the associated emotional content, and because there is no more emotional content to generate anything, you have changed your behavior.

"I'm not good enough" is a belief system. "I'm not as smart as others" is a belief system. "I'm afraid of dogs" is a belief system, and so forth. All of these beliefs are thoughts that are stuck in our critical factors. Let's look at a specific example of how the entire process plays out.

"I'm stupid."

An example of the power of hidden thoughts to derail our progress in life is illustrated by the experience of one of my sons. He was struggling in first grade to the point where his teachers told my wife and I that he would be benefitted by attending "resource," (a special class part of the day where he would be given special attention). In addition, some suggested that Ritalin, a commonly prescribed drug, would help him concentrate and focus better as well as help calm his behavior during class. Not wanting to put a label on my son, I resisted for several months the pressure to have my son join the "resource" class, and drugs were never an option for me. Finally, I gave in to the teachers' and my wife's urgings. The remainder of the school year went by without much change in my son's performance, but I do think he liked the personal attention. At the end of the school year, I also hesitantly agreed to have him tested for aptitude and ability. The results were to be available the next fall.

Sometime after my son began second grade, he came home talking about what he had been doing in resource class that day. This raised a red flag for me since he was not supposed to be in resource—parental permission was required. When I called his teacher, who was young, new to the school, and seemed capable and kind, she simply said that a mistake had been made, but he was doing well and should stay in the class.

I asked if she had the results of the tests he had taken the previous spring. After checking the file, she reported that intellectually he was in the top 10% of his school. Intuitively I had known that he had the mental capacity to do well in school, but now I understood fully that his dilemma had nothing to do with his ability. Instead, something deep inside my son's belief system was generating a response contrary to reality. I knew I needed to get to the root of the problem.

Although I had not worked with many people who needed help getting to the core of their inappropriate beliefs, I now felt a very personal need on behalf of my son, and I wanted to find the answer fast. I had just completed hundreds of hours of training in hypnosis and hypnotherapy, and it was time to prove whether the principles were correct.

After I came home from work, my son and I went into his room and just started to talk. There was no formal process (although many exist); it was just he and I having a discussion about school. Children are often in a natural state of trance with the conscious and subconscious functioning at the same time, so I began asking specific questions that would help reveal where the root of the problem was hidden.

As we visited, my son timidly admitted that he didn't really like school. Because I had a little more information on what was taking place, I pointed my questions in a manner specific towards discovering the cause of the behavior he was exhibiting.

Question: "Are you not doing very well because you sometimes don't pay attention?"

Response: "Well, yes."

Question: "Then why are you not paying attention?"

Response: "I just don't like school."

Question: "Why don't you like school?"

Response: "Because I'm stupid!"

I knew that we had discovered the foundation of it all—why my son was struggling in school, getting bad grades, being placed in resource, and feeling unhappy with his innocent little life. He had somehow bought into the lie that he was stupid and that belief had become the new him. This belief system would now control his course as long as he made it his reality.

The predominant belief system scripts logged in the critical factor belief system are the primary determining factor in how we act and behave, and he was doing a great job of being stupid. How does a stupid person act in school? He is disruptive and does not pay attention (classic signs); and for someone who was actually in the top 10%, he was doing a remarkable job of acting the part.

I knew he needed to disassociate from his incorrect belief and establish a new and correct belief in its place. So I asked him how a stupid person would act in school, and he described in detail just how he was acting. I then asked him whether he was stupid or what he was doing was stupid. The breakthrough happened as he realized that he himself was not stupid, but what he was doing was indeed stupid.

To further emphasize that point, I went to a subject we were both interested in—baseball. I asked him who the greatest pitcher of all time was.

His response: "Nolan Ryan."

My question: "What would happen if Nolan went to the mound to practice and only threw one pitch and then said, "I'm done for the day!"?

His response: "Dad that would be stupid."

My question: "Would Nolan Ryan be stupid, or would what he was doing be stupid?"

His response: "What he was doing."

My question: "If I wanted to be an Olympic weightlifter, could I go and lift one weight once and achieve that goal?"

His response: "Dad, that is stupid."

My question: "Okay, would the weightlifter be stupid or just what he was doing?"

His response: "What he was doing."

My question: "What about a great track athlete, could he run around the track once and be great?"

His response: (now rolling his eyes): "Come on Dad that is stupid."

My question: "Are you stupid, or is what you are doing in school stupid?"

His response: (hesitating just a bit, but then the golden phrase): "No, I'm not stupid, but what I am doing is."

We now had achieved what hypnotherapists refer to as a conscious, recognizable response confirming a change in the subconscious belief system. My son had moved from the reality of being stupid to the new belief that he was not stupid, but was aware that he had been acting stupid. Once the critical fact that he was bright and intelligent had replaced his negative internal thinking, we rehearsed it over again and again with examples of what I think of as light and truth.

He then came up with a further thought that he could achieve anything that he put his mind to. What had been a very discouraged eight-year-old became, in a matter of forty-five minutes, a bright boy, full of life as well as confidence that he could do anything required.

The next day in school my son apparently told his teacher that he could do anything he put his mind to. Gratefully, this wonderful teacher made that the class theme (could anything better have happened?). Wow, what a turnaround!

A few weeks later, at parent-teacher conference, my wife and I visited with my son's teacher. As we sat down across the desk, she leaned forward and asked, "What happened to your son?" She said that he had done enough good work in the past two and a half weeks to move six and a half weeks of poor performance to an average grade.

By the time we left that parent-teacher conference, all ridicule and doubt was banished, and all of the time and money I spent learning the principles of hypnosis and trance had just paid off, big time. How many tens of thousands of parents have similar questions, situations, worries, feelings, and grief, but don't know how to help their children in the way I was able to help my child? What was this worth to me? to him? to his future?

The Bane of Biology Class

Let me give just one more example from my own family. Several years ago, another of my sons was in an eighth-grade biology class where a video depiction of a diseased kidney was shown. For some reason, this son got the idea in his head that this kidney was his. Panic overtook him, and he actually passed out in class.

We thought this was an isolated incident. However, a few weeks later, a similar subject and scene came up in the same biology class, and he passed out again. This time he scraped his face on the carpet as he hit the ground, making him look as if he had crashed on his bike. I could see another pattern developing that was not good and had to be dealt with.

To be careful, my wife took our son to the doctor for a thorough exam. The doctor said that nothing was wrong with him physically and that he would grow out of this unusual response. When he passed out for the third time in the same class with more dramatic consequences, I called Dennis for a visit with my son, my wife, and I—to look further into the cause of the errant belief and to get it corrected before it rooted deeper into his subconscious and caused other problems for him in the future.

Because our son is very bright and wanted to have this thorn in his side removed, he was motivated to work to achieve that goal. He quickly learned how the mind stores information and how to correct a problem belief. For the next forty-five minutes he cooperated with the process of identifying the incorrect belief and why it had occurred. He went through the steps to disassociate from the false belief and the associated behavior, and he was able to restructure what he was experiencing in class and put it back into proper perspective.

Many times the shift the mind makes in such a situation is permanent and requires no more attention. However, my son had one more episode of passing out, so we had to work through this issue a couple more times. Another time he broke a bone in his foot and, while we were having it treated at the doctor's office, he started to feel faint—not because of the pain, but because the false belief from the biology classroom started to surface again. I recognized what was happening and we were able to go through the relaxation process, reach the subconscious, and reason through what his imagination was starting to amplify. He quickly got back into his normal thinking and was fine.

A series of behavior rehearsals can be practiced to desensitize a problem belief and practice a new behavior until it is no longer an issue, something my son has since learned. As a family, we are grateful for the knowledge we have gained over the years that has solved a tough problem that, if left unchecked, would have become more deeply seated.

Of course, things don't have to be this traumatic to cause difficulties in someone's life. The processes we are sharing in this book are meant to help people to understand, identify, and then correct false beliefs, just like the sliver removal mentioned earlier. Difficult issues do not have to persist. Problems can be solved. Solutions are available if we know how to find them.

CHAPTER SEVEN

Using Spiritual Mind Management Hypnotherapy to Eradicate Thinking Errors

Most sensitizing experiences people have during childhood and still deal with as adults are not their fault. More likely, they misunderstood something as children and thus developed "thinking errors" misrepresentations, mistakes, misunderstandings, misjudgments, belief in outright lies and so forth.

As we each mature, we become more responsible for our actions. In fact, we want to become "response-able"—able to make good decisions and choices from moment to moment. Generally, we don't prefer to continue "acting out" based on previous fixations and incorrect ideas.

Perhaps the major difference between staying a victim and being a survivor is taking action instead of constantly reacting. Once we understand the truth about our life experiences, and acknowledge our part and our responsibility, we can improve on wherever we were wrong. It is our acceptance of where we were, in fact, right or wrong that gives us the power to change. Truth does indeed make us free.

You can know the truth about your past experiences. Inside of you are lessons to learn that will contribute to your growth in wisdom and understanding. You can discover which of your past experiences still hold you back and keep you from being who you want to be. With the proper level of hypnotherapy training, someone can ask your subconscious the right questions, and the answers will come right up. Then you can deal with what the problem really is rather than what someone simply thinks it is.

The Theory of the Mind

In the last chapter, we explained the first part of what is sometimes called the Theory of the Mind. We described how behaviors are induced, beginning with the acceptance of thoughts that pass through the critical factor; how those thoughts, which are generated from four sources of stimulus, are later magnified in the imagination. They then are justified, validated and defended with specific memory which proves to yourself that your accepted predominate thoughts are true. Again, this combined imaginary amplification and memory justification is what generates the amount of accumulated intensified emotional content that we identify as our feelings.

Now we will look in more detail at how such unwanted behaviors are challenged and changed through discovery of your behavior-causing, predominate beliefs. ***The charts on the following pages summarize how unwanted behaviors are created and how we can change them with hypnotherapy processes:***

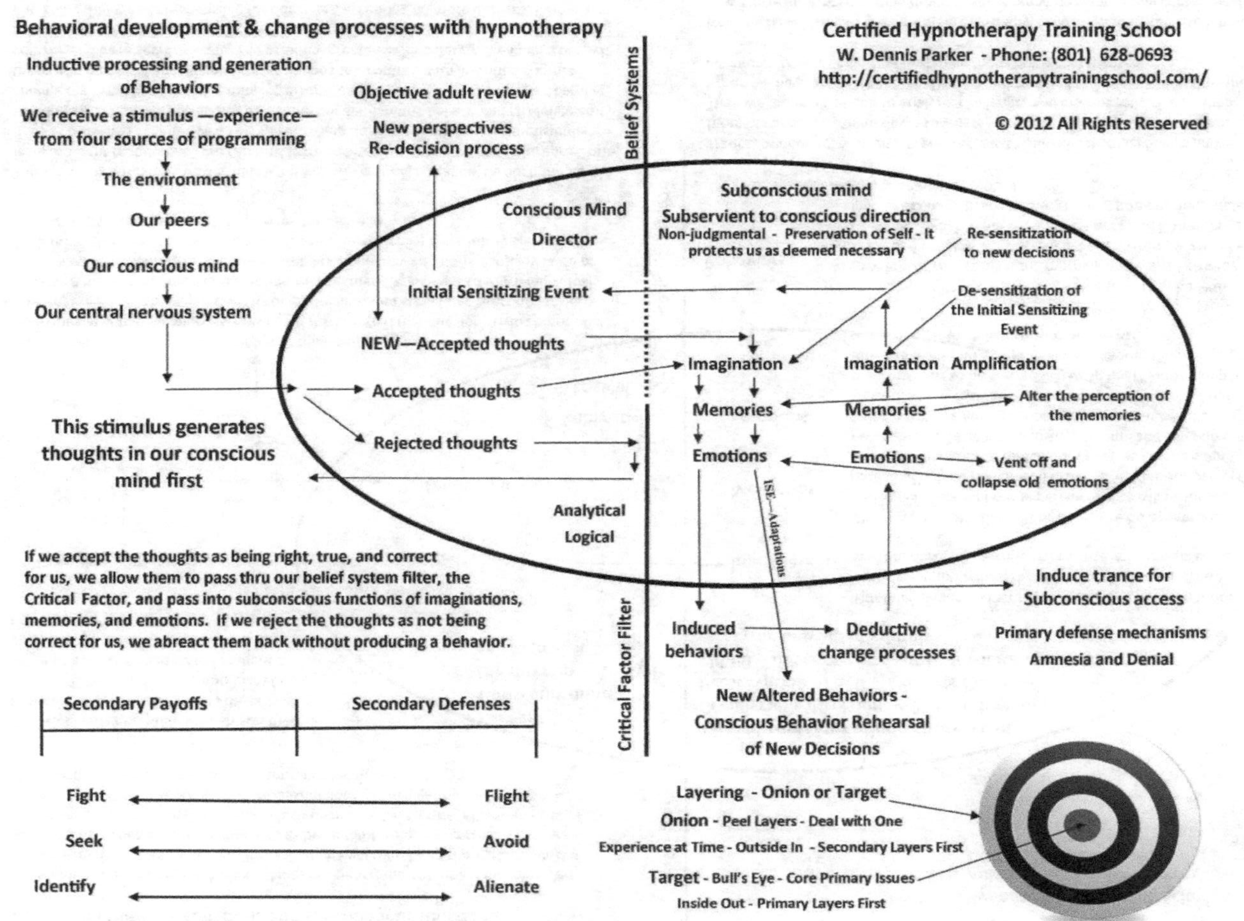

Behavioral development & change processes with hypnotherapy
Inductive processing and generation of Behaviors
We receive a stimulus —experience— from four sources of programming
The environment
Our peers
Our conscious mind
Our central nervous system
This stimulus generates thoughts in our conscious mind first
Objective adult review
New perspectives
Re-decision process
Conscious Mind
Director
Initial Sensitizing Event
NEW—Accepted thoughts
Accepted thoughts
Rejected thoughts
Analytical
Logical
Belief Systems
Critical Factor Filter
Certified Hypnotherapy Training School
W. Dennis Parker - Phone: (801) 628-0693
http://certifiedhypnotherapytrainingschool.com/
© 2012 All Rights Reserved
Subconscious mind
Subservient to conscious direction
Non-judgmental - Preservation of Self - It protects us as deemed necessary
Re-sensitization to new decisions
De-sensitization of the Initial Sensitizing Event
Imagination
Memories
Emotions
Imagination Amplification
Memories
Emotions
Alter the perception of the memories
Vent off and collapse old emotions
ISE—Adaptations
Induced behaviors
Deductive change processes
Induce trance for Subconscious access
Primary defense mechanisms
Amnesia and Denial
New Altered Behaviors - Conscious Behavior Rehearsal of New Decisions
If we accept the thoughts as being right, true, and correct for us, we allow them to pass thru our belief system filter, the Critical Factor, and pass into subconscious functions of imaginations, memories, and emotions. If we reject the thoughts as not being correct for us, we abreact them back without producing a behavior.
Secondary Payoffs
Secondary Defenses
Fight
Flight
Seek
Avoid
Identify
Alienate
Layering - Onion or Target
Onion - Peel Layers - Deal with One
Experience at Time - Outside In - Secondary Layers First
Target - Bull's Eye - Core Primary Issues
Inside Out - Primary Layers First

Behavioral change—conscious and subconscious functions

Certified Hypnotherapy Training School
http://certifiedhypnotherapytraining.com/

Consciously, we analyze, think about things pondering the potential outcomes. We examine them logically, and critically evaluate newly stimulated thoughts in our conscious mind. When we accept thoughts as being right, true, and correct for us, we allow them to pass through the critical faculty or critical factor belief system filter of our mind and stimulate our subconscious functions of imaginations, and memories. This process generates emotional content, producing behaviors.

Behaviors are generated from an accepted thoughts or beliefs that bypass the critical factor. Beliefs that become dominant become so as determined by the amount of amplification each belief receives in the imagination.

Belief system

Conscious mind, the director - Analytical, logical

The subconscious mind - subservient to conscious direction - Non-Judgmental Preservation of Self – Protects the individual – never sleeps – shuts down unnecessary or unwanted stimulus

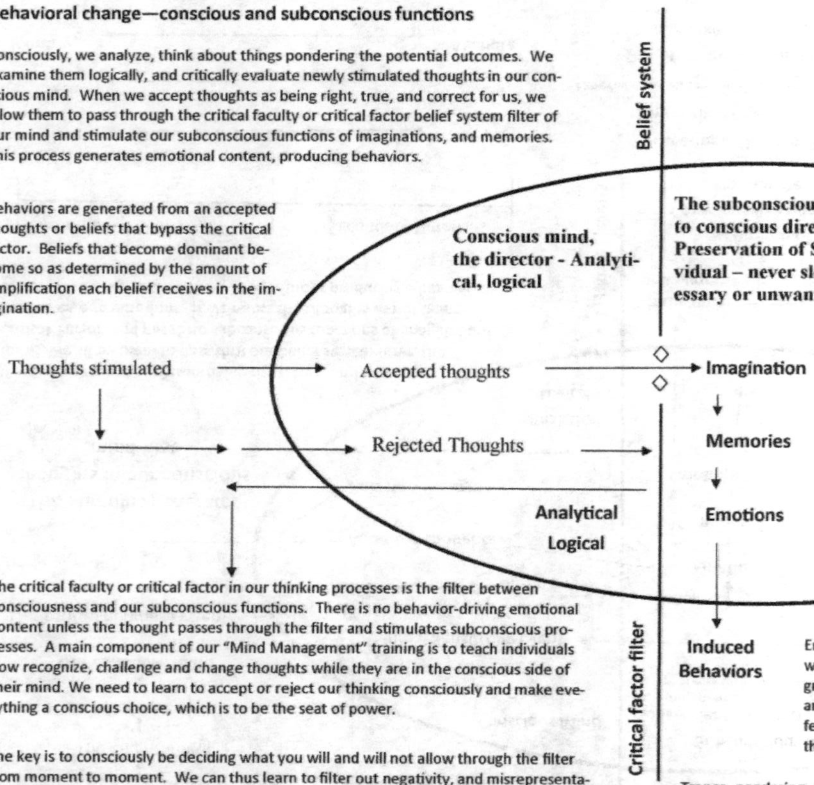

Thoughts stimulated → Accepted thoughts → Imagination

Rejected Thoughts

Analytical
Logical

Imagination ↓ Memories ↓ Emotions ↓ Induced Behaviors

Our imagination can amplify any thought multiple times, making any thought or experience as big a deal as we want to make it. Learn to desensitize your imagination.

When we accept a thought or belief, we do a memory search and look for parts of our experiences that will justify, validate, and defend our chosen belief. We skew our perceptions of experience to match our belief, as no one wants to be wrong. We attempt to justify, defend, and validate our being right. We limit our points of view, that could be viewed, and as hypnotherapists our job is to expand the points of view to be viewed, allowing the client the opportunity to learn and accept new information, thus altering the perception of the initial sensitizing, events.

Critical factor filter

Emotions generate our behaviors, as we tend to behave the way we feel. If we get up in the morning and we are grumpy, grouchy, and irritable, how do we behave? Grumpy, grouchy, and irritable, right? What we want to recognize is that those feelings are coming from specific grumpy, grouchy and irritable thoughts we have accepted.

The critical faculty or critical factor in our thinking processes is the filter between consciousness and our subconscious functions. There is no behavior-driving emotional content unless the thought passes through the filter and stimulates subconscious processes. A main component of our "Mind Management" training is to teach individuals how recognize, challenge and change thoughts while they are in the conscious side of their mind. We need to learn to accept or reject our thinking consciously and make everything a conscious choice, which is to be the seat of power.

The key is to consciously be deciding what you will and will not allow through the filter from moment to moment. We can thus learn to filter out negativity, and misrepresentations of ourselves to ourselves. This will also help us understand our earlier misunderstandings and misinterpretations, overcome our self-limiting beliefs, and challenge and change our "stinking thinking—thinking errors" before generating a behavior. Learning these processes will enable you be in conscious self-control, with intentional impulse control, and have self-discipline. The resulting greater self-mastery will enhance our self-esteem and self-confidence. When we become accountable to ourselves for ourselves and know that we are responsible for ourselves, accepting no more excuses, then we move forward in life beyond the speed of light, at the speed of thought!

Trance, pondering, or hypnosis gives access to our subconscious beliefs and thoughts and slows them down to where we can know and understand them. Then we are in a position to analyze, challenge, and intentionally change them. When we have appropriately challenged and changed the original thoughts, the emotional content being generated by those thoughts collapses.

Now we have changed the behaviors of grumpy, grouchy, and irritable to whatever we have implanted as new thoughts, generating new emotional content and new behaviors. In other words, change!

Hypnotherapy gives you the environment, the time, and the opportunity to discover and understand the sensitizing events and interpretations that are contributing to behaviors you don't like. Let's follow the entire process with a simple story about Johnny and rain.

Rain

Johnny gets up in the morning, and he sees that it's raining outside. Rain is an environmental stimulus that produces thoughts that go into the conscious side of his mind first, where he consciously thinks about rain. Analytically and logically he says, "Okay, it's raining today. That means I've got to change my good leather shoes and put on rubber-soled shoes. I'm not going to wear my leather jacket; I'll wear my nylon windbreaker. And I'd better leave for work fifteen minutes early because the traffic may be moving slower." He makes calculations and adjustments for the fact that it's raining.

But as those thought processes related to rain hit his critical factor, where his belief system is located, his belief system about rain is, "I hate rain. I hate it when it rains. I really hate rain."

Because he has logged "I hate rain" into his belief system, when a thought passes through the critical factor and hits his memories, he goes back in his mind and grabs only memories of the things that he can hate about it. So in his mind he's thinking things like, "I hate it when it rains because it washes mud down the driveway and the good dirt out of my flowerbeds. I am going to have to clean the gutters. I hate rain because it spots my car, and I will have to wash the car again. I hate the rain because it gets dirt and mud in the house from the kids' shoes. I hate rain."

He is fixated and focused only on those aspects of rain that will make his central belief right. No one wants to be wrong in their beliefs, so Johnny's mind is searching for data about rain that can justify his chosen belief of, "I hate rain." He amplifies those negative things in his imagination and makes each of them a really big deal, justifying his position of hatred for rain.

He's been doing this for a while when he turns onto the freeway, and he's now at a very high level of amplified imagination as he drives and sees cars and trucks splashing dirt and mud on his new car. By the time he gets to work, how does Johnny behave on rainy days? Yeah, he's angry. He just can't stand it.

Three doors down in the same neighborhood, same rainstorm, same kind of house, lives Mary. Mary gets up in the morning and looks outside and recognizes, the same as Johnny does, that it's raining. The thought stimulus works the same for Mary.

She has the same kind of analytical, logical conscious thinking that Johnny does, so Mary also changes her shoes. She changes her leather shoes to rubber-soled ones, and she gets an umbrella. She leaves for work early.

But when thoughts of the stimulus of rain hit up against her critical factor, against her belief system, she has logged in, "I love rain. I really love rain." Now Mary doesn't want to be wrong either. Because none of us wants to be wrong, we skew our view of the world to justify, validate, and defend our beliefs.

So Mary looks for all the things about rain in her memory to justify, validate, and defend the positive aspects of a rainstorm. As she leaves for work, she's driving and thinking, "I love it when it rains because the whole world looks like it just took a shower. I want to get home tonight and see how much greener my grass is going to be. My flowers are going to look prettier, the trees are going to be brighter, and the air's going to smell so fresh and clean."

She goes back into her memory and searches for positive things about rain. "I remember a week or two ago we had that magnificent thunderstorm across the valley with thunder crashing up against the mountains and the lightning flashing everywhere. I sat at my window and I loved watching that magnificent storm. I just love it when it rains." She drives off to work and by the time she gets there, she's amplified all of those thoughts many times in her imagination, and how does she behave on a rainy day? Happy and joyful!

Two different people who have nearly identical stimuli, but who have vastly different belief systems, go along justifying, validating, and defending different beliefs, gathering one-sided data from their memories and then amplifying it in their imaginations. In turn, their justifications determine how much emotional content, positive or negative, is generating their behavior.

Primary Defense Mechanisms: Amnesia and Denial

Now let's say Johnny comes into our office for help, and Dennis inquires, "What are you here for?"

"Well, I'd like to know why I'm always so angry, irritable, and mean on rainy days. I've been that way forever. It's really bothered me, and I want to see if you can help me to understand it, because that's what you deal with, negative behaviors, right?"

This is what is called in this chapter *deductive processing* at the bottom of the first chart, coming back in the opposite direction, following the arrows up. This means that Johnny has recognized he has a behavior he wants to change: "I am angry, irritable, and mean on rainy days."

The next step is to induce trance for subconscious access. We want to go to the fourth level of trance—to the state we call catalepsy, where a person gains access to their conscious and subconscious thoughts and functions at the same time. Right now, if I were to ask you, "What experiences have you had in life that are still holding you back, keeping you from all you really want to be?" you might have a sense of great things you are and ought to do. But you might still say, "I'm just not sure, but I think it consciously," people often can't tell us because they buried such things many years ago with what we call their *primary defense mechanisms of amnesia and denial.*

Amnesia

One way to think of our minds is that the conscious mind is the master or director, and the subconscious mind is the genie in the bottle, the dutiful servant. The genie does not judge right or wrong, good or evil, worthy or unworthy, but only attempts to carry out the wishes and directions of the master.

So when we listen to music with inappropriate lyrics, which promotes unworthy actions and behaviors, we are making conscious self-defeating, self-limiting statements to ourselves (through the lyrics), statements that the subconscious hears both with our ears and internally. Without realizing it, we are directing the subconscious to develop within us those traits.

Any personal programming we engage in works the same way. When we say things like, "I never want to think about that again!" or "That's just the way I am!" and so forth, the subconscious goes to work and attempts to impede memories to the contrary. It puts up "walls" and other mental blocks and barriers.

People describe these barriers in different ways, but the intent is always the same: to keep us from thinking painful thoughts and triggering painful emotions. If the master directs the subconscious mind to hide something from it, the genie goes to work and does the best it can to hide the painful thought or experience. It attempts to bury it in the memory, in the subconscious. Amnesia is a real thing.

Denial

We also instruct our subconscious to hide the truth of our initial sensitizing events from us, or what we perceive to be the truth. "It was no big deal." "It didn't really mean that much to me." "I didn't really want it, anyway."

Other forms of denial are lies, rationalizations, and blame-spreading: "I didn't have anything to do with it; it wasn't my fault." "You should be ashamed of yourself. I would never do something like that!" "If you had told me earlier, I would have been willing to help you, but not now!" Burying the truth in denial can be a good thing in the right "forgive and forget" circumstances, but if we are still sensitized by an experience, we need to resolve it rather than just detach from it.

Accessing the beliefs held in the subconscious through trance, and working with "what is," instead of what we or others may assume the problem to be, is powerful and enlightening. It can be life-changing to break through amnesia and denial and deal in truth. The truth empowers us. Knowing, accepting, and living in truth sets us FREE!

Trance

People will say, "I don't know why I do this. It's just the way I am. I've tried to change before, but things just don't work for me." And yet, when we go into trance, something clicks. Trance gives us access to our subconscious memories. Every thought, every touch, every smell; every sensory perception you've ever had, even every conversation you've had, from birth until now, is all in your mind and can be made accessible through trance.

Trance gives us access to the memories and inappropriate or painful thoughts we may have been avoiding for years. We all do the best we can to cope with our unfavorable past experiences, but these sensitized experiences sometimes just keep surfacing and don't go away. We need to learn the lessons that are to be learned from these experiences.

After our experiences are desensitized and viewed from perspectives of advantage instead of disadvantage they can become lessons of wisdom and understanding. We become appreciative of the opportunity of being able to learn how strong we really can be and how capable we really are as human beings. Our toughest times are the times that most reveal our character and that reveal our inner strengths to ourselves. We can go from being victims to survivors, and then, once we have new, more appropriate perspectives and viewpoints in place, we can thrive.

I have come to believe what my first hypnotherapist— Marilyn Humphreys, the one who gave me my first experiences in hypnotherapy—said: "We make all of our life's experiences good by learning to do good from the lessons learned from those experiences." When you have reached catalepsy trance, and you are asked the right questions, your personal truths will emerge, allowing you to work with what the problem really is versus what you or someone else may think it could be. Your personal truths are either promoting you forward in life or holding you back. We all have a number of deep-seated inappropriate beliefs that are inhibiting us and preventing us from moving forward as fast as we would like. Most everyone can benefit from these processes.

So let's go back to Johnny. First, we induce trance in Johnny and assist him into the fourth level of trance (catalepsy), where he would gain access to his conscious thoughts and beliefs and his subconscious memories and amplified emotions at one and the same time. We would next start the process of deductively having him go back and identify the feelings that he experiences on rainy days.

The goal would be to give the predominant emotion a name. We want to prompt for the identification of the emotional content because we want Johnny to describe it. What we're really doing is connecting the dots between the subconscious and conscious minds, between the thoughts and the emotions. The amount of emotional content Johnny brings up in the regression process shows how much he has amplified the beliefs he accepted in his imagination.

The Initial Sensitizing Event

Johnny is forty years old, and he has not remembered this sensitizing experience for over thirty years. All of a sudden in his mind and his memory, he is six years old and he has his nose pressed up against the window. It's been raining for three days. And for three days, he's been looking at his friend's house next door and at the sandbox on the side of the yard with his toys.

His buddy next door is not able to play outside either, since the belief system their mothers have is, in effect, "You'll get all wet and catch a cold; you'll track mud into the house onto the carpets," and so forth. For three days Johnny has been cooped up, and he's had it. He makes the choice and establishes it, logging it into his belief system: "I hate it when it rains. I hate rain. I just can't stand rain."

Children don't have very well-developed critical factor/belief system filters because the critical factor is mostly developed between the ages of seven to ten years old. So negative thoughts can get locked into our belief systems and amplified to a huge degree at a very early age.

Now Johnny is in trance, and he goes back to this emotional content that has been lodged there ever since he was six years old. He's been acting like he's six years old ever since on rainy days and he is now forty. He's been angry, irritated, and grouchy on rainy days because of an immature belief that his subconscious mind is attempting to prove true so he won't feel he is wrong. He hates rain, but he had forgotten all about the sandbox. Now it's about spotting his new car and washing mud onto the driveway. His whole focus has changed, but his underlying belief system and behavior are the same.

During the hypnotherapy process, Johnny realizes that he created this emotional content with a decision he made at six years old. My job then becomes pointing out to him other alternatives to this accepted original belief, in order to expand his options. By suggesting additional viewpoints and perspectives, I seek to teach Johnny personal problem-solving skills so he can solve his own problems.

Coming up with additional points of view is important while clients are in a state where they can access both their conscious and subconscious information. Yet, it is what Johnny chooses to believe next—which is up to him—that can completely alter his perception of the original experience. Johnny is now in a position to desensitize his imagination and collapse the emotional content of his earlier negative interpretations. He is on the verge of altering his behavior in a geometric way.

Johnny now sees himself as a small boy with his nose pressed against the window. We brought all of that information from the subconscious back to the conscious side of his mind to help him understand the initial sensitizing event that stimulated his strong feelings. For Johnny, it was three days of rain. Now I challenge the belief system that he's accepted in his critical factor about rain.

So I start out, "Hey Johnny, let's get real here. Don't you really like the fresh, clean smell of the air right after a rainstorm?" His response (like that of most other clients in this situation) is, "Well, you know what? I've never really thought about it." A person who is stuck on some concept in their belief system usually hasn't ever thought about alternatives because all he's been trying to do is justify, validate, and defend his belief—in this case, "I hate rain." "Don't you like the fact that your grass gets greener, the flowers bloom prettier, the trees are brighter, and the whole world looks like it just took a shower after it rains?"

"Now that I think about it for a minute, yeah, I actually do. But I've never thought about any of that before."

What so often happens to each of us is that we have this little slice of our experience pie that we're constantly trying to justify, validate, and defend. My hope is to open up thinking, to help people get a 360-degree view of life, instead of this little slice of the pie that they got themselves locked into by their original thought processes, in turn determining their behavior patterns.

Every thought I can get Johnny to accept with me here is a plus: "Yeah, I like the fresh air." "Yes. I do like the greener grass." Everything that I can get him to accept will help him to alter his perceptions of his memories. I have him go back in his mind just a little: "Think about the last storm you were in. When you came home, wasn't the grass a little greener?" "Yeah, it really was." "Wasn't the air fresher?" "Yes, it really was."

Now I am altering Johnny's perception of the memory. I'm not altering the reality of the original experience, but I can change the perception because we're simply including more information than he has considered before. And everything Johnny accepts that alters the perceptions in his memory helps to desensitize the inflated imagination. Eventually this process collapses his negative emotions and changes or modifies his behavior.

Hypnotherapy is wonderful work. I love what I do. And I like to watch the change in people's faces. The highlights are those days when somebody comes in the door burdened with a false belief that is destroying their motivation and almost incapacitating them, burdened with emotional content from a sensitizing experience that they have carried for years.

And then we teach them how to desensitize their imagination and, in just an hour or two, they're able to release two or three major negative beliefs that have been burdening them for years. They learn to challenge and change old, negative beliefs, shut down their imaginations, and free up their memories. It's like a miracle. I see people come in as victims of themselves and their life experiences and then leave as empowered survivors.

Secondary Defense Mechanisms

Secondary defense mechanisms are attempts to compensate for discomfort or pain, whether physical or emotional. They are behaviors that try to create comfort and pleasure to offset the discomfort and suffering that emerges when amnesia and denial don't work. Secondary defenses or payoffs are the benefits we each accept to justify, validate, and defend the behaviors we are exhibiting.

Some psychosomatically induced pain or illness, for example, may get us out of mowing the lawn or taking out the trash and we certainly should not ever weed the garden again. Sure we eat uncontrollably, but we are never going to intentionally be pretty or attractive again, because being overweight and unattractive is keeping us safe from relationships with others and the potential of being a target of predators.

The paradox is that these secondary actions, in most cases, are costing us what we want most. When a person denies an initial learning experience and continues to deny it through successive experiences, they continue to have similar experiences again and again because they have never learned an appropriate response to the first experience. When a client finally seeks out hypnotherapy, it is often because they have developed a rigid response to a specific type of stimulus.

It's interesting that insanity has jokingly been described as doing the same thing over and over again and expecting different results. Anger, for instance, is usually rooted in unfulfilled expectations. A person who always turns to anger in response to unfulfilled expectations can be taught the principles of spiritual mind management that are laid out in this book. They will then know how to view their expectation levels from different vantage points, see any false connections, and adjust accordingly.

A person who gets angry as a secondary defense for fear can learn to address the fear itself and thus alleviate the need for the angry response in the first place. Hypnotherapists should successfully utilize what the person brings with them to a session and help them see that they can choose to redirect it to choices that are appropriate and goal-oriented.

Everyone rebels against something, but when that rebellion is not working, a person might need to understand that a useful purpose of the ability to rebel can be to rebel against the rebellion! *"The purpose of hypnotherapy isn't so much to understand human behavior, but to show processes for altering behavior above and beyond the way someone is currently behaving." (Virgil Hayes)*

Secondary defense mechanisms include such behaviors as:

Rationalization or providing plausible but untrue reasons for conduct (We are all familiar with this one.)

Humor and laughter

Often in a session, because hypnosis accesses subconscious emotions, a person will begin to vent emotions spontaneously. These emotions may include laughter. People may even laugh while describing painful and hurtful experiences. In these instances, the laughter is actually the crying. When someone begins to laugh almost uncontrollably in a session, it most often turns to crying before long.

Intellectualization

Some people tend to keep their Intelligence in consciousness, or conscious outward observation, remaining disconnected from their subconscious imagination, memories, and emotions. This is actually a form of amnesia and denial, and is the most difficult reaction to work with in hypnotherapy as a rule. When the Intelligence is fully forward, that is, in front of the critical factor and still in consciousness, it is difficult to help the client bring up the memories, imaginings, or emotions needed for obtaining clarity. Intellectualization is likely an attempt to stay in conscious control to avoid their otherwise out-of-control subconscious emotional content—a form of denying the emotions of the past while staying in disconnect through being continually conscious.

"I tried" or "I'll try!"

Whenever we use the word try, we must come to understand that our subconscious knows that we are lying. People don't try to do anything—we either do it or we don't. Put your pencil out in front of you and *try* to pick it up. No, don't just pick it up—*try* to pick it up.

To say we are *trying* to do something puts us in a double bind between our two minds. The conscious mind is attempting to alleviate the pressure from having to make a decision, a commitment. But the subconscious mind knows we are still uncommitted. We put up a defense mechanism with those around us by making a false attempt or giving ourselves an excuse for failure in advance. We can then say we tried to make it to the event, as an acceptable excuse for not making it or doing whatever else someone has asked us to do.

I don't know

This is another example of a secondary defense statement. As little children, we did not know many things, and we got away from the responsibility of knowing by using the excuse, "I don't know." How could we be judged or condemned for not doing something that we didn't know how to do? But as adults, if the thing in question is something we ought to know as part of our job or career, or just as part of adult life in general, continuing to fall back on the excuse "I don't know" is highly detrimental.

It is not only detrimental to one's own sense of self-worth, it also undermines personal integrity. It may be okay not to know something that we are supposed to know at a particular moment. We may need to acknowledge that we will find it out or learn it. But if we really need to know it, then let's get out and learn it. Sometimes "I don't know" may mean "I don't want to bother" or "I don't want to tell you" or "I'm lying and if I answer that question, I'll be discovered."

If we don't know what no one else knows about us, then who does? How can anyone else know? Because hypnosis gives us subconscious access to the experiences, conversations, and sensory perceptions we have experienced from birth, hypnotherapy can break the amnesia and denial of "I don't know." Like parents who allow their children to use "I don't know" as an excuse ("Johnny, why did you hit your little sister?" "I don't know—it just happened.")

We do our clients a disservice when we do not ask them to take responsibility for their actions, but allow them to continue on in amnesia and denial by using this excuse. The correct challenging statement is, "You mean you don't know yet. Allow yourself to go a little deeper into relaxation and find out what you really do know."

I can't

This is still another secondary defense statement, one that really means, **"I won't."** "I can't learn that." "I can't decide that now." "I could never do the kinds of things they do—I can't change." "I can't remember." "I can't get along with them." And so forth. It's amazing how we all *can* do what we really want to do or what we have to do when what we care about is jeopardized. How do we know we *can't*, when we haven't prepared, and practiced, and practiced again until we *can?*

We may find we have all kinds of hidden abilities once we make a new choice, a commitment, and say, "I will." "I will learn that." "I will decide now." "I will do whatever it takes to accomplish the changes I want to make." "I will remember that in just a moment, I'm sure it will come back to me." "I will change—I can do whatever it is that I need to do." Then, to make our commitment even more powerful, we can say the statements in the present tense: "I am learning." "I am deciding." "I am doing everything that it takes."

The above list may give you some ideas as to what to look for in yourself or as a hypnotherapist with your own clients. A number of other secondary defense mechanisms and behaviors exist, but these are the ones our hypnotherapists deal with most.

Through hypnotherapy, we provide clients with processes for identifying their sensitizing or original learning experiences. From their accumulated lifetime of experiences, we give them the opportunity to re-decide how to interpret those events. In this process of discovering what the stimulus was that developed the behavior in the first place, they may experience confusion. Learning does not occur without confusion; it is the feedback we are looking for as hypnotherapists that indicates that we have successfully challenged the client's fears and motivations. Then we are able to show them how to make new choices and alternative decisions—in other words, to have new responses to old stimuli.

A Client Learns to Master her Emotions

Many people experience a sense of feeling out of control, of not being in charge of themselves when they are just responding to life with learned, rigid response patterns, rather than making conscious choices from moment to moment. At Certified Hypnotherapy Training School, we want our clients functioning from consciousness in the here and now.

We teach people to make decisions from conscious choice from moment to moment, based on current stimuli rather than on past memories or imagination or emotions. As noted earlier, when your Intelligence is in emotions, you will become aware of feeling it from the top of the back of your head going down the back of the head almost to the shoulders. Here is one example of a client who learned this valuable lesson:

Dennis: Okay, the other thing we want to do is to teach you how to go into your emotions. To go into your emotions deductively lock into your emotional content with your Intelligence. We have people look down to the left, because that's the physical cue that we are locking into our emotions. Look down to the left. I want you to find a very happy time; maybe Christmas or a birthday party or one of those happiest times in your life, one of those most pleasurable times for you. Tell me when you feel that feeling right there. Go find it.

Speaker 2: Okay.

Dennis: Now what I want you to do at this point is recognize that the part of the emotions you are experiencing reacts with your imagination. I want you to understand that you're in control of your feelings and emotions. I want you to really be happy; so double that feeling you have now. I want you to double that feeling of happiness, and then double it, again and again.

Speaker 2: Seriously?

Dennis: Seriously. How does that feel?

Speaker 2: Feels good.

Dennis: Do you want any more, a little more?

Speaker 2: Sure.

Dennis: Double that again.

Speaker 2: That's a good thing.

Dennis: Double that again. Okay just enjoy that right there for a minute and in a second I will count to three, very quickly, and then I want you to look at my hand. Okay 1, 2 and 3, right here. Right here, look right here, right over here, outward at my hand. What happened to those emotions you were locked onto?

Speaker 2: They just faded.

Dennis: They just faded? Now the way we describe this is that you have detached from them. That part of your mind that you feel moving around there; we call it your Intelligence, the thing that actually moves within us, and inside our spirit. We actually sense it moving, so we can either attach to our emotions or we can detach from them. Some people use the words "associate with them or dissociate from them." Is that the way you would describe what you just did?

Speaker 2: Yeah.

Dennis: Okay, you just let that memory go?

Speaker 2: Uh-huh

Dennis: Okay one more time. Look down to the left, lock on to that feeling again. This time though, I want you to double it, and double it again. Let me know when you have doubled it three times. Are you there?

Speaker 2: Yes.

Dennis: Only this time I want you to come back slowly, and bring that feeling back into the room with you. Bring it back very slowly, hang on to it, bring it back, bring it back, and just be here happy in the current moment. Are you happy to be here?

Speaker 2: Yes.

Dennis: Now you know how to be happy all the time. Does it feel good?

Speaker 2: Feels good.

Dennis: The point here is that our Intelligence can attach to our emotions, or we can detach from them. What most people have done, when they come in for hypnotherapy, is that they've allowed their Intelligence to be fixated into or onto old negative emotions. They've brought those old emotions forward to the current moment in time, and they're reliving those old feelings and thoughts constantly. Does that make sense?

Speaker 2: Yes.

Dennis: So you now know you have the ability to attach or detach from feelings. Look right here at my hand again; let it go, look right here at my hand. Is the memory gone?

Speaker 2: Yes.

Dennis: Okay, but if you wanted to reattach to something at any time you chose, you could do that. You could choose to bring that feeling back into the current moment in time. Or you could choose to let it go. This also applies to any negative feeling or thought—you can attach to it or detach from it. You have that same ability if you consciously think about it and choose to do something different; true or false?

Speaker 2: True.

Dennis: Valuable?

Speaker 2: Valuable!

Dennis: Okay, well what I want you to recognize again is that if we have the power to turn our emotional content up, then we also have the power to turn our emotional content down. And if we were to turn it all the way down, we can also learn to turn it off. We worked on some of that before, true? I want to practice that with you a couple more times. Look down to your left, lock on to that happy feeling, and let me know when you have it.

Speaker 2: Okay.

Dennis: Double it, and double it again. I'm going to count to three and then I want you to look at my hand immediately. 1, 2, 3, Look right here;

look over here, right here. Where did that feeling go?

Speaker 2: Gone.

Dennis: It's gone. Now once again it's not that it's gone, it's that your Intelligence inside your mind, that piece of you that is moving around in there, that is you, is not attached to it. So it's not that it's gone forever, it's just that you have chosen not to attach to it. Does that make sense?

Speaker 2: Yes.

Dennis: Okay, now lock on to that feeling again and look down to the left, please. As you look down to the left this time, I want you to amplify that feeling, double it, and double it again. I want you to be really happy this time, so double it again then let me know if you have it amplified. Now this time I want you to come back into the room with it. Bring it back slowly. We're not going to go 1, 2, 3, and jerk you out of it. I want you to move 1, 2, and 3 very slowly. Bring it back with you. Even amplify it a little more, bring it back with you into this place. Got it?

Speaker 2: Yeah.

Dennis: Now I wish you could see how bright your eyes are and how happy you look right now.

Speaker 2: Hey, I want to cry, it's weird.

Dennis: Because?

Speaker 2: I'm really happy.

Dennis: You're really happy?

Speaker 2: It's weird.

Dennis: Now you know how to be happy all the time.

Speaker 2: Yes, I'm getting silly.

Dennis: Isn't it great to be happy?

Speaker 2: For sure.

Dennis: Now this is a real key point for you, because in the past what you've been doing is that you've been going down and locking onto old negative experiences, old negative emotions, and bringing them to the current moment in time. And that's how you've been letting the past ruin the current moment, the present. You got it?

Speaker 2: Yeah, right!

Dennis: You understand it now?

Speaker 2: Yes.

Dennis: Now you can choose to hang onto old emotions, positive or negative, at this point, because you now have control over your own mind. You can choose to hold on or let go. Look at my hand, 1, 2, and 3; look right here, let the emotion go, let it go. Tell me when it's gone. Is it gone?

Speaker 2: Yeah.

Dennis: How cool is that?

Speaker 2: Really cool.

Dennis: So have you been learning to be more in control of your mind, or less in control of it, in these processes?

Speaker 2: More, a lot more.

Living with Freedom of Choice

There are many ways we can enjoy life free of past fixations, free to consciously make good choices. One client we saw, for example, was a 78-year-old woman who had never been in therapy of any kind. She was getting ready to go on a cruise and was rather concerned about this, even experiencing fears about going.

Her daughter, whom I had worked with previously, brought her for a session of hypnotherapy. When we started the session, we started right back when the woman was three and four years old. She was afraid of going to school—the newness of the experience provoked natural fears of the unknown. She also did not want to be away from mom and family.

Her husband was not going to accompany her on the cruise. She was just going to be with her sisters, so she had similar fears of the unknown and of a completely new experience. Anticipating the cruise was a symptom-producing event that triggered her original response to her initial sensitizing event of going to school for the first time.

As is often the case when we do subconscious work like hypnotherapy, this woman had not thought about those initial childhood experiences in many decades. Yet during hypnosis her personal truths came up, and she was able to recognize that she was responding as a child and not as an adult. When she reprogrammed her younger self with her present viewpoint of now being an adult with many years of experience, the emotional content of her apprehensions collapsed, and she enjoyed a wonderful new experience by going on the cruise fear-free.

These hypnotherapy processes also create intentional control over the impulse to do what we ought not to do—for example, the temptation to look at pornography due to a suggestion from a line from a song or an image setting off scripts that go through our minds. Hypnotherapists can teach techniques to combat them. This also applies to food impulses. You could say that whenever you make a decision to do something, you have hypnotized yourself. You decide something consciously and your Intelligence fixates upon it, so you act upon it. Your Intelligence locks onto a specific decision when given a particular stimulus. Perhaps a person's character, personality, and behavior are the sum of these accepted predominant thoughts. *Self-hypnosis may well be defined as an improved decision-making process.*

In the reverse, addictions might be viewed as simply a string of continuous wrong choices, as predominant thoughts that have captured or locked onto our Intelligences as we consistently misapplied our power of choice. Making a series of consistently wrong choices may be where cravings and addictions originate. Perhaps all hypnotherapy, NLP (neurolinguistic programming), and other forms of mental health therapies are simply attempting to help people become clear and free-minded by freeing up the proper and full functioning of their Intelligences.

Since a person with a free-functioning Intelligence enjoys the power and freedom of agency and choice, they can accept responsibility and accountability for their choices and actions. This means no more excuses. They can live in truth, which not only makes them free, but keeps them free! *Everything then becomes a conscious choice, from moment to moment!*

CHAPTER EIGHT

Make Conscious Choices with Truth Balanced in the Center

I have discussed the concept of an inner Intelligence and how it moves to different locations within our spiritual minds. I have also explained that those locations include consciousness, imagination, memories, and emotions, and I have provided descriptions and examples of each area. In this chapter, I will explain why it matters *where* our Intelligences are in our minds. You will learn how recognition of where it is at influences what we think by giving us the opportunity to view different viewpoints and gain personal insights and understandings into whatever we are considering. This is a major part of what we are calling personal problem solving.

Finding Balance within our Minds

Most of us want truth and balance in all areas of our lives. Water is a good example of this need and desire for truth and balance. We must have water to live, as up to 70% of our body weight is water. Yet, if someone were to try to obtain as much water as possible by dunking his head in a five-gallon bucket of water and breathing in all the water he can, he would either come up coughing and sputtering or he would drown. If, realizing that water could drown him, he then decided never to drink water again, he would eventually begin to dehydrate and become seriously ill. Eventually the individual would come to understand that no water at all could also kill him. The truth about water, then, is found in balance—in the center. We each must have enough water to live healthily—not so much that we drown and not so little that we dehydrate.

> *The truth will most often be found in balance in the center, not at either end or extreme.*

A balanced view of things is usually the best view of whatever we are thinking about. It puts us in the position of being "response-able"—able to make new choices that are right for us. Balance is the point at which we can consider different options from multiple vantage points in our own minds, and then make a conscious choice of what action to take.

When your Intelligence is centered in your mind, that is, when you can feel it in the middle or central position on top of your head for each of the four areas (conscious outward observation, imagination, memory, and emotion), then you are learning, imagining, remembering, and feeling your emotions in balance. You should then be able to enjoy living a balanced life where your decisions are consciously chosen.

The real Key to "Intelligence Mind Management" hypnotherapy is not just in the Suggestion structure, the depth of trance, and other processes and procedures, but in asking the Right Questions in the Right Verbiage to elicit the Right Information from the Subconscious!

"It's all in there"!

When the "Intelligence" is Centered in the positions of Conscious Outward Observation, Imagination, Memories, or Emotions, you are Learning, Imagining, Remembering, and Feeling your Emotions in Balance.

We are to enjoy living a Balanced Life!

The more the "Intelligence" is fixated, is positioned, or moves, to the Right Side of the Head Downward, the further into Seeking, Identifying, and Fighting for the Predominant Thoughts or Scripts being ran in the Subconscious, Imaginations, Memories, or Emotions.

The more the "Intelligence" is fixated, is positioned, or moves to the Left Side of the Head Downward, the further into Avoiding, Alienating, and Flight from the Predominant Thoughts, Images, or Scripts ,being ran in the Subconscious, Imaginations, Memories, or Emotions.

Right and Left Mean Fight and Flight

When your Intelligence is in the area of balanced imagination, you will be aware of it in a range that covers from the top of your forehead back to the center of the top of your head. The more the Intelligence is fixated, positioned in, or moves to the right side of the head downward, the greater the amplification you will experience—seeking, identifying with, and fighting to maintain the predominant thoughts or scripts being run in that area of the mind. In other words, the further you're Intelligence sits or travels down on the right side of your head, the more you are fighting for, seeking, and identifying with the thought, experience, or visualization now in your imagination. The further your Intelligence sits or travels down your head to your left, the more you are fleeing from, avoiding, or alienating from that same thought, experience, or visualization.

The Mind Management skill the authors wish to teach here is that anyone can learn to move thoughts, experiences, or visualizations from one side of the mind to the other. Doing so allows you to see a single thought or experience from different perspectives inside of your mind. You will come to realize that when your Intelligence is at the crown of your head, in the area we designate as imagination, your ability to think is in balance. From there you can make a conscious choice as to whether you choose to amplify a particular thought, experience, or visualization in a positive or negative direction. *Knowing how to do this makes you capable of seeing everything as a conscious choice, giving you ultimate control of your own mind.*

To use an example of something that we are all exposed to in the media, a sexually suggestive image, that you think about or dwell upon the image with some excitement, lust, or desirable light, you would identify it as being in the area of the imagination on the right side of your head. If you intentionally moved it to the crown of your head, you would see the image change. It would lose some of its lifelike qualities. However, if you took that image further to the left, all the way down to the left side of your imagination, it would grow dimmer and dimmer until you could watch it completely disappear. Learning this mental skill can give you the freedom to immediately walk away from behaviors such as involvement in pornography. You can willingly bury such pictures with amnesia and denial to manage your mind and prevent them from returning.

One client identified an image in his mind when his Intelligence was all the way to the right side of the front half of his head, reporting that he saw an image of a naked man and woman. As I had him move the image slowly up to the crown of his head, the naked couple now had clothes on. Then, I had him move this image down to the far left of his head to the point that it just disappeared.

Amplifying Memories in Fight or Flight Mode

We can go into the extremes of fight or flight mode with virtually any stimulus, depending on how much amplification in the imagination we choose to give to the impulse, the image, or the memory. An individual can identify with or alienate from food, for example. We each have associations that trigger old feelings of "eat this, and it will make you feel better" behaviors. So we can find ourselves using food as a means of feeling good and to alienate ourselves from the thoughts that make us feel "not good enough." Depending upon which side of this equation we choose to make our most predominant thought, we can choose to become obese or bulimic and anorexic, or we can choose to be balanced in our use of food.

A person who has had early sexual encounters, depending on their interpretations of those experiences, can either identify with or alienate themselves from overly sexualized thoughts. They can either seek or avoid sexual encounters in the future. How they amplify the memories and emotions of those experiences will determine whether they become promiscuous or frigid. A person who has experienced violent physical encounters may also choose either to seek out or flee from that kind of situation in the future. Depending upon which side of the equation they choose to amplify, they may become angry or fearful.

I teach the introductory concepts of the spiritual mind and our Intelligence, such as discerning the movement of an inner Intelligence shifting from place to place; much the same way I learned it from Virgil many years ago. The movement we felt in our spiritual minds at that time was shown to students to help us gain an awareness that something like our Intelligence does exist. Again, at the time it was called, "I am of Self." The main purpose was to teach us that we could live conscious lives and make conscious choices.

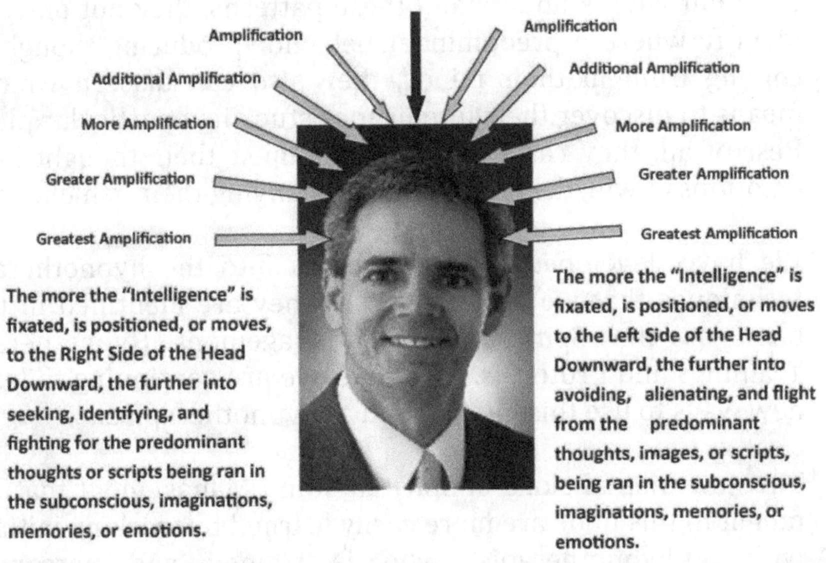
When the "Intelligence" is Centered at the crown of the head you are in balance in the positions of Conscious outward observation, imagination, memories, or emotions.
This is where you can imagine, remember, or feel things in Balance.
We are to enjoy living a Balanced Life!
Amplification
Amplification
Additional Amplification
Additional Amplification
More Amplification
More Amplification
Greater Amplification
Greater Amplification
Greatest Amplification
Greatest Amplification
The more the "Intelligence" is fixated, is positioned, or moves, to the Right Side of the Head Downward, the further into seeking, identifying, and fighting for the predominant thoughts or scripts being ran in the subconscious, imaginations, memories, or emotions.
The more the "Intelligence" is fixated, is positioned, or moves to the Left Side of the Head Downward, the further into avoiding, alienating, and flight from the predominant thoughts, images, or scripts, being ran in the subconscious, imaginations, memories, or emotions.
Certified Hypnotherapy Training School - http://certifiedhypnotherapytrainingschool.com/ - © 2014 All Rights Reserved

I am now able to use and teach the additional knowledge I have gained over many years of observing client responses to the fight–flight and imaginary amplification patterns described above. We use this information to do de-hypnosis of natural somnambulist clients, more rapidly produce pain control results, and many other behavioral modifications that we will continue to explain.

The ability for clients to understand the effects of where one's Intelligence is found in these patterns is a huge leap forward in assisting them. In addition, we can identify both the volume and intensity of that emotional content and its attendant behavioral effect. This information helps us better guide people through changes in their internal perspectives of themselves by quickly desensitizing the events responsible for their fixations. We literally give them new ways to view their personal thoughts, something that improves their internal problem solving.

Once our clients understand these patterns, they not only can identify where a predominant behavior-producing thought is coming from in their minds, they also can discern what it means to discover their Intelligence stuck in a particular place. Best of all, they can learn how to adjust their thoughts and emotions at will, the key to quickly changing their behaviors.

We have developed these processes into the hypnotherapy techniques that we use and teach. They are identified in this book as the Spiritual Mind Management Hypnotherapy Trainings and Protocols. Of course, we are continuing to learn new ways to use this information as hypnotherapists.

The new mental skills of Spiritual Mind Management that are taught in this book are more easily learned by working initially with a hypnotherapist who is trained and personally experienced in these processes. However, our hope is that many people will take this information and continue to figure out their lives in new and different ways. Thus, our goal remains to give our clients the knowledge and tools to change their own lives in positive self-reliant ways.

Examples of Teaching Mind Management to Clients

The following are additional examples of how we teach mind management concepts and skills to our clients.

Dennis and Client/Speaker 2

Dennis: Let's move back here [to the back left side of memory]. It's where you found your address. Is that true? Point on your head, where it actually was—that was it, right?

Speaker 2: Uh-huh.

Dennis: Okay, so now with your address, the question is, if you put it back here [on the left side of the head, in memory, halfway down], the question is what address is it that you're thinking about? Since its back there I suspect that you really don't want to be in that location.

Speaker 2: It's where I live right now.

Dennis: So you have a desire to move out of where you live right now?

Speaker 2: Yes, sir.

Dennis: That's indicated by where you're at in your mind with that particular address.

Speaker 2: Yes.

Dennis: I want you to visualize, maybe not the exact address, but the place where you would like to live, the place where you would like to move to, and put your finger on your head where you feel, or see, or hear that place in your mind, where you like to be.

Speaker 2: Here… [Imagination, right side]

Dennis: Okay, so over here we're identifying, seeking, fighting for the new address, a new place where you want to be, and you notice that that's over here in the right side of your mind. Now what did you just learn about yourself?

Speaker 2: That I understand where my thoughts are, and that emotions are attached to them.

Dennis: Now if you want to go back and feel that, you can come back over here to the old address (left side). Be back over here, move your intelligence back over here, and have you now locked into the old memory, the old feeling there? And if you come back over here to the new thing, how does that feel different again? We're practicing this. See the difference? Feel the difference right there?

Speaker 2: Uh-huh.

Dennis: Now what would we want to do if we say, "I want to live my life in balance?" We would want to be happy where we're currently at, and to not over-emphasize where we want to go someday because that could set us up for anger and feelings of "I'm deprived," and so on, if we over-amplify the positive to too great a degree.

What I want you to do right now is to see the address where you live right now and bring it back into balance (top center of the head in memories) because it may not be really all that bad. It's just where you want to move away from someday; what's making it bad is the fact that you have this other thought. Bring it back right here into the balance and tell me what your present address feels like, looks like, when you see it right there.

Speaker 2: It's just normal.

Dennis: Yeah, so it's not negative, it's not positive. It's just kind of in balance right here?

Speaker 2: Uh-huh.

Dennis: Now take the image of where you want to go someday and kind of get it back in balanced perspective. Put it right here [top, crown of the head, in imagination]. What just happened?

Speaker 2: It's just normal as well.

Dennis: Yes and how does that feel?

Speaker 2: Peaceful. I know where I could go, but it's not tying me up.

Dennis: So you're at peace where you're currently at. That's different than what you were feeling just a minute ago, true?

Speaker 2: Uh-huh.

Dennis: And the other place is not so compelling that you are uncomfortable where you are. You've kind of brought them both back into a state of balance, true or false?

Speaker 2: True.

Dennis: So what does that look like, sound like, and feel like, for you now?

Speaker 2: Everything is okay; it's just wonderful.

Dennis: So we're back in reality, meaning conscious balance, true or false?

Speaker 2: True.

Dennis: What do you think about that?

Speaker 2: Feels better!

Dennis and Client is speaker 3.

Dennis: You're far down on the left side of your imagination now. There, right there. You're totally alienating your imagination from your old girlfriend, True or false?

Speaker 3: True.

Dennis: Now, feel that feeling. Bring that feeling to the crown of your head and take a look at it there. Bring it up. Learn to view things from a different viewpoint inside your own mind. Bring your Intelligence; bring that feeling right to the crown of your head. Put your finger on where you're at when you do. Now how does she look and sound different right there [at the crown of your head] than over there, on the left side?

Speaker 3: She looks better, that's what happens.

Dennis: Well, she might be better. Do you really want to look at her? Now bring her right over here and identify her on the right side.

Speaker 3: I don't even want to. I want her to look ugly, and let her go.

Dennis: Well, then bring her image back down on the left. Flee from it, alienate from it, and let her go. Take it back down, take her back down; just shove her right off down there, to the far left side of imagination.

Speaker 3: Okay.

Dennis: Now you've used amnesia and denial. You've used alienation intentionally for your own purposes. You got it?

Speaker 3: Yeah.

Dennis: It's okay to keep her over there. In this same way we can shut off images of pornography we may have seen, or other things that we don't want to remember. We have the ability and power to take those thoughts, put them over there [on the left] to where we flee from them, alienate them, and avoid them. We just put them over there to where we can't even see them. They don't even matter; we just don't care anymore. You got that?

Speaker 3: Yeah.

Dennis: Now for your own Spiritual Mind Management learning purposes, I'm teaching you how to manage your own mind in the future. I want you to practice this yourself because that's a good point of reference; right there [the far left]. Take your hand and put it where she is in your mind, where you turned her off, over there on the far left. I want you to practice and see the difference, what happens in your mind, as you bring her back to the crown of your head again. What just happened right there, when she's at the crown of your head, in imagination?

Speaker 3: She got bigger and brighter.

Dennis: She got bigger and brighter. Now if you want to amplify your imagination, increase it, now bring her image back to the far right and go identify with the image. Now what just happened?

Speaker 3: She looks like a goddess.

Dennis: Now, what did you just learn?

Speaker 3: Not to imagine stuff you can't have anyway; and that you can control the balance.

Dennis: Exactly! I'd like to note something about what you just learned. We're working with more and more people who have problems with pornography and those kinds of things. Your issue of being fixated on the image of your old girlfriend in your mind is exactly the same as what people do when they're obsessed with pornography. They're over here on the right. They've amplified the images to be goddess-like when the truth is something entirely different.

Weeding the Garden of Your Mind of Pornography

Have you ever asked, "How can anyone do such a thing to someone else, or to themselves?" Or, "Why do I keep doing what I do, even when I know I ought not to be doing it?" What are the keys to real behavioral change? How would learning the skills of behavioral modification that are being offered here change yours and your loved ones lives? What if you had the knowledge and skills to assist others to: have impulse control managing unwanted emotions, be free of pornography, have enhanced learning abilities and test taking relaxation skills, enjoy increased self-esteem and personal self-confidence, enhance sports performance, be free of fears and phobias, stop smoking, loose that unwanted weight once and for all, enjoy pain control reducing your pain levels, living a more enjoyable life, and change a myriad of other personal behaviors and attributes for the best?

A key principle of positive behavioral modification and change is that we teach students and clients how to overcome double mindedness. James 1:8 says, "a double minded man is unstable in all his ways." We propose the double mindedness spoken of here is the incongruent predominant thought thinking errors that we have logged in our subconscious mind, that are in opposition to the goal achieving desires that we have in our conscious mind. When we have incongruent thinking and opposite beliefs at our conscious and subconscious states of mind it creates opposing forces within us, "instability." We want to move forward, achieve new goals, and be our best self-consciously and yet as we hold opposing, incongruent thoughts and beliefs in the subconscious mind. We experience inhibitions, hesitations, and we procrastinate. We are unstable in all our ways!

There is an area between the two minds called the Critical Faculty or Critical Factor which is the area of our belief systems. It is a filter to the subconscious mind. When we do conscious critical, analytical, logical thinking, and we accept a thought as being right, true and correct for us, we allow it to pass through the critical factor into our subconscious functions of imaginations, memories, and emotions. Once the belief is in the subconscious it will generate a behavior. The extreme to which the behavior is demonstrated depends on how much amplification of our imagination we apply to the thought, and how much justifying and validating data, we can come up with in our memories to prove to ourselves that we are right in our chosen belief. The amount of amplification and justification is the amount of emotional content we experience as our feelings; drive our behavior because we behave the way we feel.

The "KEY" is that it requires hypnosis, trance, or pondering, (all three are synonymous to us) to penetrate the critical factor filter barrier and access the incongruent thinking errors being held in the subconscious. It requires skills and training in trance to know which hypnotic level (because there are seven observable states of mind that we utilize in hypnotherapy) is going to work best for the chosen hypnotherapy procedure, to challenge and change the newly found thinking errors. Once these thinking errors are challenged appropriately and brought into alignment with conscious goal driven thinking, being single-minded, people now move forward in life fulfilling their dreams and goals more rapidly than ever before imagined possible.

We use the metaphor that what we are doing is weeding the garden of our mind. Let's say we have a major thinking error, a big weed in our garden. In conscious or cognitive therapy, we may whack away at the leaves above the ground, we may break off branches, and with sufficient time, we might even chop it down to the ground. Without hypnosis or trance access to the subconscious root and the training to know how to actually pull it all the way out resolution is extremely difficult. When the individual experiences a similar stimulating event that generated the behavior producing thought process in the first place, the weed is stimulated and simply grows back, and so does the behavior.

A major key to behavioral modification hypnotherapy is overcoming double mindedness instability by having subconscious access through trance and pulling out the root causes of the behaviors. The following two of stories give insight to how these processes are utilized in overcoming the maladaptive behaviors of pornography.

Man age 25 shares his story about pornography

One of the most significant blessings in my life has been to learn about and receive hypnotherapy. Outside of my religion, nothing in my life has been as satisfying, encouraging, enabling, or uplifting. I am a 25 year old man who has struggled with depression, anger, and other effects of sexual abuse from another male. Some of these effects include impulses towards pornography and self-abuse. My life was in serious straits when I was first introduced to Dennis.

When I was 23, I was on the verge of throwing my life away to sexual addictions. I am a religious man, and I have felt ashamed of my emotions and actions, and I didn't understand why or how my life had turned into such a mess. I had struggled for years to overcome my feelings of resentment towards myself and the bad habits I had developed. I had gotten to the point where the burdens felt unendurable.

I felt that for the most part my therapists were unable to help me, that my family was let down, and that my religious leaders were shaming and condemning, and my God either uncaring or unhearing. It was at this point in my life that I actually *decided* to throw in the towel on living the life I wanted (having a wife and family) to live a life of self-abuse and pornography. Feeling isolated with no family, no church, and no God. As the old saying goes, "if you can't beat 'em, join 'em!" My mother ignorant of my plans must have had a stroke of inspiration and somehow convinced me to go see Dennis. She wanted me to see what I thought of his mind-management classes of which she had previously attended.

I will admit I was not overjoyed with my first visit with Dennis. I learned he does not believe in the traditional definitions of addiction. Dennis took away my excuses, with challenging and logical questions and explanations. He clearly explained how my repeated actions and behaviors developed from concepts that originated from my stimulus experiences. He taught me that whatever we have learned to do, we can challenge and change, that I could learn to do things in new and different *healthy ways.*

He taught me that through choice and accountability in my thoughts, beliefs, and concepts, I can choose which thoughts I allow to formulate into emotions, which then transfer into my actions and behavior. He taught me that I am responsible for becoming response – able. I am now better able to respond to the generated thoughts that come from the stimuli' I receive. He believes that "regular pornography involvement" is a consistent misuse of our agency, a string of inappropriate choices, giving way to spontaneous impulses which were ineffectually challenged and left unchanged. He taught me new mental skills which are personally revitalizing and empowering. When I take the time to use these tools, I am able to have self-control and see my misconceptions for what they are which then lead to understanding myself better. Dennis took away my ability to say "That's just the way I am," as well as all my other ways of saying "It's time to give up," because all my excuses were grounded in my misconceptions, and he helped me see them for what they were falsehoods and fears.

I gradually began to see that my inappropriate choices were giving me new ways to grow and change my entire vision of life. I grew more comfortable expressing my feelings and struggles, and I found that happiness began to permeate my life in a way I had not experienced for years. Giving my emotions a name and a voice helped me see my emotions as something more concrete than abstract chemical processes in the brain. This concept helped me connect my emotions with the thoughts that were generating my emotional content in the first place.

Hypnotherapy gave me a way to manage my inner voice that generated my emotions, as opposed to suffocating or trying to ignore my thoughts and feelings. I learned that my emotions do not define me, that my emotions are coming from my accepted thoughts, and are not me (that was a game changer for me) I am *not* my emotions, and I have real control over them! I have the ability to change my mental template, and immediately dissolve old emotional content, thereby allowing for new emotions based on the new more truth-full thoughts. This knowledge has helped me to escape so much of the shame that I felt, and the anger and depression that I felt to such extremes have now vanished almost completely.

I want to be clear; hypnotherapy is not a magic pill that gets rid of all your problems. I still have to fight the battle of choice whether or not I will accept inappropriate thoughts from time to time about pornography is still mine to fight. But I now understand my power better. I still get angry, I still get confused and depressed sometimes when I am not managing my thoughts and actions well, but I know how to fight now.

While I have received help from other therapists that I have been to over the years, I feel that I have gained most from hypnotherapy because it permeates the deepest part of myself my inner voice and emotions. I don't need to spend the rest of my life running and hiding from problems, or talking endlessly about them either. I don't need to give in to my problems, be they past, present, or future, because as I have learned through hypnotherapy that I have the ability to choose what I will become and who I allow myself to be. I choose what voice I listen to, what decisions to live by, what actions I choose to allow. I can choose to live by truth, and that is what sets me free.

To close, I also want to note that hypnotherapy has blessed my spiritual life as well. I was led to Dennis when I felt most abandoned by God, and I intended to abandon Him. Ironically, hypnotherapy has expanded my view of God, and drawn me closer to Him. I am better able to see the beautiful and fearsome powers and abilities that He has granted each one of us in our lives. I am learning that my spiritual life is more complete, more satisfying, more efficacious, and more beneficial to those around me when I take the time to use the gifts God has helped me find in hypnotherapy.

I am a different man when I use these skills, and I am able to use some of the same procedures and ideas expressed in hypnotherapy to bless the lives of my family and friends when they face trials and difficulties of their own to better see things as they really are. I am now planning on going to graduate school in therapy, as well as becoming certified in hypnotherapy so that I can pass on the emboldening and inspiring tools that have forever changed me.

A middle aged father of four

To start at the lowest point:

I was completely without hope... I had a plan in mind of how to end my life. It would have been easy, appearing accidental, with even a feeling that, "He died doing something he loved!" There would have been plenty of insurance money for the kids and wife, I would finally be able to rest from the affliction of pornography and its accompanying ills that hounded me and held me captive for 25 years of my 32 year existence here.

While it wasn't the only reason, pornography was among the biggest contributors to the other two huge problems staring me in the face that I couldn't resolve: a marriage that was a disaster despite my best efforts and a business that was crumbling after years of giving it the best I knew how. I felt like my inability to keep pornography in check was the reason my business and marriage were in such desperate straits. I felt like a complete failure!

Except for the day described above, I always knew deep within me I was not meant to live like this, I had a higher purpose. I just never knew when I would get through it and I never would have believed how. I am a father of four young children, and I had tried desperately for decades to make my actions conform to my beliefs.

I hated what I did. I could never figure out why part of me wanted something so intensely that the rest of me hated and punished myself for constantly. I sought help in twelve step groups for years. I counseled with every ecclesiastical leader who had stewardship over me from the time I was about thirteen. I was more prayerful and studious than 99 percent of people my age. I attended seminary in my teenage years with enough consistency and extra study to letter in seminary. I attended Institute of Religion courses for four years of college, waking up early or staying up late to excel in religion courses as well as in my career studies to graduate summa cum laude from college and with honors from the Institute of Religion.

Outside of religious education, I served as a leader in church programs, boy scouting, and FFA club during high school and after high school. I was always asked to lead others when I served a religious mission for twenty four months on the other side of the world (as the twelve steppers would say, "I white knuckled it for that entire duration), and when I came home I was unable to maintain abstinence from this dreadful habit. It seemed that the minority of my desires was ruling over the majority.

I abstained for nearly a year while I courted and started a marriage, but returned to the dreadful practice after being injured and laid up for several months early in our time together. I again counseled with ecclesiastical leaders and found strength to abstain for 18 months even when my wife refused to be intimate with me for months and even for over a year at a time.

At year four or five we sought professional help with one therapist who was supposed to be the best at treating pornography addiction. I experienced little or no progress in the three or four times I met with him. At year six we were referred to a therapist who, we found on good authority, was the very best in our area. He focused intensely on true principles of life and helped me truly believe that pornography is not an addiction but a reinforced habit. I learned later that *what* reinforced my habit was not at all what I believed it was. Through his counsel I was able to understand all the whys and why not's and I had nearly a year without incident, but there were close calls and a lot of white knuckling.

Part of me still wanted the porn so badly. I spent thousands of dollars with this great counselor who helped us make great strides forward as a couple and individually. After my lowest point I tried to go on anti-depressants to get me in a better place and relieve me from the temptations to view pornography. I tried three different medications, all of which made me worse to the point where I felt like my brain was burning and all I could do was lay in bed twitching from medication side effects. I still couldn't be free from this constant temptation.

I blamed my seemingly unconquerable desire for pornography on an early exposure at age seven. I used to believe that the exposure lead to heightened curiosity and lead me to view a lot of pornography over the subsequent years.

I always had the feeling there was something that needed to be unlocked, or unwound back to my childhood that contained the root of this desire. Until I experienced that first hypnotherapy session, I didn't think it was possible to even remember what this was, indeed many told me to just move on, that I would never be able to recall what it was that started this in me. I believed them and tried to move forward without fixing the past.

I was so scared to try hypnotherapy. I thought of the stage performers I had seen, I wondered if I would be looked down upon by my ecclesiastical leaders, I was scared of what I would say if I wasn't in control of my mind, and perhaps the greatest fear was that it all sounded too good to be true, another failed attempt waiting to happen.

I had nothing to lose; my wife had decided to divorce me by this time. I was truly seeking to solve my own problems and fix me so I could move on and be rid of the prison cell of pornography that I kept choosing.

In my first hypnotherapy session (I really didn't believe that I was even hypnotized at the beginning because it felt so natural), one of the first instances that came out of the session were a couple of memories I had of stealing toys when I was 7 years old. I learned that I had decided to never trust myself because of those actions. I believed the lie that I simply could not be trusted. I found through hypnotherapy that *this lie was what was reinforcing my habit of pornography indulgence.* As Dennis guided me through the process of learning the lessons I was supposed to learn from those experiences, and making proper restitution for my actions, my desire to view pornography immediately diminished. I became more and more single minded.

In visit after visit, more and more layers were removed to clear up lies and misunderstandings I had kept deep inside my mind from my earliest years and even very recent times. Perhaps the most important insight came during a session when Dennis pointed out that the enemy of our happiness speaks to us in the first person to make us believe it is us who wants to do what is contrary to what we know is right and good. That principle has been as a shield to my mind against negative thinking.

The Spiritual Mind Management principles I have learned through this process have allowed me to address a myriad of experiences on my own. I have used the triangular conversation gestalt technique, which really helps me to clear up lies, negative thinking, and interactions with others that have troubled me. I have also used the empty chair gestalt to banish negative personality parts I had allowed to enter and influence my personality. I am learning to control my intelligence for clearer thinking and decision-making, and even to enhance my creativity in problem solving at work. (Gestalts – See Chapter 10)

I highly recommend you give this process a chance. It will change your life. You have nothing to fear inside your own mind; you have everything to gain from becoming a unified whole person. I worried at times that this would impact my faith negatively. I have found that I have never been more faithful, optimistic, and hopeful. When I think back on that dark day when I lost all hope and nearly sought to end my life, I see those dark hours served to get me to a place that I could overcome my fears of trying something very different and for me that was hypnotherapy.

Now back to further understanding our imagination

Dennis and Client/Speaker 4

Dennis: Okay, so what I want you to do now is close your eyes, and I'll take your hand, and right here in your hand I will put the stem of a rose. Take this rose. Don't squeeze it too tight; you might get a thorn. I want you to very slowly bring that rose to your nose, and as you do, notice that the fragrance increases, gets clearer, stronger, fresher. Tell me when you have that rose, a very beautiful rose. Tell me when you smell the fragrance of that rose.

Speaker 4: I smell it.

Dennis: Now what color is your rose?

Speaker 4: Red.

Dennis: Take your left index finger and put it on your head where it is that you're seeing that red rose.

Speaker 4: Right here. [Top – center above the forehead]

Dennis: Okay, and as you're seeing that red rose right there, describe what it looks like. Can you give me any detail?

Speaker 4: Yeah, it's very soft—the petals look very soft—and there is a couple of dewdrops on them. The image is very detailed.

Dennis: Okay, now what I want to do is teach you where the positions of your mind are. I'm going to use my finger to indicate positions on your head, but now you know how to keep your Intelligence right there, with the details?

Speaker 4: Yes.

Dennis: Now I want you to continue to see and smell the rose. Only I want you to bring it up, your Intelligence up, and I want you to see and smell it from right here in your mind. What just happened? Put your Intelligence right here, on the right side. See and smell it from right here. What just changed inside your head?

Speaker 4: It went from more of an imagination to reality.

Dennis: Meaning what?

Speaker 4: It got more realistic looking.

Dennis: Excellent. Now move your Intelligence over here and see the rose over here. What's happening over here to the rose? (left side)

Speaker 4: It's turning plastic.

Dennis: Put it down here; what's happening down here to the rose?

Speaker 4: It's tainted and plastic and ugly….

Dennis: And down here….

Speaker 4: It doesn't smell good. It smells terrible and I just want to get rid of it.

Dennis: Okay, let's come back here again. Bring it back up here [to the center of the crown of your head, in imagination]. What does it look like here again? Bring it back here.

Speaker 4: A wonderful, real rose.

Dennis: Now bring it over here, to the right side. Now what's happening?

Speaker 4: It's like I can't smell it, and I can't really feel like I'm holding it. I can see it in a place like in a garden.

Dennis: Okay, so now it's a rose in a garden.

Speaker 4: It's a bright one. It's the brightest rose in the garden.

Dennis: Bring it right over here [further down to the right] does it get any brighter?

Speaker 4: It's getting like a brighter, richer color.

Dennis: Some people tell me that when they're seeing the rose over here, on the left side, it kind of looks like it's not real. What's it like over here?

Speaker 4: Plastic and disgusting.

Dennis: And on this side it looks like the brightest rose in the garden?

Speaker 4: Yes.

Dennis: Now what are you learning about your imagination, right there?

Speaker 4: It's as if it was a real rose on the right side and a fake and ugly rose on the left side.

Dennis: Now we have never discussed this before, done any of this, have we? This is all new experiential learning for you?

Speaker 4: Yes.

Dennis: The reason that I'm doing all of this is that I want you to recognize that you have your Intelligence, and we can learn to live in balance. Right here in the center is what I call balance. Put the rose back here. Now it's real. It's not plastic, but it's not the brightest thing in the garden, either. Put it right here and you will see it in balance. Now I want to propose that this is the right place for you to examine your thoughts from, so you can live your life in balance. Is that starting to make sense?

Speaker 4: Yeah.

Dennis: Your aim is to have your Intelligence right here in balance so that you're not alienating or fleeing from things, because the left side is flight. You avoid and alienate as you come down here, and as you alienate from the rose, it turns plastic and clear. Down here it turns…ugly

Speaker 4: Yuck!

Dennis: Yes, but on this side you're fighting for the thought, you're identifying with the thought, and you're increasing your imagination, and over here now it's the brightest…

Speaker 4: Rose in the garden.

Dennis: So you could take any thought and do this to it, and that's what people do. We can amplify the thought many times in the positive or many times in the negative. Now you're going to learn something else about this and how you can manage your mind. I want you to say the word "Dad,"

Speaker 4: Dad.

Dennis: Tell me where you go in your head when you say, "Dad."

Speaker 4: Here [the left side memories].

Dennis: Okay, learn something new, stay with me. Take Dad right here; bring him up here to the crown of your head in memories. Keep your Intelligence under your finger, and bring Dad up, put Dad right here. What just happened?

Speaker 4: He's standing in front of me, but I'm very, very angry at him.

Dennis: Yeah. This is what?

Speaker 4: This is reality. It's not too positive, and it's not too negative.

Dennis: Yeah, now see what happens. Bring Dad over here. Now what happens? Move your Intelligence over here, to the right side memories.

Speaker 4: Now I see him being all happy and cheerful like he's supposed to be, but I don't feel that way.

Dennis: Okay, so we've gone from what over here, on the left....

Speaker 4: From just being irritated at him

Dennis: To being kind of angry at the center [crown or top of her head], to being happy and giddy over here [on the right].

Speaker 4: Well, that's what he's doing. I'm not happy and giddy over here.

Dennis: Okay, but that's what Dad is doing?

Speaker 4: Yeah.

Dennis: But in your mind, how have you just adjusted your thinking in your own imagination around Dad? Do you not have some control now over what you think?

Speaker 4: Yes, I could either go to the very negative, thinking that he's the worst person on the planet, to he is not the worst person on the planet, but I still don't have any good feelings toward him. Or he could appear as what I wish he would be, but then I definitely know he is not going to ever be that way.

Dennis: Good, but what did you just learn about your thinking and your thought processes?

Speaker 4: I can see one simple thing in different areas as a good thing, a bad thing, and an extra-good thing. I can see in different points of view; I have different points of view.

Dennis: Inside your own head?

Speaker 4: Yeah.

Dennis: Excellent. How can you use that for personal problem-solving now, to view a problem differently inside your own head?

Speaker 4: Well, when I want to say something because my brother made me irritated or angry or whatever—probably it will take me a while to get used to this—I can stop and think do I want to make this negative, or do I want to make this a positive? So it could go either way, depending on what I choose.

Dennis: Good for you. Now does that give you more personal power and control, or does that take power and control away from you?

Speaker 4: Gives me more power and control.

Dennis and Client is Speaker 5

Dennis: Tell me just a little bit of what you have noticed, what you have done since the last time we've met. You've mentioned a couple of situations where you were applying the Spiritual Mind Management principles and you were able to attach and detach from things at will. Is there anything particular that comes to mind?

Speaker 5: Well, I think something that would be huge for people who can't sleep, is that when I wake up in the middle of the night or early morning and something starts going through my mind, it has been enormously helpful to be able to make it really large, and realize where it is in my mind. Then I bring it back to center and even though at times your mind starts running like a hamster on a wheel, where the same thing runs through in your mind over and over again, even though I haven't perfected the Mind Management processes so that I can accomplish them in two minutes, I can tell the difference. Because I can bring whatever is troubling me back into balance. Then if my thought processes and my Intelligence start going again, I can tell where they're going and be able to sleep. I am able to say to myself, "It really isn't that big of a deal. You're making one little statement or one little thought into your whole life."

Dennis: So you are able to adjust your imaginings?

Speaker 5: Right. It is huge, being able to see things in perspective!

Dennis and Clients/Speakers 6 and 7

Dennis: The next thing I want to teach you about is your imagination, okay? So I want you to close your eyes for a minute, and take your right hand and with it I want you to feel the stem of a rose. Lock your hand around that stem, not too tight, you might poke yourself with the thorns. Once you have that rose in your hand, I want you to pretend and imagine that you have the most beautiful rose you've ever seen. The absolutely most gorgeous rose ever. What color is your rose, Debbie?

Speaker 6: Pinkish red—the petals are pink with a red tip.

Dennis: Okay, Kevin, what color is your rose?

Speaker 7: Darker.

Dennis: Okay. Very slowly I want you to bring that rose up to your nose. The closer it gets, the stronger the fragrance becomes—the fresh, sweet, pure smell of that beautiful rose. Bring it up until you have the strength of fragrance that you would like and enjoy the most. Now take your left index finger and put it on your head. Where on your head do you actually have the awareness of smelling that rose? [Left side imagination] Excellent job. Now with your hand right there, I want you to recognize that area your mind as being in your imagination—the top of the forehead to the center of the top of the head. Now Debbie, how do you normally think about roses? Do you like roses?

Speaker 6: Not particularly.

Dennis: Kevin, do you like roses?

Speaker 7: Not really, I'm kind of indifferent to them.

Dennis: Okay, now here's what I want to teach you next. You've been learning where your consciousness is, which is forward. You're in your imagination there, as you remember thoughts. Stay right there for me, please. Stay right there. You have your arm on the left side of your head, and right here is full conscious focus; right in the middle of the forehead is consciousness. The imagination is right here, from the top of the head to about the center where you're both at. The center from back is memory, to the back of the back of the crown of the head, and then back down to the back of the crown of the head is emotions, where emotions run down the central nervous system. The further we get off into the left, the further people go into flight, alienation, and avoidance. The further people come over to the right, when their Intelligence comes over to the right, the more they go into fighting for something, identifying with it, and seeking it.

When I asked you both, how do you really feel about roses, and Debbie answered, "Well, I don't really care for them," where was she in her imagination? Off to the left, because she's avoiding, not really into the rose thing much, and Kevin's the same. Now both of you stay locked onto the rose and that feeling, and now I want you to move your finger to the top of your head, and keep your Intelligence right under your finger, right to the crown of your head. Notice how the rose changes in clarity, color, and other perceptions right there. You got it?

Describe that change right there. Debbie, let's start with you. What just happened inside your head?

Speaker 6: It changed. It became clearer, the color's a little clearer. I'm refusing to smell it; I don't like the smell of roses.

Dennis: That's okay, go ahead and see it.

Speaker 6: It became clear, very clear. It wasn't as fuzzy. It seems like it might have been fuzzy before, but it became clearer as I moved my finger, and my Intelligence to the top center of my head.

Dennis: Kevin, how would you describe it? Similarly or differently—what would you say it?

Speaker 7: The rose actually changed a little. When I imagined it at first, it had some imperfections and the scent wasn't really strong and now, I noticed the scent more than anything being stronger.

Dennis: In that position?

Speaker 7: Uh-huh.

Dennis: Okay. Now if we identify with it, if we seek it and we're fighting for it, what will actually happen is that the Intelligence will come further down in the imagination on this side (the right side of the head). I want you to slowly, intentionally, move your finger over to the right side, bringing your Intelligence to that area underneath your finger and allow the color to get brighter and clearer and see if that is your experience? As you identify with it, you fight for it. You want to see the most beautiful rose you've even seen and understand roses in a new and different way. Keep going until you've brought that to full, high definition clarity in your mind. See it, Debbie?

Speaker 6: Wow!

Dennis: Say that again, Debbie?

Speaker 6: Wow!

Dennis: Wow what?

Speaker 6: It's not exactly what I thought it was. I'm able to handle the smell a little bit better now. I choose to handle the smell a little better. I can tell the shape.

Dennis: Kevin, how would you describe it?

Speaker 7: There's actually a glow around it.

Speaker 6: Yeah.

Dennis: You concur with that, Debbie?

Speaker 6: Yeah, I do.

Dennis: There's a glow around it now. Now watch what happens. Have your Intelligence lock on to that rose and go right back to the top of your head, back just to the crown, right there. Now you're living life and viewing things in balance. If you want to alienate from something in your imagination, you can go all the way down to the left where you can shut it all the way off. Turn it down to your left; take your finger back down to your left, keeping your Intelligence under your finger until you hardly even see the rose, maybe just a faint glimmer. Got it?

Speaker 6: Uh-huh.

Dennis: Kevin, you got it?

Speaker 7: Uh-huh.

Dennis: Now feel that experience again as you exercise your imagination, come put it back over the right side and watch it brighten up and tell me that experience as you come all the way across again. What did you just learn? Debbie, what did you learn?

Speaker 6: You can change things in your imagination to like them, dislike them, or to just be in balance.

Dennis: You mean you can actually have everything as a choice inside your own head?

Speaker 6: Yes!

Using These Insights as an Aid to Hypnotherapy

When a person is really stuck and very rigid in their response to something, and they can't get their Intelligence free, the real secret to helping them with hypnotherapy is not necessarily making the right suggestions. It is being able to ask the right questions.

When you have the client or yourself identify the awareness of where are they seeing, hearing, or feeling the thought the most in their mind and point to it on their head, it gives you immediate access to the information you are seeking, their personal truth. I'll ask something like, "Where is it that you're feeling that thought, or the pain of that thought, on your head? I want you to just point out where your awareness of the experience is on or in your head. Where are you feeling it, seeing it, or hearing it?" I want to know if we are working with an imagination amplification problem, or a combined memory-imagination problem or an emotional issue amplified to what degree in the imagination.

Where the person points, indicates to me (the hypnotherapist) the location of the problem-behavior-producing thoughts in the spiritual mind. This information reveals to me the information needed to start challenging the problem and teaching the individual personal problem solving skills assisting the client to change as they view the experience from different internal perspectives.

Another example is that people come in for assistance with fixated memories and emotions around former relationships. Perhaps there is a memory of a very loving time and experience with their first spouse and they are still fixated on it, but they are now in their third marriage. They want to know how they can forget the first relationship, so to speak, move on and focus on obtaining the same feelings for their current partner. They want to be in love again, to the same degree as they are in the current emotionalized fixated memory of their first marriage.

The process is to have them identify where on their head they are aware of the fixated experience. Usually somewhere off to the right side of the head, back and down amplified many times in the imaginations. Once this identification is accomplished and an understanding of where they are at in their spiritual mind, then the process of separating the person from the emotions, detaching from the experience, is the next step.

This is done by having them view the loving experience again in their mind. Then have them identify the emotions and sensations of the experience, such as they feel safe, loved, accepted, wanted, sensual, approval, important, and all the things we all want to feel as human beings. Then have them separate the feelings from the individual recognizing that it is the feelings they want, and not the fixation to the association of the individual. If this were not true they would not be here in my office attempting to disassociate and detach from them in the first place. Move the image of the individual all the way over to the left side of the mind in alienation and avoidance. It will completely shut down the old memory and feelings.

Now have them see the new partner in their mind and have that image overlaid on the wonderful feelings we all want to experience, and even associate the feelings again of the first experience with the current partner. Now have them move this image and the positive emotions further to the right side into identification or seeking. People are always amazed that they can have such control of their minds and are delighted to realize that they are truly in control of them. They can now move the desired behavior of loving and caring for their current partner to the same degree of intensity or greater than they were experiencing with the first. These are some of the wonderful mental skills we assist clients to develop and utilize on a daily basis.

A story of a middle aged wife, mother of two children, and a student in Certified Hypnotherapy Training School tests these concepts with her daughter:

The other day I realized that I would have no opportunity to do a hypnotherapy session with my daughter before she would be going to a Halloween (CANDY) party. The party was after school and I would be in class the remainder of the afternoon/night. She has a weight-management issue that we have been working with for the past several, frustrating years. I had the brilliant thought to try the Spiritual Mind Management techniques with her, as we were driving to school.

We were stopped at a red light and I asked her, "What is your favorite food?" She answered, "Candy... And cake! Yes! and cake!" she said. "Good. Go ahead and think of your favorite candy and cake." I asked her to point to the place on her head where she felt that thought resided. She pointed to a spot a couple inches behind her right eye. I asked her to describe her candy and cake. She told me how much she liked them. (She seemed to really enjoy this exercise!) "Good. Now see what happens if you move that thought up here to the center of your head." She did that and then told me that she was less excited about the candy and cake. Then I had her drag the feeling, down to the left side. She did and said she noticed that the thought of candy and cake became even less appealing.

We practiced this back and forth, moving the thought around her head and noticing how it changed. The final time, I asked her to again bring the thought down and to the left. She did, and she told me that there was now an ant crawling on the cake! We were both amazed. I hadn't given her any explanation of the process. I had given her no pre-talk or description of what I expected her to experience. The conversation proceeded just like I have written above. Later that day, I called and reminded her father to remind her to try the techniques while she was at the party and confronted with temptation. We called the technique the "Temptation Tuner" or "Temptation Tamer." Later that night, her father said that she had described the technique to him in detail. That made me happy. The next day, I asked her about the experience. She told me that she, indeed, had used it at the party and that she felt it had worked for her. Hope this helps inspire others."

My wife's experience with Spiritual Mind Management

During the 3rd week of Hypnotherapist Certification school we were introduced to the idea and process of Spiritual Mind Management. I was excited to get home and experiment with my wife. I didn't tell her anything about the process to make sure the experiment was "blind". I asked her to close her eyes and name a food she doesn't like. She said "fish." I asked her to think about eating fish and to point to the place in her head where the thought was. Without hesitation she pointed to the part of her head indicating strong dislike or avoidance, her facial expression clearly showed she didn't care for the thought. (I don't want to tell you where she pointed so you can conduct your own experiment without the possibility of being influenced by knowledge of where the sections are located.)

I then had her move her finger (and the thought) to the area indicating neutrality and asked her what she now thought of eating fish. She said, "I guess it wouldn't be so bad if it was breaded." That was cool! So far, so good. Then I had her move her finger and the thought to the place on her head indicating where one would like or identify with the thought and she said, "That's not too bad." Now you have to understand she really does not like fish, especially if it smells like fish, so that response was a very dramatic change from her original expression of disgust.

Without any previous knowledge or coaching at all about the process, she had completely validated the training I had received that morning. She and I continued experimenting with other uses of the Spiritual Mind Management processes and found the results to be consistent with the trainings in our hypnotherapist course work.

I use the following technique with migraines and for other pain control:

When someone says, "I've been to all the doctors, I've been everywhere. There is nothing wrong with me; nobody's finding anything wrong with me," then generally the problem is psychosomatically induced. So I may ask, "Where do you feel the pain the most?" The answer will give me the clues of where to go so that I can start to ask the right questions, like, "Okay, what is it over here in your imagination that you're alienating from, that you really don't like, or don't want to feel, or what are you avoiding knowing about yourself?" I start on the types of questions that will elicit the right information from them, so we can deal with their behavioral issues faster. It is an exhilarating experience for both the hypnotherapist and the client as we use hypnotherapy to connecting the dots between the thought, the emotion, and the behavior, (the behavior in this case is the migraine) literally at the speed of thought.

> *We want to bring our awareness of the stimulus to the middle of the behavioral scale intentionally, (the crown of our head) to make a conscious choice with each new experience or stimulus. We must decide in each situation if it is appropriate to fight for something or to flee from it, to seek it or avoid it, to identify with it or alienate ourselves from it. We are to make everything a conscious choice, using agency appropriately, being responsible and accountable for our actions and behaviors. This is personal empowerment!*

When someone's Intelligence is not where we would normally expect it to be for a particular function to take place that indicates to the hypnotherapist that a thinking error needs to be adjusted, challenged, and changed. The goal is to help bring the client back into balance for the particular stimulus or experience.

Another client comments: Female: age 25, married, 2 kids, pregnant with 3rd

I was terrified of hypnosis and thought it was creepy and didn't have any clue what it entailed. The only exposure I'd ever seen of hypnosis was that of entertainment as people in an audience volunteer and go up on stage and proceed to "make fools of themselves. It was funny to watch, but terrifying to ever be a part of. It's so much more than just "talking about your problems." It helps solve them and you can implement the truths you learn into your daily life. Hypnotherapy, for me, is a lot of pondering and discovering truths that help me to be a better person.

I'm sure it's different for everyone. At first, for me, it was about discovering lies I had believed my whole life were true and discovering the actual truth and reprogramming myself to know and believe the real truth. Then the later sessions were about learning techniques I could do by myself so I can take what I'm learning and apply it to my daily life and not be dependent on Dennis the rest of my life. But I can learn mind management and how to control my thoughts and mind. It's really hard to explain in writing and I don't want to limit your experience with what mine was.

Here is what I explained to my brother in a text message about my experience with hypnotherapy.

Hypnotherapy has helped me more than any other thing I have tried. People in my life, like my mother for example, have told me they can see improvements and positive changes happening to me, as an outsider looking in. That means a lot to me and made me realize it's not just me that is noticing a positive change, but people around me have noticed. I like that because I feel empowered and know I can make a difference for good. And as I improve myself, it opens the door for others to do the same.

After I had my 2nd baby, I was in a dark place emotionally I felt so depressed and, more times than not, I found myself feeling like a failure as a mother and wife. I was so wrapped up in being a mom and wife I forgot who I was as a person. I was desperate for some help but felt hopeless in finding any. Just at that time, I was invited to a "self-improvement" class. I wasn't told any details, but thought it would be a nice break from the kids, and I'm always open to becoming a better person and learning new things.

Once I got to the class, the big projector on the wall, presented in PowerPoint form, said something about hypnosis. As I read that to myself I thought, "I've got to be in the wrong place. Hypnosis is scary and I am not ok with having someone control me like a puppet or read my mind! Do I leave? What do I do?" Just then the class began. I decided to stay and if I felt uncomfortable, I would excuse myself from the class. I'm so grateful I decided to stay. I am grateful the teacher Dennis Parker was willing to educate the public and me on what hypnosis really is and what it can do for you. I loved what he had presented and taught us.

After the class I made an appointment for an individual session and since then my life has not been the same. It has improved drastically and I'm no longer in a dark place, but loving life. My double mindedness had me so confused and lost, but, as I discovered the truths, it set me free. I am free to live my life in the way I truly want to. It has allowed me to be the amazing person I knew I was, but would too often trick myself into believing I wasn't. When I would discover the lies and find the truth it always felt so empowering and peaceful. It just felt right. It made sense. I am able to have better mind management skills and it feels good to better myself and keep learning and growing as a person and a much happier, wiser, confident woman."

In Summary

It is when we are clear and free-minded that we can be in our conscious mind at will. There, when we are also in balance consciously, we can view a situation clearly from all angles and are most able to discern the truth. We are then centered or grounded, as I like to call it. *When the right information is always understood by the client when they come to a place of peace, which is the sign that they are in a place of personal truth. They sense true closure and are in a place of pure knowledge. They do not doubt anymore, but are full of understanding and have a clear view of themselves and their life experiences. They are happy, and are experiencing joy and peace.*

When you learn Spiritual Mind Management, you will understand these concepts from the inside out, at deep internal levels. You can know what you are choosing and why you are choosing it. You can make every choice a conscious one, with total awareness of the process you used to do so.

CHAPTER NINE

How to Hypnotize Yourself and Others

This book is not meant to be an all-inclusive work on hypnosis and hypnotherapy. There are plenty such books available already. We are teaching some of our own discoveries, things we do that are new and different.

We hope you find some of the information we have included enlightening, or if you are still a novice with hypnosis you may find it useful. This chapter is a very basic guide to inducing trance in yourself or others.

The processes of self-hypnosis and hypnotizing others include several components. They are discussed below in the order in which they would be used.

The induction

There are four basic components to any hypnotic induction: pre-conditioning pre-talk, fixation and focus, relaxation, and suggestions.

Preconditioning Pre-Talk

The first step in inducing trance is pre-conditioning. A pre-conditioning talk educates yourself or others as to what hypnosis or trance really is. Once it is understood to be the natural processes of mind that we all go in and out of as we go in and out of sleep, people become more amenable to following the suggestions and they generally achieve trance easily and comfortably.

One simple explanation that I use is telling clients that they are going to be as though they are half-asleep. Again, it needs to be understood that *all hypnosis is self-hypnosis.* Each individual needs to learn to go in and out of hypnosis or trance themselves. I teach clients that should they choose to follow the directions given, they will immediately, easily, and comfortably achieve the trance levels and depth required for the therapies being done.

Some individuals may require a great deal of information about hypnosis and hypnotherapy, and about the hypnotherapist, before they have the confidence to move forward. The information coming from you and your experience will build rapport and trust. The number one ingredient of a successful hypnotherapy session with any client is the feeling of trust between the client and the hypnotherapist. Once adequate trust is achieved, then it's time to go to work.

I also tell clients that they will be in a deep level of relaxation, and yet they will still be able to hear and understand everything I say in this extremely relaxed, comfortable state. It will be as though they were drifting off to sleep while watching a TV show. Just as they are aware of the voice on the show in that situation, they can continue to be aware of my voice even as their mind is drifting downward into rest and relaxation. They will always be able to hear, understand, and respond to my voice.

Since all hypnosis is self-hypnosis, people can resist going into trance if they choose to, and then they cannot be hypnotized. But that is not why they have come. So I tell them, "Let's not waste your money and my time—please simply follow the directions given and you will be very successful at this process." Hypnosis is not something that we do to them; it is something that clients learn to do for themselves. We instruct them that as they follow the prompts we give them, they will immediately and easily be able to drift off into trance and be able to do their hypnotherapy work.

The pre-talk educational information may include such things as:

- The history of hypnosis
- The nature of hypnosis
- What hypnotherapy is and what it isn't
- The differences between stage hypnosis and clinical hypnotherapy
- A description of the six observable trance states
- The basics of the therapeutic processes in hypnosis and self-hypnosis
- The personal programming called affirmations
- What autosuggestions are and the rules of successful autosuggestion
- How recordings can be used to aid the process

The Theory of the Mind

- How behaviors are generated
- The conscious and subconscious minds
- The critical factor or belief system filter
- How the imagination can magnify things by several times
- Emotional release techniques

Answer all of the person's questions and concerns before inducing trance. Ensure you and the client's success by preparing them in advance what to expect and how to assist in the processes. Some questions you might ask the client to put them at ease may include: Have you ever been hypnotized? Have you ever seen a stage show or someone else who has been hypnotized? What have your impressions been?

Our purpose here is not to give you long, detailed explanations of various inductions, as that can be found in other hypnotherapy books. People have come up with hundreds of ways to do hypnotic inductions, choosing different items to fixate on and achieve focus. The only limitation to hypnotizing is the creativity of our own imagination. We will give you some simple directions below, and if you or your client chooses to follow them, you/they will immediately drift off into deep trance.

Fixation and focus

You will want your own or the client's eyes, hearing, sense of touch, smell, and other sensory perceptions to fixate and focus on a particular object, sound, feeling, or fragrance. So start by bringing them into a singularity of focus. You can choose anything you like to focus upon.

One of the simplest things is to choose a spot overhead, looking up with the eyes without moving the head. The intention here is to tire out the tiny muscles in the back of the eyes. Since this is an unnatural position, those muscles tire quickly, and the eyes soon want to shut. Take a couple of deep breaths, and when your eyes are very tired, simply close them and continue to breathe deeply. Now intentionally lock on to that feeling of tiredness and relaxation in your eyes, and begin to extend it to other parts of your body. Allow your neck to become very limp, loose, and tired, just like your eyes. Allow your head to begin to float, just like a helium balloon, as if it were attached by a string to your shoulders, and so forth.

Relaxation

This can be accomplished by breathing with the diaphragm. Focus on breathing. You would normally have the client breathing through their nose, and release the breath out through their mouth. Again, breathe in through their nose, out through their mouth, and so forth. Simply have them notice that as they breathe in, they should be pushing their stomach out, and as they release a breath, their stomach should be coming in. This also helps to accomplish fixation of focus, by tying the deep breathing together with paying attention to these movements. Continue to have them focus on their stomach area, noticing that the stomach should be pushing out as they breathe in, and coming back in as they breathe out. This is the proper movement of the diaphragm.

Many people have who are stuck in shallow fight/flight breathing need direction in this breathing method. They may need to push the stomach out as they breathe in, and allow the stomach and diaphragm to come in as they breathe out. Instruct the client to continue to breathe fully and rhythmically as they begin to relax, allowing feelings of relaxation to fill their lungs and chest. They should do this for a minimum of four to six deep breaths or more. Instruct them to look for the subtle relaxation in the body that begins as the diaphragm stimulates the Vegas nerve and the body naturally begins to relax.

Suggestions

Begin to give the client or yourself relaxing suggestions. Here are a few that have proven to be successful most every time:

> Have the person fixate and focus on different body parts, and relaxing and releasing tensions and cares from them. You can have them start from their head and then move downward or with their feet and move upward.

Don't allow your eyes to close until they are very tired and very relaxed. Allow them to become "stuck shut"—with every breath becoming more so. Imagine that the harder you try to open them, the tighter they want to stick.

Allow your head to float like a helium balloon.

Allow your jaw to sag and your shoulders to do the same.

Allow your arms to become limp and loose like a wet towel.

Allow your mind to relax and release all tensions and cares.

Now focus on different parts of the body again, making relaxation suggestions, going from head to toe or toe to head.

After an additional number of deep breaths, while staring and gazing at the object chosen overhead, have the eyes close tightly. "Allow your eyes to just become stuck shut; the harder you try to open them the tighter they want to stick, to stay stuck shut." Repetition of suggestions builds responsiveness.

Tie suggestions to natural bodily functions: "Every breath you take takes you deeper into relaxation. Every beat of your heart takes you deeper, deeper down into relaxation," etc.

Identify the predominant signs of trance as they are exhibited. The slight fluttering of eyelids, dryness in the throat, an urge to swallow, the pulsation of blood flow up through their neck, with the suggestions that, "you are going deeper and deeper into trance," creating an expectancy of deep trance.

Hypnotic Script for Inducing Trance

You want to learn to instruct your subconscious mind to receive the right, true, and correct thoughts and actions for you. You can do this with affirmations. Affirmations are statements and directives of what you want your mind and body to do, of what you want to happen in your life, affirming such desires to yourself, for yourself.

Repeating your affirmations several times in your mind, or better yet, out loud, with real intent and emotional conviction, establishes new predominant thoughts and beliefs, producing the desired right, true, and correct thoughts and actions for you.

Repeat in your mind the following: "I receive and accept all the right, true, and correct thoughts and ideas that come to me as my new predominant thoughts and beliefs. My mind discerns and understands truth. I open my mind to truth. It is my desire and nature to understand all truth. I choose positive, happier, more productive, correct thoughts and actions for me. I choose to direct my life in successful, meaningful paths. In every aspect of my life I am doing better, being an individual of integrity, with a strong sense of mission and purpose in life."

I want you to think of a steering wheel. Whenever you see a steering wheel, all of the new ideas and affirmations of truth given here, or truths that come to you while in this state, are automatically renewed in your mind.

Whenever you see a steering wheel or someone driving a vehicle, your resolves to improve are automatically strengthened in the many ways you choose. Say in your mind: "I choose to act automatically in new and more appropriate ways. I choose to make new and more appropriate decisions, from moment to moment, and day to day, always."

Seeing a steering wheel will bring positive, comfortable feelings to you from your personal commitment to do things right. These enjoyable, peaceful, yet exciting feelings that come to you when you see steering wheels or have your hands on one confirm the rightness of your daily new decisions, thoughts, and actions—you are steering your life in new and important ways.

Steering wheels represent to you that you are now doing the things you have always known you wanted to do. "I am moving towards the positive, happier, more productive, correct thoughts and actions for me." Choose to direct your life in successful, highly meaningful paths. In every aspect of your life you choose to do better, being an individual of integrity and understanding the purposes of your life. Steering wheels remind you of your new directions and goals in life and invigorate and strengthen you with positive thoughts.

You are automatically aware of your new decisions and improvements throughout your daily routines, each and every time you see a steering wheel or use one yourself. You are steering your life right—doing things right.

Be in a comfortable, relaxing place where you can rest from the cares of the day. You are aware that life is still going on around you, but you give this time to yourself for relaxation and thoughts of personal improvement. Decide that no sounds or noises or other activities will bother you. You may find that any sound takes you deeper into relaxation, such as the tones of my voice. You may allow each sound or noise to take you deeper into this wonderful state of relaxation we call hypnosis.

Please focus on a spot overhead, and in time as you learn to relax instantly, automatically going deeper into relaxation, you may prefer to simply close your eyes from the very beginning.

Focus on a spot overhead or on the inside of your eyelids. We want to intentionally tire out the small muscles on the back of your eyes. Turn your eyes up, looking overhead, not necessarily tilting your head back. Just look up with your eyes. As your eyes become tired, we are going to associate and transfer that tired feeling to other parts of the body, to have each area relax instantly throughout all of your body. Your entire body is to go into a state of rest and relaxation. Allow all of the systems of your body to rejuvenate and renew themselves and function better, each and every time you go into this relaxed, comfortable state.

All of your glands, organs, muscles, and every part of your body automatically rebuilds, rejuvenates, renews, restores, and repairs itself, easily and instantly, each and every time you go into this relaxed, comfortable state.

Continue focusing overhead or on the top of the back of your eyelids, and I'll begin counting from three to one. With every number I say, allow yourself to go just a little deeper into relaxation, become a little more comfortable, more peaceful. With each number, please take a deep breath, and breathe with your diaphragm. Your stomach moves out as you breathe in and moves in as you breathe out. Take a deep breath now and practice—diaphragm moving out as you breathe in, stomach and diaphragm going in as you breathe out. Now take another full breath and just relax as your eyes become even more tired, and you feel drowsy.

Excellent, you want to continue this full and rhythmic breathing whenever you take time for yourself to relax and learn. Relax and learn new things now. Deep, full, and rhythmic breathing will assist you to relax and become more comfortable. As you bring in fresh oxygen, it renews every cell and improves every function and system in your entire being. Your health and strength improve every time you go into this relaxed and comfortable state.

Counting now. Three. Take another full, deep breath and continue to focus, inhale, and exhale. With every breath you take, begin to gather in from your entire body, mind, heart, and spirit, all the tensions and cares and concerns of the day. Learn to release them by drawing in those feelings into your chest, and just blow them away every time you breathe out.

Let those feelings go, a little more each and every time you breathe out, just blow them away, simply blow them away, each and every time you breathe out. Any noises you hear simply tend to take you deeper into relaxation; any sound becomes pleasant to you, relaxes you. The sound of my voice helps you to relax. Go even deeper, even deeper into relaxation now.

Two. Your eyes are tired, very tired. You're drowsy and your eyes want to close now. Don't close them yet, unless you already have. Another full, deep breath. Stomach goes out as you breathe in, and comes in as you breathe out. Breathe in fresh, rejuvenating oxygen. Oxygen calms you, cleanses and purifies, improves every cell, and the quality of your entire being.

As you breathe in fresh, revitalizing oxygen, go into a state of cleansing and healing, healing and improving every part of your body. Draw in more of the tensions and cares of the day, and then release them, incrementally, a little more, a little more, each and every time you breathe out. Let them go, release them now. All the tensions and cares of the day let them go with each easy breath. Allow the sounds around you to take you deeper. My voice relaxes you, as you go deeper now, twice as deep into relaxation.

One. Take another full, deep breath, and when you breathe out completely go ahead and close your eyes, if you haven't done so already. This is your time to contemplate, meditate, and make new and more appropriate decisions. Any sound or noise you hear simply takes you deeper into relaxation as you realize that life is still going on around you. In fact, all sounds or noise simply tend to take you deeper and deeper into relaxation. The pleasing sounds of the tones of my voice take you further on this pleasant journey into this comfortable, wonderful state of relaxation.

You might feel a slight fluttering of your eyelids. Maybe even have dryness in your throat, an urge to swallow. You may experience some tearing of your eyes. These are physiological signs that you are going into deep relaxation. Going deeper and deeper down now concentrate; focus on those little tiny muscles, right on the back of your eyelids, and as you do it feels so good just to have your eyes closed. With the drowsiness in your eyes, you go deeper and deeper down into relaxation. You feel drowsy, comfortable, and peaceful.

It would take more energy to open your eyes now than it would be worth. And as you notice this, they feel as though they're stuck shut. Release tension and cares by breathing deeply, releasing all of the tension in your face, and facial muscles. Release it now, and let it go.

Allow your jaw to sag, and your scalp and the back of your neck to relax and release all the tensions and cares of the day. Your head feels lighter and lighter, and seems just to float on your shoulders like a helium balloon. Your neck and head are relaxed, and feel as though they are just floating on top of your shoulders.

Allow a wonderful feeling of relaxation to go down through your neck and into your shoulders. As your shoulders sag, your lungs and chest feel a wave of cleansing, healing relaxation. Allow a wave of cleansing, healing relaxation to enter your arms. Your arms relax, and become very loose, very comfortable, and very limp now, just as though they were wet noodles hanging off of your shoulders.

Allow your arms to feel as though they are wet dishtowels, just hanging off of your shoulders, limp and loose. Allow yourself to become like a Raggedy Ann or Raggedy Andy doll, very limp, very loose. Arms and hands now feel limp, loose, relaxed. Just let them go as limp as possible. Your shoulders sag, your jaw sags, and your breathing is full, cleansing, and rhythmic. With every breath you take, just go a little deeper, going deeper, more relaxed. Let go, twice as deep now, twice as relaxed with every easy breath.

A wave of comfortable, pleasant relaxation goes down through your stomach and midsection. Release all worries, all tensions, and all cares. Incrementally release, one by one, each uncomfortable feeling. Breathe deeply, and blow them away. Quietly and peacefully, take this time for yourself, to improve personally in the many ways you choose.

Allow your stomach muscles to relax and release, become stronger. Your midsection becomes peaceful. All of your body's functions improve minute by minute. Your digestive system is now working better. Your stomach and all of the organs and glands in your midsection are functioning better, improving moment to moment.

Feel a wave of healing, cleansing relaxation go down through your waist. All of the muscles throughout your back relax and release. You know they support you in all that you do. You are supported, and your back and abdominal muscles become stronger and stronger, supporting you in each new decision to improve your life. Relax and release all tensions and cares in your back, all the way down through your waist. Relax and release every tension and care.

Your eyes and eyelids feel very comfortable, very relaxed. Notice now, that it would take more energy to open your eyes than it would be worth. It would take so much energy to lift your hands. Your eyes, your arms and hands, feel as though it would be almost impossible to lift them. And as you try to open your eyes, or try to lift your arms and hands, they feel so relaxed it is not even worth doing. Your eyes feel as though they are stuck shut. The harder you try to open them, the tighter they want to stick. They are staying stuck shut. Stop trying now and just go deeper.

Take another full deep breath, as a wave of relaxation goes all the way down, down, deeper down, all the way down through your legs and thighs. They release, become relaxed. Feel free of stress, cares, and worries with every breath you take. In this very comfortable sleeplike state, you rejuvenate, restore, and repair all of your body's functions and systems.

Be as though you are in deep sleep at night, when your body has time to cleanse, purify, heal, rebuild, and repair itself. All of your body's systems and functions do so now in a more effective way with every passing moment. Take in cleansing, healing oxygen. Every gland, every organ, every muscle, every fiber, every cell, every part of your body is now improving. Your entire body utilizes this time to renew itself, just as you are using this time to renew your mind, heart, and spirit.

Say in your mind with conviction, or out loud, "I am steering my life in new and important directions. I am doing things right for my body and my body does right for me. Moment to moment, day-to-day, oxygen burns fat, cleanses all my systems, and I am becoming clean, healthy, and strong. My heart beats firmly and strongly, my lungs are breathing fully and rhythmically, becoming stronger, healthier, with each deep breath. My circulatory system is functioning better, flowing freely."

You may even feel a slight pulsating sensation, possibly in the side of your neck, as all the fresh oxygen and blood flow to your brain, opening up your mind to new and more creative thoughts. Your mind and your brain relax, releasing the cares of the day.

Be more relaxed. Allow a wave of cleansing, healing relaxation to pass over you. Feel this relaxing wave go deeper and deeper, more relaxed, to the bottom of your legs and your toes. Your toes relax, your feet relax. Just let them go, as comfortable as the rest of your body.

Your entire body is now very limp, loose. Melt; melt, like a pat of butter on a hot stove, just melt. You are more relaxed than ever before; deeply, deeply relaxed, feeling healthier and stronger every day. Your mind is clear, peaceful, comfortable, and relaxed. See, hear, and feel steering wheels—I am steering my life right, I am doing things right. I do things right for my body, and my body does right for me.

All the muscles in your legs unwind, loosen up, and become limp. Your entire body is now relaxed. Let go. Let go twice as deep, deeper down, twice as deep now. Steering wheels—I am steering my life in new and more goal orientated directions. I am doing things right!

Predominant Signs of Trance

People will demonstrate one or more of the following as an indicator that they have entered some stage of trance or hypnosis:

- Fluttering of the eyelids
- Dryness in the mouth and throat and an urge to swallow
- Pulsation of the jugular veins on the side of the neck
- Deep relaxation of the body
- Warm hands
- Eyeballs may roll up toward the top of the head

- Tearing of the eyes
- Emotional release through physical abreactions such as a jerk or spasms
- Physical responses may slow down or become robot like
- A change from regular breathing to deep, rhythmic, full breaths
- Redness of face and neck
- Redness of Eyes
- Limp, loose, lethargic muscles

Please remember that various signs and characteristics of trance change at the different observable levels or states. Check the list of characteristic on the trance chart for more detail.

Once you or the client is in trance, it is time to use one of several ways to reestablish more goal-directed, selective thinking. Remember, the reason for hypnosis or trance utilization in the first place is to achieve subconscious access, a bypass of the critical factor, where we choose to intentionally become more hyper suggestible, more susceptible even to our own suggestions.

These ways are discussed in detail in the next chapter. They include: positive self-talk, affirmations, auto-suggestions, age regressions, gestalts, guided imagery (stories, metaphors, or scripts), and pain control methods and procedures.

Any additional post-hypnotic suggestions should be given at this time, while the person is still in trance. Future rehearsal and future pacing are also done at this time as well, reviewing in your mind how you're going to respond in different ways when you receive old familiar stimuli.

Awakening techniques

Bringing yourself or the client out of trance in the proper way is important. There are several things that ought to be included in this procedure. Remember, when using a counting method for bringing a person into hypnosis, we always want to count down, from five to one (for example). When bringing them up or out of hypnosis, count up—from one to five. This is an effective time to intersperse some further positive and posthypnotic suggestions. Here are some examples:

1. "As you come back up out of this state, you remember and accept every positive and right suggestion that has been given to you, for your benefit, and you have decided to make them your new reality. If this is acceptable to you, just take another deep breath and take each suggestion deeper within you, as each suggestion now becomes your new and automatic reality. Now begin to wiggle your fingers and toes, and rotate your head in different directions."

2. "With every number I say, as you come up just a little more, adjust your bodily functions of blood flowing from your brain, thus avoiding any temporary dizziness or headache. Take deep breaths of rejuvenating oxygen, breathe fully and deeply as you stretch your arms out. Move your legs—stretch, stretch, stretch."

3. "You find you are becoming more energized and excited to go forward in life, making new exciting, meaningful, worthwhile changes daily. Stretch your entire body out now, arms overhead, just like a cat waking up in the morning."

4. "You are feeling refreshed, invigorated, and full of life and energy, ready to accomplish your new goals and desires. Take big, deep breaths—you feel energized, invigorated, revitalized, excited to go forward in life."

5. "You are now fully alert." After a client has had several sessions and experiences with the process, if you feel no need to use this time for further reinforcement of post-hypnotics, you can simply instruct them (when they are ready) to adjust their awareness, feeling wonderful in every way, and to open their eyes and be here with you. In a few moments they will be fully alert, and naturally come to full consciousness.

CHAPTER TEN

The Techniques at the Heart of Our Hypnotherapy

As noted earlier, we at Certified Hypnotherapy Training School teach many processes, techniques, and protocols, all which are called hypnotherapy when they are utilized with the client being in an induced state of trance. Hypnotherapy is a general term that is applied to such techniques and processes such self-talk, affirmations, auto-suggestions, age regressions, gestalts, indirect associative focusing, (metaphors, stories, and scripts) and the latest in pain control techniques for both acute and chronic pain. Then we teach students and clients how to do personal problem solving by managing their own spiritual minds with these Spiritual Mind Management processes and techniques. As explained they are taught to view their behaviors and problems from different viewpoints within one's mind.

Again, all these processes when utilized appropriately at the correct trance levels or states of mind for maximum effectiveness desensitizes amplified imaginations they alter perspectives of past sensitizing experiences, which then collapses old unwanted accumulated emotional content which now alters and changes behaviors because we feel different, being released and free from past fixations.

We use hypnotic trance for access to the subconscious mind in order to obtain the positive or negative personal truths or mental thought scripts and beliefs of the client. We are to assist the client as a hypnotherapist to develop thought alignment at both the conscious and subconscious levels overcoming double mindedness and instability. Individuals then move forward with a new understanding of themselves as a survivor of past behavior-producing events. They learn how to continually challenge and change incorrect thinking errors and place their goal-directed beliefs and purposes in harmony in their own thought processes at all levels of mind. They then move forward and achieve great things faster and easier than ever before without hesitation, inhibition, and procrastination.

The process of self-hypnosis or hypnotherapy is the establishment of new self-decisions. You might say that it is enlightened decision-making.

The methods we use most often in self-hypnosis and hypnotherapy, listed in alphabetical order, are briefly described below:

Affirmations and Positive Self-talk

In describing the relationship between the conscious and subconscious mind, people use many metaphors. One that I mentioned earlier and particularly like, is to think of the subconscious mind as a genie in a bottle and the conscious mind as its master. The master, the conscious mind, is the analytical, logical, reasoning mind and makes judgments, compares, and decides. The genie, the subconscious, only attempts to produce what it perceives to be the most predominant wish of the master. The genie doesn't judge right or wrong, good or evil, its only intent is to fulfill the wishes of the master.

When the master directs the genie correctly (with clarity in the accepted thoughts sent to the subconscious) then the genie sets about to do the bidding of the master. However, when we hold two opposing views in our mind, consciously wanting to do one thing and subconsciously having a set of beliefs that would call for the opposite kind of behavior, we have "double-mindedness" and "become unstable in all our ways."

We do this when our conscious mind instructs our subconscious mind, which is the subjective mind containing our memories, by saying things like, "I don't want to think about that ever again," or "I never want to feel that way again," and so forth. Or we may make other instructive statements to our subconscious like, "I am just no good at remembering names. I have the hardest time ever remembering a person's name." By saying this, we have instructed our subconscious memory to hide things from us.

Therefore, the statements that we make consciously to ourselves make a difference. Affirmations and positive self-talk are an attempt to instruct our genie, which does its job by fulfilling our wishes, in a way that will develop a singularity of focus, connecting the conscious decision-making mind to the subconscious functions of memory, imagination, and emotions in ways that penetrate the primary defense mechanisms of amnesia and denial.

However, once we have developed long-term habits, and our genie is used to responding in certain ways, it requires some real effort at new instruction to get our genie to fully understand and do what we now desire. We may have to direct it numerous times to get it to believe that we are serious about wanting to create new habits and new behaviors replacing the old, longtime, fixed, existing behaviors.

There are several ways to do this. One is to use positive affirmations on cue cards. This is where you simply write down a positive statement that affirms a new direction and course in life that we wish to take. Repeat this affirmation to yourself several times each day, and especially at night just as you fall off to sleep, that natural trance state.

Many people are successful with simple positive affirmation cue cards when they are determined to make changes and are consistent and diligent enough in the constant reading of them to plant the seeds of thought in the subconscious. To make a cue card, write out your affirmations using the three principles of personal programming. They are: **1.** The affirmation has to be positive. **2.** The affirmation has to be personal **3.** The affirmation has to be stated in the present tense.

An affirmation should be based on what you want, not what you don't want; what you are for, not what you are against. It should enact the "as if" principle—choosing to think and act "as if" you are already a certain way until it becomes natural and automatic for you to be that way.

An affirmation for health and weight management might be: "I choose to be lean, healthy, and strong. I do what I know I must do each and every moment of each and every day to be lean, healthy, and strong. I am lean, healthy, and strong. Each and every day I am healthier in every way."

You would repeat this affirmation several times each morning, just as you awake, and at night just before going to sleep. Again, these are times when we are in a natural state of trance and our subconscious is more susceptible to our direction in the form of suggestions. You may do this for 30–90 days or longer and find that you have successfully directed your genie by doing things differently, almost automatically becoming lean, healthy, and strong. These processes are the "21 days to change habit" techniques. There are faster ways to induce change or make new decisions at what we call the *speed of thought.* Please read on.

Age regression techniques

The regression process, which is also described in earlier chapters, is used to access the subconscious mind and discover the underlying accepted misunderstandings, misinterpretations, and misrepresentations of oneself to one's self. It also helps uncover outright lies that are accepted as whole or partial truths that were developed from an original stimulus from initial sensitizing events. The age regression process is a very powerful tool for making behavioral modification changes, at the speed of thought, when done in the appropriate trance level for maximum effectiveness as before explained.

Auto-suggestion

These are groups of suggestions and affirmations that are brought repeatedly into the subconscious mind by the stimulation of a symbol. We can have numerous thought affirmation suggestions, all brought into the subconscious by a symbol, a color, or a key word. The hypnotic induction routine in the previous chapter is *an auto-suggestion induction and auto suggestion combination* that is built around the symbolization of steering wheels. Each and every time someone who has repeatedly been hypnotized with this routine touches a steering wheel, sees a steering wheel, or in any way thinks about a steering wheel, the above positive suggestion affirmation programming should repeat through their mind, stimulating them in the direction of the affirmations.

This is how we make use of the fact that our mind is a computer and we can program into it with what we choose. Auto-suggestion is a more powerful process than single affirmations because the suggestions and instructions are repeated more often. Thus stimulated by symbolization, it has a compounding effect, with the potential for trance-facilitated bypass of the amnesias and denials that we are attempting to challenge and change.

Auto-suggestions with a recording

Auto-suggestion is the basis for most hypnosis recordings. Most people are very successful with such recordings, especially when they diligently listen to them and make a point of repeating the positive affirmations out loud or in their minds several times each day. Our *White Series* of CD's use the word and color white to mean, "I am doing things right," so we are continually setting ourselves up to make better choices each and every time we see something white or hear the word white.

I personally believe that, for the most part, we can all become our own best therapist by learning to listen to and discern the truths and errors of our own thoughts and thinking. Therefore all of my recordings contain what I call therapeutic prompts. These therapeutic prompts are the times during the recording when I will say half of a sentence, a stem sentence, or ask a stem question. You are to complete the sentence with the first words and images that come into your mind, from your very own thoughts and beliefs. This helps you learn to listen to and come to understand your current predominant thoughts and beliefs, both at a conscious and subconscious level.

This feature makes the recordings in our *White Series* different from other hypnosis programs containing simple positive suggestions and affirmations, even though you will receive many of those as you listen. The therapeutic prompts will allow you to gain wisdom and understanding about yourself from your subconscious mind and your conscience, somewhat similar to a hypnotherapy session.

These recordings are meant to help you come to know the tremendous benefits of pondering and meditation so that you can discern truth from error in your life. You will experience divinely granted gifts of spiritual enlightenment, and receive wisdom and understanding more frequently, when you seek insights on the experiences of your life from a higher source.

Programming while you sleep

Listening to chosen recordings for your goal directed learning purposes when sleeping can be an especially effective way to program your subconscious mind. Because the critical factor is more easily bypassed during sleep, which is a conscious mind function as the subconscious mind never sleeps. Our subconscious is more open to suggestion and learning as we dream, imagine, and visualize deeply, without conscious distraction or interference from analytical processes.

Suggestions made through lyrics put to music are a powerful predominant thought programming method in either a state of self-hypnosis or sleep. Some seek to learn new languages by listening to the pronunciation and definitions of words and phrases on a recording at night, over and over again as they sleep. Other educational subject matter can also be recorded and played repeatedly at night. It will be taken into our subconscious memories, as again, our subconscious mind never sleeps.

Some people choose to program themselves for entirely new subject matter as they deeply relax or sleep. Entire learning programs have been created for what some call hypnosis-learning. It is an excellent way to memorize material for instant recall. Again, repetition is one of the best forms of learning, and what better way to utilize our full day and maximize our time management than to learn while we rest and sleep? This is why our *White Series* recording programs are so successful, because users process the suggestions and therapeutic prompts at various trance levels and hypnotic states as we go in and out of sleep.

Therefore, listening to these recordings several times at night— leaving the recorder on repeat—provides the desired suggestions at various trance levels of suggestibility. You may notice that you enjoy listening to these recordings at any level of relaxation. Many people report that they sleep better than ever as they listen and are amazed over time at their seemingly natural changes and desired improvements.

Listening repeatedly to a recording designed to promote a desired behavioral change can also provide the time for you to come to an understanding of your current predominant thoughts and beliefs and the opportunity to challenge and change any nonproductive or inappropriate thoughts. Instead you can establish new, more productive predominant thoughts and beliefs, leading to more desired behavioral changes.

We suggest listening closely to the *White Series* of CDs as often as possible during the day and several times at night during sleep for 30 to 90 days. You will know when you have achieved predominant thought changes since your new behaviors will be automatic. You will also want to listen to the CDs occasionally consciously to achieve conscious and subconscious thought alignment. This CD listening process is an integral part of our behavioral change program as illustrated by the three stories below:

Dear Mr. Parker,

I am writing you in response to the inspiration your CD on personal improvement and self-esteem has been to my 17-year-old niece and me. My niece moved in with me after being misplaced from several other homes. She felt as though she was at the end of her rope, with no place else to go. I let her move in under some very strict rules and guidelines. One was that she begins listening to your CD on self-esteem. She had been having trouble sleeping and was very cranky in the mornings. Not much joy to be around.

I explained to her that I wanted her to give your CD a try for at least one week, and if she felt it was not helping her she could stop. Since she began listening she has slept better than she has ever slept in her life. She tells me that her stress level has dropped to almost none. I can see several changes in her, all are very positive.

She has started dreaming of her Olympic dreams again, and is working hard to once again get back to the shape that will someday get her there. She has gone on to finish her schooling and is currently employed. Her life has made a complete turnaround. She refuses to go to sleep without the CD in, and tells me that when she moves out that she would like to take it with her. I, of course, told her she will have to get her own.

Thank you for making a difference for so many. Sherry

Dear Dennis,

I was shopping at Walmart late one night and I went to the candy aisle as I do every time I am in there, I walked over and got a pack of 10 miniature candy bars. Every time I go shopping I get these and then, on the way driving home, I eat all 10 of them. It is like my little (big) treat for myself. I went through the entire store telling me how I shouldn't be eating them and having a battle in my head. Thanks to the weight loss CD I had been listening to, all the scripting kept going through my head about taking care of your body, etc.

I made it through my shopping trip and was up at the register to check out and I just couldn't do it. I had to leave them at the register. It has been at least two weeks since I have had a candy bar. I also go to the fridge always looking for something to eat and the thought scripted from the CD, "are you really hungry or are you feeling an emotional hunger with food." Then I stop myself and get a drink of water instead and move on to something else. I find myself doing this at least several times a day. The CD is wonderful.

My husband has been drinking at least 4-8 soda pops a day since he was a teenager. He starts out his 4:30 a.m. day with a large Mountain Dew or Coke; it is a daily ritual for him that is followed by several more throughout the day. He very rarely drinks water and never drinks juice. I started playing the weight loss CD at night while he was sleeping. He didn't know what the CD was saying because he is always asleep before I turn it on. After a week or two of listening to it, he started making the funniest comments to me, unaware of where they were coming from.

First, he came home from work one night and told me that he was trying to cut back on soda pop and would like it if I would keep more juice in the house for him. Then another time we went out to eat and I was ahead of him in line at Subway and they asked what we wanted to drink and I ordered him a coke just like always and he came over quickly and asked me what I got him and then had the gentleman change his drink to lemonade. This went on for quite some time, we would go out to eat and he would actually ask for water to drink instead of a pop. But the second I stop playing the CD he is back on soda pop.

Cheri

Dear Mr. Parker,

I am dropping you this note to thank you. I have been listening to your CDs for several months now and will not go to sleep without them at this point in my life. I started listening to your self-esteem CD and found it so helpful in not only creating a happier frame of mind for myself, but for my niece as well.

After seeing the turnaround in her I decided to try your weight loss CD. Since I began listening to it four months ago I have dropped 25 pounds. I don't have cravings for those comfort foods anymore. My life is heading in the far greater direction today than when I first started your CD listening course. The positive attitude that I have found in myself, I owe partly to you.

I am getting married in the spring and I know today I have the confidence to put on that "white" dress and feel as beautiful in it as I will be. My self-esteem and my determination to get to the size I want to be for this wedding grow stronger every day.

Again thank you!
Sunshine and Smiles,

Jill

Catching "thinking errors" about ourselves or others in our conscious critical factor filter is important. Pay close attention to self-denigrating statements that go through your thought processes: "I'm not good enough!" "I'm not smart enough!" "I could never do the things they can do!" and so forth. How do you catch and challenge these types of thought in your critical factor filter and not allow them through to stimulate subconscious behavior-producing functions? You can simply bounce them back out, do not allow them through, and reject them telling you the opposite truths. "I am good enough to accomplish whatever I choose to set my mind too, and so forth.

Understand the action of your conscious filter as you reject these false thoughts and ideas. Ponder the following: what is the first thing that came into my mind? How did I react to that thought? That laughs? Or that face? What physical abreaction did I experience to reject the statement? *You just learned to use a therapeutic prompt to discern errors or lies and then tell yourself the truth by challenging an inappropriate thought.*

We will use the same process to challenge other lies as well as uncover other misunderstandings and misinterpretations of your life's experiences that may come to you as you listen to the *White Series* recordings.

De-Hypnotizing

Today, more and more people live in a chronic state of trance that is generally identified or assessed to be somnambulism which means "sleep walking or sleepwalkers". We refer to them as *natural somnambulates as a group or a somnambulist as an individual.* These are people, by dictionary definition, that are sleep walking, stuck in a chronic state of hypnosis or trance, and by characteristics are identified as being highly imaginative and vulnerable to the suggestions of others. They tend to be very fixated in imaginative creative roles. We find them in some of our most creative positions as musicians, artists, actors, writers, graphic designers, architects, scrap bookers and so forth.

This use of the imagination for productive output in these fields is the positive side to this level of trance. But being constantly in it unaware is dangerous to them as individuals, because it leaves them extremely vulnerable to the suggestions of others, where they will allow others to do their critical thinking and decision making. They allow others to take control of their agency replacing their own consciousness and conscious choices. The live life in a somewhat "spaced out condition."

They talk in absolutes. "This ... always happens to me!" "This is just the way I am!" There is nothing I can do about it" "They tend to give up their agency easily, going along to get along. It additionally is an attempt to avoid personal responsibility and accountability because they did not make the decision; they just did as they were told. Therefore when it doesn't work out at times, the consequences of their actions are now excusable as not being their fault, in their misguided, misdirected, thinking errors.

The goal we have in hypnotherapy is to train individuals in all of the observable levels of trance so they can make a conscious choice as to when they choose to go into somnambulism for creative purposes, and yet come out of it at will. Intentionally, not staying vulnerable to the suggestions of others and allowing others to take the place of their consciousness, agency, and choice.

Somnambulists are being produced out of so many of our young people and some adults by constant imaginary stimulation in all of its modern media forms. Stage hypnotists seek these people out for the benefit of the illusion of mind control for the entertainment value of the show. Since those who volunteer to go on stage are already in trance, they don't have to be hypnotized. They are willing participants to come up and act out as directed. They are the prey of every stage hypnotist. In our hypnotherapy practice, we de-hypnotize natural somnambulates and teach them how to come to full conscious awareness so they can start functioning from conscious recognition of their own agency and choices. We want the conscious mind, conscious choice, and conscious decision making, to be the seat of power within the individual. Yes, we want everything to be a conscious choice.

Being stuck in and living in their imagination makes them extremely sensitive to "what if" scenarios, or amplified judgments of "I should have..." It creates negative expectations in their intended outcomes of their future experiences. It generates needless fears and phobias, such as fears of heights, flying, bugs, snakes, and so forth. Teaching them about their imagination, how to recognize when their Intelligence is in it, and how to go to a place of balance is a huge step for them.

They need to be taught how to stay out of their imagination and live in consciousness, except when they choose to be there intentionally for creativity. Then, with awareness they can live their lives in the current moment, consciously, except when they choose to be somnambulistic for the purpose of creative goal oriented endeavors. I can't overemphasis these points enough, or maybe I just did.

When dehypnotized these individuals are always amazed at the differences they experience when they finally become fully conscious. They look around at the world in a new ways. Some describe it as coming out from a fog or a cloud in their minds, or as looking past a wall. Their view of the environment around them is sharper, clearer, has more detail, brighter colors, and greater awareness of reality.

We have and are raising generations of over-stimulated, adrenaline junkies. Young people receive so much media input that to keep the stimulation going no explosion is big enough or car chase fast enough; no plane, train, or multi-car and truck freeway wreck is massive enough; no fight or battle is violent enough because it requires more and greater excitement stimulation to really stir them up and keep the adrenaline and other stimulating hormones flowing.

Sensory-stimulating events like these have been viewed so many hundreds of times that it is difficult for their adrenaline to shut down as they are living most consistently in over sensitized amplified imaginations. So, the entertainment media keep raising the sensory bar in an effort to further stimulate the "wow" factor and have people keep buying the next level of stimulation.

This generation of youth who are adrenaline junkies, are so used to constant stimulation, to being in "fight or flight" mode, that they function as if this state of adrenaline rush is normal. Whenever they are not stimulated to the extreme of adrenaline and other chemical imbalances, they are likely to use the "B" word—boring! They not only find ordinary, everyday life boring, they feel that somehow they are entitled to or deserving of constant stimulation. When this adrenaline stimulation no longer satisfies them, they often seek greater stimulation in drugs, sex, violence, and even murder.

In fact, authorities are alarmed at the trend of murders committed by youth who claim they were simply looking for something to do. Recent incidents include three boys ages fifteen to seventeen who shot and killed an Oklahoma college athlete as he was jogging to his girlfriend's house. One of the three teenagers apparently told police that they were "bored and didn't have anything to do, so we decided to kill somebody."

According to NBC News, juvenile homicide expert Phil Chalmers, author *of Inside the Mind of a Teen Killer*, said, "I don't think it was an excuse. I think they are being honest about being bored." Chalmers, who at that time had interviewed more than 200 teen killers, called it "a gang killing by thrill killers" and explained, "Thrill killing is killing someone to experience the act of murder "just for fun."

Dave Cullen, an in-depth researcher of the Columbine High School massacre, suggested that blaming boredom might be masking other motives. "What I hear from that statement is more like, 'People mean nothing to me,' or 'I enjoyed this.' What I hear is an extreme lack of empathy, an extreme callousness that people can't even conceive of . . . " Other murders where young killers blamed their acts on boredom include the fatal stabbing of a 25-year-old pizza chef in New London, Connecticut in 2010 by six teenagers, the 2008 suffocation of a college student by a 22-year-old in Manhattan, and another fatal stabbing in 2006 in the UK when a 19- year-old attacked a nurse taking a break from her hospital job.

In the above scenarios of where people went to violence as their path to escalate sensory stimulation, even murder, Lt. Colonel Dave Grossman explains in his volumes of written works on the subject of video game simulation of killing and murdering people, which continues to be more graphically enhanced, and more stimulating to the imaginations of the inclined, that these young people are being trained in a conditioned response fashion to kill just as they train people to do so in the military.

He explains that in the investigations of recent school and others shootings that the objective of these shooters is to obtain the highest head count possible. Dead body head count is how they will get the most notoriety, points on the board so to speak, and win the game. The effect of these video games ought to be scrutinized by every parent. (In my hypnotherapy work, I do as much de-hypnosis as I do hypnosis, indicating the need of this information in the public domain.)

I personally believe by my observations that the constant bombardment of overstimulation of the imagination is a major source of what is called ADD. I also believe the constant release of the emotional content into the central nervous system in the form of physical abreactions is a major component of ADHD. I believe that these concepts are not well understood or researched at this point. While I admittedly do not have a lot of experience in this area, I find that young people who learn to understand their spiritual minds and begin to control their amplified imaginations immediately begin to demonstrate different behaviors and to express how different they feel. They are much more comfortable and peaceful as they learn and utilize these mind management techniques.

We need hypnotherapists, parents, grandparents, teachers, ministers and clergy, councilors and so forth who understand trance at its different levels so they can begin to teach people how to live quietly and peacefully in their own minds. The goal is to have and enjoy peace of mind. Many children are being raised on a steady diet of media stimulation do not even understand what peace of mind means. When they finally experience consciousness being de-hypnotized, they then have actual experience of the difference for themselves, being disconnected from their subconscious functions of imaginations, memories, and emotions.

Again, just like the man whose hand twitched every time the thought, "I never should have signed that check" went through his subconscious mind, young people may be experiencing incessant subconscious mind chatter consisting of mental scripts from their many media influences. Being exposed to such an endless bombardment of media stimulus keeps them overactive and physically abreacting to the subconscious thought scripts. They need to be exposed to being fully conscious to have a chance to recognize what it is to experience peace of mind.

As we learned earlier, one person's hand tic was stimulated by a single mental script. Imagine how a child or youth would act with 20, 30, 40 or more such scripts constantly rolling around in their head as mind chatter. These mind management skills are highly useful for children who are hyperactive and need to stay focused to do their schoolwork. Teaching children to enjoy living quietly in their own minds, free of mind chatter, ought to be a goal of every hypnotherapist.

Such mind chatter can be accessed through hypnosis or trance, which slows the thought processes down. Then the individual can recognize, understand, and deal with each one. Perhaps in the future, as others investigate the Spiritual Mind Management methods we are proposing here, along with our other hypnotherapy processes, recognition will be given that these are indeed answers to many of the serious attention deficit disorders of our young people.

A story to help explain these points:

I had a father bring his 14 year old son to me at the clinic explaining that he was being asked to get his son some help. Teachers and counselors at a recent back to school night told the father that his son was not focusing on his school work, and always seemed to be daydreaming, looking constantly out the windows and doors. He was also considered to be somewhat rebellious as no matter how many times they asked him to pay attention; he just seemed to ignore their directions.

We brought the son in and induced the appropriate level of catalepsy trance for subconscious access to the root thoughts causing or stimulating these behaviors. I utilized techniques to have him isolate and identify the feeling that he was experiencing each and every time he was looking out the windows and doors. He identified it as FEAR! He became emotional and started to vent (cry), rapid short shallow breathing, lacrimation of the eyes, and tense muscles throughout his body. I then had him listen to the voice, or identify the script in his head that was creating these feelings. What was the voice saying to him? In trance he could connect the dots between the thoughts and the feelings that are generating the behaviors.

He said, "It is my dad's voice!" What is he saying to you? "We are having a conversation where he is telling me to watch out for my little sister at school so that nothing ever happens to her like what happened to Elizabeth Smart. Every day as we leave for school my dad says to me, 'Take care of your sister!' I am so afraid that something is going to happen to her and that it will be my fault. I will disappoint Dad and he will be so angry at me! That it is all I can think about throughout the day is wonder if she is okay? I am constantly looking to see her on the athletic field, playground, or in the halls to know that she is alright."

Children are exposed to so many distractions in our society now that give them concern for their safety, and well-being. Their minds are so full of stimulating imagery that they do not even know what normal is. Yes, I am proposing that what they have going on in their imagination is more important to them than what is going on in the current moment of time in their school work and the imagination is winning.

Of course, we went on with dad there to challenge and change the son's thinking of who is really responsible for the care and safety of his little sister. Dad obviously had to take responsibility for her overall safety and well-being and had no idea that his statements were being taken in so literally by the son as to not pay attention to his school responsibilities. We went on to dehypnotize the young man from the somnambulistic state he was living in and brought the situation back into balance in his mind. Yes, he came out of his amplified imaginations. The young man understood what he had been doing with his imagination, took conscious control and could focus again on his school work. He went on to excel in school.

Example of a de-hypnotizing experience

Dennis with Speaker 2

Dennis: Do you want to tell people about your de-hypnosis experience?

Speaker 2: What? Being dehypnotized?

Dennis: Yeah, that whole process we took you through.

Speaker 2: Well, how long did it actually take to do it? How long was the therapy?

Dennis: You had probably four or five sessions before you became fully aware that you were conscious. Remember that day when you finally looked around the room and…

Speaker 2: I remember that session being so easy, though.

Dennis: Well, it wasn't traumatic like some of the other stuff we've done. It was more you learning Mind Management.

Speaker 2: Okay. When I came out of trance, I opened my eyes and I felt more whole, I felt more complete. Things were bright, things were clear. The room was actually brighter. The walls didn't have like a grey tint. Before it actually felt like I had a dark glaze over my eyes my whole life.

A week later, I drove to my grandma's house. She's been living in the same house my whole life, and this time I saw blue road signs on the way. I thought they were all green before, but I found that some of them were actually blue. It was really weird. Since I've been dehypnotized, I also haven't had people's suggestions influence me whatsoever. Somebody can say something nasty, and okay, I really don't care. Before, I might put a smile on my face, but inside it made me sick and hurt. Then I would find reasons why I actually was whatever that person called me.

Dennis: So you're doing what we talked about, you're doing Mind Management

Speaker 2: Yes!

Detaching from negative emotions

We can detach from negative emotions temporarily (or help others do so) as we visualize, pretend, and imagine that we can take hold of a negative thought, emotion, or experience by mentally putting it in our hand. We pretend and imagine that it is a lump of sand on the beach and that we are crushing—disintegrating the lie, the misunderstanding, or the negative experience. You notice that, as the sand falls to the beach, all negativity, sorrows, or other unwanted feelings begin to fall from your mind, your heart, and your spirit, as your hand releases the sand and you let go.

You see, hear, and feel the sand falling to the ground with all past negative thoughts and feelings in it. The ocean immediately washes over it, and it is gone. It is now a part of the past. Finished!

You also take deep, full breaths, and pretend and imagine that you are drawing in any negative feelings of a particular experience or lie. You draw those feelings in, then visualize them going back out, being released from you, each time you exhale. Those old feelings of the past are caught up in the gentle breeze and blown away, far away from you.

As you practice this process, your mind gets clearer and your heart becomes more peaceful. Each and every time you utilize this process, you find you can process thoughts and feelings this way both in hypnosis and during your daily routine in conscious reality. You will find that this system works easily and effectively for you even though you may still need to do the deductive hypnotherapy processes to achieve final resolve.

You will feel safe, secure, and comfortable, knowing that you are now more in control of your thoughts and feelings than ever. You will also feel confident, self-assured, and more powerful as an individual. Anytime you sense an uncomfortable, self-defeating feeling, simply take several deep, full breaths, and incrementally, piece by piece, just blow it away.

Crush the thoughts again; questioning how much amplification you may have done in your imagination. Sometimes it may be helpful to visualize that you have a dial on your amplified imagination and emotions and that you can see, hear, and feel yourself in your mind turning the dial down. Let the imagination go, let it go. It's getting weaker and smaller.

You are letting the feelings and strong emotions go. Let them go now. Turn the dial down, turn it down again, and turn it all the way down now. Every easy breath takes you deeper and deeper into relaxation. Inhale, exhale—let it all go. You're more comfortable, peaceful, going deeper into relaxation, twice as deep now, deeper and deeper, down into relaxation. Your mind gets clearer, and your heart becomes peaceful.

Emotional release techniques

Our Mind Management hypnotherapy programs include ongoing reinforcement of impulse control techniques and emotional release processes through the use of our *White Series* CDs. You will learn here how to use emotional release techniques to let go of pent-up emotions. Repeated listening will help you to understand subconscious scripts and give you the opportunity to clear up any "stinking thinking."

We have all accepted some misrepresentations of ourselves to ourselves—misunderstandings, misinterpretations, or even outright lies about ourselves and our many life experiences. We may, in fact, at one time or another, truly have been a victim of some of life's most difficult tests and trials. But we now choose to move forward in life as an understanding survivor.

In trance, you can more easily understand how your imagination amplifies thoughts and beliefs. When utilizing our imagination positively, you can amplify your creative abilities and create enthusiasm and excitement. This, in turn, develops positive attitudes and positive thoughts. Attitudes come from our expectations about outcomes. If we expect things to turn out poorly, we have a poor or negative attitude. If we expect things to turn out positively, we have a positive attitude. Our expectations come from our beliefs.

Another time, I had a college student come in to work with me on test-taking relaxation and sleep issues. During our conversations, one of the things he complained about was that his nose twitched every few minutes and had done so for as long as he could remember. I watched this happen consistently while we visited. I explained to him that what he might have is a mental script, which is a thought pattern that he generates in his mind on a regular basis, and the emotional content or the electrical energy of that thought might be dumping off into the muscles of his nose. This script was playing at a subconscious level below his conscious state of awareness. We did the trance work and challenged and changed his thought processes. His nose stopped twitching immediately and has not done so for several months.

Spiritual Mind Management techniques will have you identify where on your head you are feeling the emotion and then intentionally move it to the crown of your head in balance or over to the left side into alienation and avoidance and shut it down or off.

Gestalt techniques—as we use and teach them

Gestalt is a German word that means to organize or arrange, to create an organized whole. Gestalt therapy addresses secondary defense mechanisms and secondary payoffs, which are learned responses to primary core experiences. Both need to be dealt with to accomplish complete and permanent change. Gestalt identifies and deals with the emotions and ideas that tend to reinforce amnesia and denial of an original and negative sensitizing event.

Gestalt therapy was developed by Fritz Perls, Laura Perls, and Paul Goodman in the 1940s and 1950s. Perls perceived many personalities as lacking wholeness and being fragmented. He claimed that people are often aware of only parts of themselves rather than their whole self. The aim of Gestalt therapy is to help people become whole—to help them become aware of, admit to, reclaim, and integrate their fragmented parts. The idea is that this integration helps a person make the transition from dependency to self-sufficiency, from authoritarian outer support to authentic inner support. A person with inner support is self-reliant.

Methods common in Gestalt therapy:

- Role-playing
- Exaggeration of symptoms or behavior
- Use of fantasy
- Staying in the immediate moment, the experience of "being in the now"
- Becoming aware of bodily senses, and learning to "stay with feelings" until they are understood and integrated

At Certified Hypnotherapy Training School, we utilize some of the original Gestalt techniques taught when I went to school, but have modified others to suit our new purposes incorporating mind management principles as well. We will explain some of the methods we see as being the most effective in achieving our goals with clients.

One of the most important uses of Gestalt hypnotherapy is to assist clients in overcoming *double-mindedness. Double-mindedness* is a lack of alignment of consciously chosen goals, desired achievements, and supporting beliefs due to opposing thoughts or beliefs in the subconscious that cause opposing forces within the individual. Double-mindedness encourages self-limiting beliefs, self-defeating behaviors, inappropriate habits, and maladaptive behaviors.

Double-mindedness

Double-mindedness is the state of holding opposing beliefs in the conscious versus the subconscious levels of our mind, causing opposing forces within us. Thus we start something and then stop. We try to move forward and then we hesitate. We need to overcome our double-mindedness. As the Bible says, "A double-minded man is unstable in all his ways" (James 1:8).

Eliminating double-mindedness will bring stability to our lives and help us make more consistent, intelligent choices. Our actions will be more positive. We will be able to overcome (fill in the blank here) that we want to address or any other problem

Eliminating double-mindedness will clarify the difference between good and evil, right and wrong, worthy and unworthy, and we will become more stable in all of our ways.

Typical inner conflicts or double-mindedness

Consciously, we may know we ought to be healthy and physically fit. However, in the subconscious mind we hold opposing predominant thought behavior-producing beliefs that create opposing forces within us and require hypnosis at deep levels in order to access, challenge, and change them, and bring the minds into alignment.

- What is it that you are fighting for and at the same time fleeing from that is costing you what you want most?
- What is it that you are seeking and at the same time avoiding that is costing you what you want most?
- What is it that you are identifying with and at the same time alienating yourself from that is costing you what you want most?

Most of us will continue in a state of instability, of unawareness of being double minded until we achieve subconscious thought access through trance or hypnosis.

When our "double" minds become aligned, we move forward without hesitations, inhibitions, and procrastination. We move forward seemingly automatically, and both comfortably and confidently towards our goals. We achieve more than we ever imagined possible when we are in harmony within ourselves.

When full alignment is achieved and we have our new Mind Management mental skills in place, we move quickly towards our desired achievements.

Gestalt Empty Chair Technique

We use Gestalt methods as one tool in the toolbox to help our clients do the kind of personal problem-solving that brings an end to double-mindedness. Whether a predominant belief currently resides in consciousness or in the subconscious, it will be revealed in the Gestalt process. We then assist the client in moving the seat of power back to consciousness by aligning the subconscious with the consciously chosen objectives and goals.

We want the client to learn to act out of choice, rather than to react with learned rigid responses held in the subconscious and given power by misapplied amplifications of the imagination or misinterpretations of experiences in memory. Gestalt therapy usually leads to an "aha" moment that reveals incongruent thought patterns and allows for alignment of the conscious and subconscious minds.

Because playing both roles of being both the conscious participant and the younger representation of ourselves or various other persons in a sensitizing experience (your imaginary self in the memory of the initial sensitizing event) allows the client to understand their own perceptions of a behavior-stimulating experience both consciously and subconsciously, Gestalt's empty chair role play can reveal disconnects between conscious and subconscious thoughts and beliefs.

We therefore ask the client to be themselves consciously, and then to isolate whatever they perceive as the influence on their behavior in the problem—the other person's pain, the new job, their younger self, etc. They are then instructed to put those behavior influencers in another position, such as on an empty chair or by their knee out in front of them. If the individual feels the need for protection in their mind, such as imagining themselves confronting a molester or an attacker, you can place the perpetrator behind bars or bulletproof glass in front of them, keeping them safe in their imagination as they start to desensitize the experience with the conversation that follows next.

Change comes about by recognition and resolution of what their accepted beliefs are for the initial sensitizing events. No one wants to be wrong, so we all attempt to justify, validate, and defend our chosen beliefs. The following method can reveal the beliefs someone is defending.

The client pretends to have a conversation, a dialogue between themselves (as the older, wiser, smarter, more mature person) and whatever imaginary representation they have put in the other chair. Sometimes it is also useful to have them change chairs and act as the behavior influencer speaking to them in the other now-empty chair. The purpose is to reveal to the individual what their thought processes and beliefs are, revealing themselves to themselves, clearing up incongruence and nonalignment of thought and belief, overcoming double-mindedness and instability.

See the Empty Chair Gestalt illustration on the next page

Empty Chair Gestalt

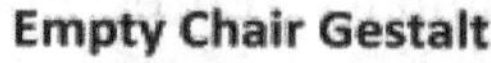

Have your younger-self in the empty chair in your imagination, at whatever age you experienced your initial sensitizing event. Subconscious Perspective!

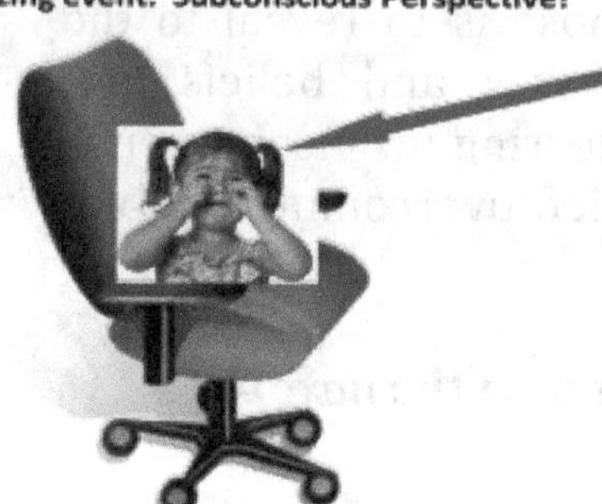

Conscious Adult Perspectives

The client (or you if you are doing it as self-hypnotherapy) sits in one chair and faces another empty chair.

Pretend and imagine isolating your younger self when you first were sensitized, or the other persons, pain, emotions, gland, organ, muscle group, disease, new job, other person in a relationship, or whatever they perceive as the influence of the behavior in the empty chair.

Or, pretend to isolate the other persons, pain, emotions, gland, organ, muscle group, disease, new job, other person in a relationship, or whatever they perceive as the influence of the behavior to be.

Have a conversational dialogue between the client (or you as the client) being the older, wiser, smarter, more mature person, (representing current conscious thoughts and perspectives) and whatever imaginary representation they have put in the other chair (representing former subconscious thoughts and perspectives). Sometimes it is useful to have them change chairs (go from the conscious chair to the subconscious chair) and be the representation of the behavioral influencer speaking to the other now empty chair representing them in their conscious mind. This reverse role playing is to reveal to the individual what their thought processes and beliefs are at both a conscious and subconscious level, gaining revelation of themselves to themselves, clearing up incongruences in thoughts and beliefs, developing alignment overcoming double mindedness and instability. This is a component of personal problem solving Mind Management.

You may have the conversation between older, wiser, smarter, more mature you, and younger you, having the adult teach and review again what they both have learned from the conversations. Have the older conscious person finish up the conversation with younger them. You will know when you have resolve, as releasing emotional content is over and younger you will be ready to come back and be with older you. You are to pretend and imagine them coming back and putting them in your heart and reintegrate, as you consciously bring them back and gain the feeling and confidence that they are now with you. Then have older conscious you say what you need to say to younger them again as they are now back with you. (I am old enough, wise enough, smart enough, mature enough, to protect you and take care of you, I have missed you, I love you and I will do the best I can for you from here on out, and so forth.) You will know when you or the client has reached closure as there is always a sense of peace, happiness, and joy. They feel as though there has been a burden or weight lift off of them, they feel lighter and free. CLOSUER!

Triangle Conversational Gestalt

We also teach what we call the "Triangle Conversational Gestalt." First, we induce catalepsy trance. Again we have you isolate the other person's pain, the emotions, the muscle group, the disease, the new job, the other person in a relationship—whatever you perceive as the influence on your behavior in the problem situation. Place the influencer off to your left knee.

Put your younger self off to your right knee, at whatever age you first had your initial sensitizing event. Start the conversation between the younger you and the other influencer of your behavior. Continue the dialogue until there is a sense of full disclosure and closure is achieved.

Then have the conversation between older, wiser, smarter, more mature you, and the other behavior influencer. You will know when closure has been reached as you (or the client) usually sigh, letting the rest of the emotional content finally release, and the perpetrators will either leave or disappear. Have the conversation between the older, wiser, smarter more mature you and the younger you, having the adult you teach and review again what you both have learned from the conversations.

Have the older conscious you finish up the conversation with the younger you. You will know when you have resolved the issue as the release of emotional content will be over. When the younger you is ready to come back and be with the older you (to reintegrate), bring the younger you back and put them in your heart. Say what you need to say to younger you again. ("I am old enough, wise enough, smart enough and mature enough to protect you and take care of you. I have missed you. I love you, and I will do the best I can for you from here on out," and so forth.)

See the Triangle Gestalt on the following page

Conversational: Triangle Gestalt

Conscious Adult Perspectives

Pretend and imagine that you have your younger-self off to your right knee, at whatever age you experienced your initial sensitizing event.

Pretend and imagine that you have the other persons, pain, emotions, your younger self, gland, organ, muscle group, disease, new job, other person in a relationship, or whatever you perceive as the influence of the behavior, off to your left knee.

Start the conversation between younger you (subconscious representative) and the other influencer of the behavior, (subconscious influencer representative/s). You be the voice for each of the patries as it comes to you from the your subconscious memories. Allow both bottom end of the triangle representatives converse, until there is a sense of full understanding and discloser. You will know when you have completed the conversation as their will be a strong sense that closer is achieved.

Then have the conversation between older, wiser, smarter, more mature you, and the other behavioral influencer first. Let each party say what they need and want to say. Have the conversation until full understanding and closure is achieved. You will know when closure has been reached as you will usually sigh letting the rest of the emotional content finally release. The other gestalt representations and/or the perpetrators just leave or seem to disappear.

Then have the conversation between older, wiser, smarter, more mature you, and younger you, having the adult teach and review again what they both have learned from the conversations. Have the older conscious person finish up the conversation with younger them. You will know when you have resolved the problem, as younger you will be ready to come back and be with older you, and reintegrate. Then have conscious you bring younger you back. Pretend and imagine, put them in your heart. Tell your younger person what you want and need to say to them again as reinforcement, now that they are back with you. (I am old enough, wise enough, smart enough, mature enough, to protect you and take care of you, I have missed you. I love you. I will do the best I can for you from here on out, and so forth.) You will know when you have achieved integration and alignment of thought processes, as the emotional content is gone, and you have a strong sense of happiness and peace. Everyone describes that they feel like a huge weight has just been lifted off from them.

Emotional Gestalts

The third most popular Gestalt method we teach is called an Emotional Gestalt. As we have discussed previously, there is no emotion without the accepted thought crossing the critical factor filter into subconscious functions. You can use this technique the next time you are experiencing an unwanted emotion or you become aware that something is troubling you although you are not aware of a conscious reason for feeling that way.

Step One: Go somewhere you can be quiet and still for a few moments. Accomplish your self-hypnosis techniques of focusing, deep breathing, and relaxation.

Step Two: Feel the emotion that is at issue; then intensify it in your imagination. Double it and then double it again. The stronger you make the emotion; the easier it is to connect the dots between the emotion and the thought or thoughts that generated it. You'll also learn that in amplifying the emotion, you have the ability to turn the emotion up as high as you like, which indicates to the subconscious mind that if you have the power to turn the emotion up, then you also must have the power to turn it down. And if you have the power to turn it down, you can turn it all the way down, and then simply turn it off.

Step Three: Give the emotion a name, such as anger, fear, guilt, greed, and boredom, fear of rejection, fear of failure, fear of the unknown, and so forth. The Gestalt then is to have the conversation between your conscious mind and the subconscious emotions, connecting the dots to the thoughts creating and generating the emotional content. Separate out the feeling from your consciousness. Separate your conscious mind from the emotion, recognizing it as negative energy or as something separate from you.

Step Four: For our example, let's say the emotion involved is fear of rejection. Maintaining the feeling of *fear of rejection* as something separate from you, do a conversational Gestalt. Ask the fear of rejection, "What is it that you are doing for me or attempting to provide me with?" Listen carefully in your mind for the voice of your subconscious emotions to answer, connecting the dots to the thoughts.

Step Five: The answer generally is an excuse not to have to experience something new or different, an excuse not to have to change, or some way of attempting to protect you from something or someone. If this fear of rejection has to do with creating a new friendship or business relationship with someone, the voice may be saying, "They wouldn't give me the time of day, so why should I even try?" or "I'm not good enough to do this," or "I am afraid of rejection, and it's just not worth the effort." These are examples of subconscious scripts that may be invalidating our conscious efforts and desires to develop new relationships, both business and personal.

Step Six: Consciously start to challenge the feeling and the thoughts coming from it by asking yourself and the emotion questions. Are these lies, misunderstandings, and excuses for failure "in advance" that I have bought into, that I have allowed to inhibit me from going forward, keeping me from accomplishing what I know I want and desire?

Step Seven: Now go back and challenge each of the subconscious scripts with what you want to acknowledge, recognize, and accept as the conscious truth. Start reprogramming your subconscious with statements opposite to your negative scripts. Your positive self-talk and affirmations in this example would be, "If these people only knew what I had to offer, they would be more than willing to give me enough time to explain it to them. I am well prepared and good enough to accomplish this task of explaining myself to people and making new friends. I love people; I enjoy friendships. Making new friends is easy for me. I know that as I smile, people smile back. I know that as I am friendly to people, others choose to be friendly as well. I know how to control the outcome of my experiences, as I know the natural law is that I will get back what I give out. If I am friendly, they will be friendly back," and so forth.

Step Eight: Continue to challenge the negative scripts with opposite positive statements from the conscious mind to the subconscious until the old emotions have collapsed because you have replaced the subconscious negative thoughts with new positive ones. Continue to tell yourself the truth: "I am good enough! I am capable! I am smart enough to do this! I am likable! I like myself!"

When we have challenged the old thoughts and replaced them with new positive thoughts, the negative feelings automatically collapse and new energized feelings emerge, changing our behavior. It really is about what we choose to believe, as we act out of our most predominant thought and beliefs.

See the Emotional Gestalt diagram on the following page

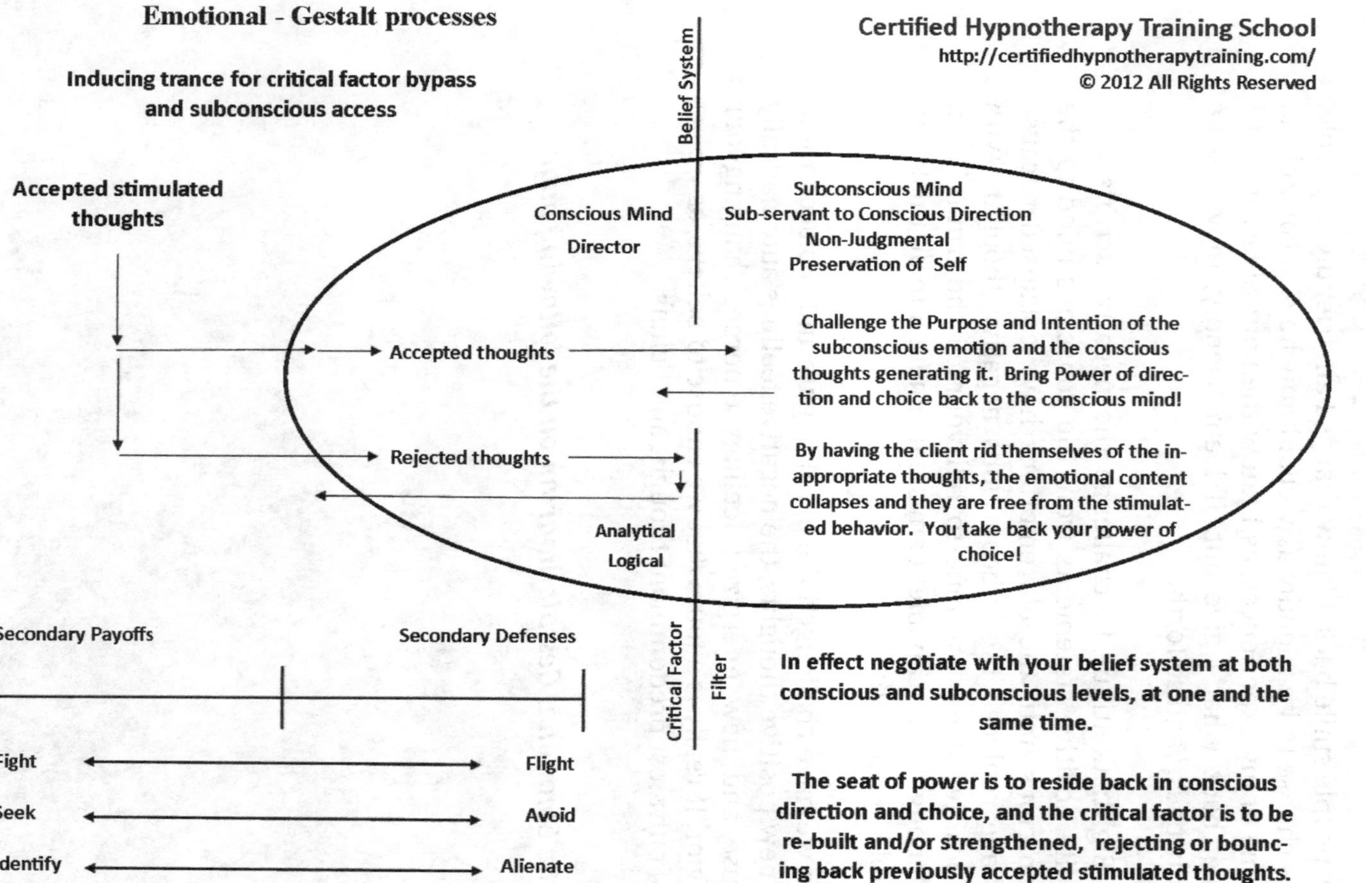
Emotional - Gestalt processes
Inducing trance for critical factor bypass and subconscious access
Certified Hypnotherapy Training School
http://certifiedhypnotherapytraining.com/
© 2012 All Rights Reserved
Belief System
Accepted stimulated thoughts
Conscious Mind
Director
Subconscious Mind
Sub-servant to Conscious Direction
Non-Judgmental
Preservation of Self
Accepted thoughts
Challenge the Purpose and Intention of the subconscious emotion and the conscious thoughts generating it. Bring Power of direction and choice back to the conscious mind!
Rejected thoughts
By having the client rid themselves of the inappropriate thoughts, the emotional content collapses and they are free from the stimulated behavior. You take back your power of choice!
Analytical
Logical
Secondary Payoffs
Secondary Defenses
Critical Factor
Filter
In effect negotiate with your belief system at both conscious and subconscious levels, at one and the same time.
Fight
Flight
Seek
Avoid
Identify
Alienate
The seat of power is to reside back in conscious direction and choice, and the critical factor is to be re-built and/or strengthened, rejecting or bouncing back previously accepted stimulated thoughts.
Generate new and changed behaviors!

Guided imagery—stories and scripts.

Guided imagery uses the subconscious functions of imagination, memories, and emotions to offer suggestions and thoughts that are goal directed. It is a method of indirect associative focusing that utilizes stories, metaphors, or scripts. It is an indirect method because it does not confront the client and their problem directly or personally attack them. It allows the client to visualize and associate their personal problems with the problems of the characters in the stories, metaphors, or scripts.

Imagery from stories, metaphors, and scripts focuses attention and awareness on solutions and resolutions to problems portrayed by the characters that are similar to them. It is a relaxation technique that can help people quickly and easily manage stress and reduce tension in the body. It's as easy as indulging in daydreaming for visualization of creative new ways to solve old problems. Guided imagery can be used to help lower blood pressure, reduce weight, stop smoking, manage pain and promote healing, enhance athletic performance, and overcome fears and phobias.

Doing guided imagery self-hypnosis does require some training and an understanding of self-hypnosis principles and processes to be most effective. It is considered an alternative therapy and is one method or form of hypnotherapy.

First, relax your client. The person may be directed to remember their favorite time at the beach or if they have never been to a beach, to imagine what it might be like to be on the beach on a bright and sunny day with a warm, gentle breeze blowing through their hair and gentle waves lapping up against their feet from bright, clear, blue water. Such imagery is utilized to engage all of the senses, including the smell of the salty air and so forth.

The idea is to guide people into their imagination for purposes of deep relaxation. As you continue to develop the imagery, have them start to imagine how they can do things new and differently. Begin to utilize their memories and imagination to do personal problem-solving. They can achieve relaxation and stress reduction as they visualize being in a comfortable, safe, secure place, surrounded by their favorite loved ones and friends.

If you are Hypnotizing Yourself

1- Get yourself in as comfortable a position as you can for the circumstances in which you are doing this. Begin doing deep breathing from your diaphragm. Close your eyes and focus on your stomach moving out as you breathe in and your stomach moving in as you breathe out. The diaphragm stimulates the Vegas nerve in the central nervous system and you automatically begin to feel physical stress relief and relaxation after several full deep diaphramic breaths. Be in a very pleasant, comfortable place in your imagination, the most pleasant, comfortable place you have ever been.

2- Start adding additional sensory detail to your imagery. It may be a bright, sunny beach and you are resting on the warm sand with a gentle tropical breeze blowing through your hair and birds chirping in the palm trees that line the beachfront. Or you may be floating down a pleasant, gently flowing river on a comfortable raft. You may even enjoy pretending and imagining that you are taking a walk through a wonderful mountain forest and you love the fresh, clean smell of the pine trees with wildlife all around you and squirrels scampering from tree to tree.

3- The more of your senses that are involved, the deeper you will go into relaxation. You may smell the salty sea air and feel the warmth of the healing sun all over your body. You may feel the fresh, warm breeze blowing across the landscape. You may enjoy the sounds of the ocean as the waves roll in or the lapping of the water from a gently flowing brook or river. Involve all of your senses and see what the scene looks like in great detail. Smell the flowers in the landscape all around you, feel the warmth of the sand and the sun. See the amazing scenery in every direction and listen to the birds sing happily in the trees.

4- Stay in this comfortable, pleasant, wonderful place for as long as you like. You are not in a hurry to leave this environment since you are enjoying every minute. As you breathe fully, deeply, and rhythmically you notice that it's very easy and natural for you to breathe in any stressful emotional content and then just begin to blow it out of your body with every easy, deep, full, rhythmic breath. Enjoy deep breathing and oxygenating your entire mind and body. Deep breathing is pleasant, comfortable, invigorating, revitalizing. You realize that stress is being released with every breath, and you simply blow any negative emotion, any negative thought, far away from you.

5- When you are ready to return from this imaginary but most pleasant journey, you simply begin to count from one to five. By the time you get to five, you allow yourself to be fully alert, wide-awake, invigorated, revitalized, and ready to enjoy the rest of your day's activities. You feel as though you've slept for a long period of time.

Examples of Stories

If you are the hypnotherapist and you have the client in deep trance, you would now simply read them an appropriate story from a book or other source in an enthusiastic voice (or whatever the story seems to call for). Put the emphasis in the script on the right suggestions so the client may ponder and consider the meanings and moral of the story in the script, relating it to their personal problem-solving.

Let's say the behavior problem at hand is that the client allows everyone else's opinion to be more meaningful to them than their own. Sometimes we like to confront clients who think this way with the question: Are they worshiping at the altar of the God of what other people think? The following Aesop's fable might be a good choice for this particular problem.

The Miller and the Donkey

A miller and his son were driving their ass to a neighboring fair to sell him. They had not gone far when they met up with a troop of women collected around a well, talking and laughing. "Look there," cried one of them. "Did you ever see such fellows to be trudging along the road on foot when they might ride?" The old man, hearing this, quickly made his son mount the ass, and continued to walk along merrily by his side.

Presently they came up to a group of old men in earnest debate. "There," said one of them. "It proves what I was saying. What respect is shown to old age in these days? Do you see that idle lad riding while his old father has to walk? Get down, you young scapegrace, and let the old man rest his weary limbs." Upon this the old man made his son dismount, and got up himself.

In this manner they had not proceeded far when they met a company of women and children: "Why, you lazy old fellow," cried several tongues at once. "How can you ride upon the beast, while that poor little lad there can hardly keep pace by the side of you?" The good-natured miller immediately took up his son behind him.

They had now almost reached the town. "Pray, honest friend," said a citizen, "is that ass your own?" "Yes," replied the old man. "O, one would not have thought so," said the other, "by the way you load him. Why, you two fellows are better able to carry the poor beast than he you." "Anything to please you," said the old man. "We can but try." So, alighting with his son, they tied the legs of the ass together and with the help of a pole endeavored to carry him on their shoulders over a bridge near the entrance to the town.

This entertaining sight brought the people in crowds to laugh at it, till the ass, not liking the noise or the strange handling that he was subject to, broke the cords that bound him and, tumbling off the pole, fell into the river. Upon this, the old man, vexed and ashamed, made the best of his way home again, convinced that by endeavoring to please everybody, he had pleased nobody and lost his ass in the bargain. (*Aesop's Fables,* translated by George Fyler Townsend)

Parables

Parables are another good way to do indirect associative focusing. An example:

The Sower (Matt: 13:3-8, Mark 4:3-8, Luke 8:4-15)

(New Testament | Mark 4:3-8)

4 - And when much people were gathered together, and were come to him out of every city, he spake by a parable:
5 - A sower went out to sow his seed: and as he sowed, some fell by the way side; and it was trodden down, and the fowls of the air devoured it.
6 - And some fell upon a rock; and as soon as it was sprung up, it withered away, because it lacked moisture.
7 - And some fell among thorns; and the thorns sprang up with it, and choked it.
8 - And other fell on good ground, and sprang up, and bare fruit a hundredfold. And when he had said these things, he cried, He that hath ears to hear let him hear.
9 - And his disciples asked him, saying, what might this parable be?

10 - And he said, Unto you it is given to know the mysteries of the kingdom of God: but to others in parables; that seeing they might not see, and hearing they might not understand.
11 - Now the parable is this: The seed is the word of God.
12 - Those by the way side are they that hear; then cometh the devil, and taketh away the word out of their hearts, lest they should believe and be saved.
13 - They on the rock are they, which, when they hear, receive the word with joy; and these have no root, which for a while believe, and in time of temptation fall away.
14 - And that which fell among thorns are they, which, when they have heard, go forth, and are choked with cares and riches and pleasures of this life, and bring no fruit to perfection.
15 - But that on the good ground are they, which in an honest and good heart, having heard the word, keep it, and bring forth fruit with patience.

A Story of Forgiveness

"To err is human; to forgive, divine." This quote from Alexander Pope can be applied to the following true story.

Op Ed, page Christian Science Monitor - Tuesday, Oct. 2, 2007
Upside Down Forgiveness - Donald B. Kraybill

On October 2, 2006 a shooter shattered a cloudless day in Amish country at Nickel Mines, PA. After dismissing the boys and adults in the one room school, he tied the legs of ten girls and then in execution style fired off thirteen shots in eight seconds, killing five and injuring the rest before shooting himself. Within days of the massacre, hundreds of news accounts reported that the Amish had forgiven the killer and his family. News of the instant forgiveness stunned the outside world. Many pundits lauded the Amish but others worried that hasty forgiveness was emotionally unhealthy.

What the news stories did not explain was why the Amish forgave. In dozens of interviews with Amish people after the tragedy I discovered that Amish forgiveness is upside-down in many ways. The father of a slain daughter explained, "our forgiveness was not our words, it was what we did." Of the seventy five people at the killer's burial over half were Amish, including parents who had buried their own children a day or so before. They hugged the gunman's widow and other members of his family. They also brought food and flowers to the killer's home. Amish people also contributed to a fund for the shooter's family. There were a few words, but it was primarily hugs, gifts, and presence—acts of grace—that communicated Amish forgiveness."

The Rev. Schenck reports a grandfather of one of the murdered Amish girls said of the killer on the day of the murder: "We must not think evil of this man."

Jack Meyer, a member of the Brethren community living near the Amish in Lancaster County, explained to CNN: "I do not think there's anybody here that wants to do anything but forgive and not only reach out to those who have suffered a loss in that way but to reach out to the family of the man who committed these acts."

Dwight Lefever, a Roberts family spokesman, said an Amish neighbor comforted the Roberts family hours after the shooting and extended forgiveness to them.

Dozens of Amish neighbors attended Charles Roberts' funeral on October 7, 2006. He was buried in an unmarked grave in his wife's family plot behind Georgetown United Methodist Church, a few miles from the one-room West Nickel Mines schoolhouse. One mourner stated that Roberts' wife was touched by the outward gesture of forgiveness by the Amish community. The schoolhouse was torn down eleven days after the tragedy and was re-built in a nearby location. (Wikipedia)

True stories like this have a strong impact

Such stories, scripts, or parables can be played on a recorder as the individual is in the relaxed state described above or read to them by another individual or by a hypnotherapist as part of a hypnotherapy session. Many books of scripts can be purchased and thousands of metaphors, stories, and scripts can be found for free on the internet. You can start building a library of stories to have ready to use with your clients. You first want to understand the specific problem, habit, or behavior your clients wish to overcome so you can choose wisely the story, script, metaphor, fable, or parable you think will have the most impact. If you are not sure, then use several stories, metaphors, and scripts as time in the session allows.

Pain control and relief techniques

Dennis does individual sessions of pain control on a regular basis as a contract hypnotherapist at the Advanced Health Clinic in Farmington, Utah. He mostly works with long-term chronic pain relief, and has developed very successful unique protocols of hypnotherapy utilizing the Mind Management principles taught here. We also do advanced pain Mind Management control training in our Certified Hypnotherapy Training School Programs. Our pain control methods are not going to be discussed in this volume, as the intention of this book is to focus on understanding the spiritual mind and the personal skills development of being able to instantaneously accomplish and achieve behavioral modification with these new techniques. However, we will include our unique pain control methods and techniques in future books.

Peeling the onion

We've said a number of times now that we want to recognize, challenge, and change current predominant thoughts and emotions that are generating undesirable feelings. These feelings, when acted upon, produce maladaptive behaviors, such as unwholesome cravings. Since each inappropriate thought needs to be challenged and changed, we sometimes compare this thought-switching, thought-changing process to peeling an onion, one layer at a time. One thought after another, one feeling and experience after another, is being changed and improved.

When people go into a state of trance, their minds, spirits, and bodies are free to choose what they will deal with first, next, and each time after that, one experience after another. The individual client thus directs what the hypnotherapy session is going to be about, not the hypnotherapist. You simply have to facilitate and maintain the proper trance state and be prepared to apply the processes to whatever comes up, then the next thing after that, layer after layer, sensitizing experience after sensitizing experience, until each experience has been properly understood and learned from, until the mind is finally clear of sensitizations and is fixation free.

The idea is to one day become free of negativity and in control of our minds and hearts, having intentionally chosen and programmed ourselves to receive peace of mind.

As a hypnotist, you rarely know what a session is going to be about in advance. This keeps things interesting, to say the least. Specific issues can be probed for, but are best handled in turn when they appear as the next layer of the onion to be peeled, so to speak, by the client. There are primary behavioral causes and secondary behavioral causes. Some clients will come in and will go straight to a primary event and once that is resolved, will then work outward to resolve the secondary supporting event layers.

Others will come in and start with their secondary events and then, layer by layer, work from those secondary outer layers towards the primary event. They gain additional mental, emotional, and spiritual strength each time as they take on the next issue or layer, freeing up energy once used to hold onto past problems. The next layer comes up automatically when they are ready to deal with it.

Addressing Primary and Secondary Experiences

Our Mind Management hypnotherapy peels away negative layers of self-limiting beliefs, eliminates inappropriate habits, and conquers maladaptive behaviors. We deal with one experience and belief system after another, one layer after another, until we have peeled the entire onion. Then the person has a clear and free mind, where they have awareness of their Intelligence and its functions and can receive the benefits of effectively managing their thought processes.

The entire process, from starting to obtain a clear mind, takes several sessions. But each session is a building block of sequential training and experiential learning that empowers the client to continue to work on their own, in between sessions. Thus most of the change process is accomplished by the client him or herself as they learn to apply Mind Management principles in stages. They eventually become self-sustaining and their own best behavioral therapist. The goal is to create independence, not dependence. Virgil always reiterated the idea that "powerful people create independence and weak people create dependency." We assist clients in becoming self-reliant and independent.

Target: the inner layer of the onion

Bull's-eye: core or primary issues (initial sensitizing events)

When the client begins their personal problem-solving work from the outside in they are dealing with maladaptive habits and behaviors first known as secondary issues or layers (symptom-producing or symptom-intensifying events).

As hypnotherapists we often think we want to deal with core or primary belief issues first (such as the thought, "I am not good enough," amplified many times). We like hitting the bull's-eye, or the center of the target.

But we also understand and teach that it is better to use processes that allow the client to choose the direction of each session and bring up what they are willing to address. Probing for primary, core belief system, behavior-causing thought processes before the client is ready to deal with them can potentially release volcanic eruptions of strong emotional content and physical abreactions. These can be avoided if the client chooses to work on less disruptive experiences first. Although doing strong emotional release work is not necessarily a bad idea if you are trained for it and know how to handle it, otherwise can be uncomfortable if you are not experienced and don't know what to expect.

The authors prefer allowing each client to start with whatever issue comes up first in hypnosis and then work on the experience they choose second, then third, and so forth. We clear each sensitizing event one at a time, allowing the client to bring up experiences in any order they choose. In this way, they are encouraged to clear up experiences that have bothered them for many years, and most new clients initially go to childhood experiences.

Each layer a client clears up releases emotional, psychological, and mental energy that has been taken up with maintaining that experience in the mind. The individual then has more strength for tackling the next layer. Eventually, when they come to the bull's-eye, it will be within their "new" (now normal) capacity to deal with it. They can break the amnesias and denials of the past, release the fixations of their core issues, and experience a clear and free mind.

Spiritual Mind Management training comes after general hypnotherapy—after the sensitizing events have been desensitized and the fixations released. Clients are then ready to learn about the movement of their Intelligence and the benefits of knowing and utilizing "Spiritual Mind Management" skills to maintain the freedom of enjoying peace of mind.

Addressing primary and secondary experiences with hypnotherapy

Certified Hypnotherapy Training School
http://certifiedhypnotherapytrainingschool.com/

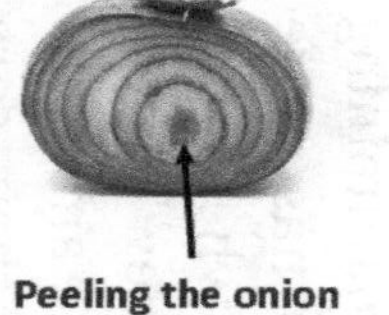

Peeling the onion

In hypnotherapy we peel away one layer or experience at a time, assisting the individual client to learn the lessons to be learned from each of their life's experiences. Lessons learned through the personal problem-solving skills we teach release fixations of the Intelligence that are holding them back, binding them down, and keeping them from being all they want and wish to be.

Our "Mind Management "hypnotherapy peels away negative layers of self-limiting beliefs, eliminates inappropriate habits, and conquers maladaptive behaviors. We deal with one experience and belief system after another or one layer after another, until we have peeled the entire onion and the person has a **clear and free mind, where they can have awareness of their Intelligence and its functions and receive the benefits of managing their thought processes with effectiveness.**

This process takes several sessions, but each session is also a building block of sequential trainings and experiential learning's that empower the client to continue to accomplish their own work in between sessions. Most of the change process is accomplished by themselves as they learn to apply "Mind Management" principles in stages, becoming self-sustaining and their own best behavioral therapist. The goal is to create independence not dependence. Virgil always reiterated – hypnotized us if you will, 'powerful people create independence and weak people create dependency. We assist clients to become self-reliant and independent.

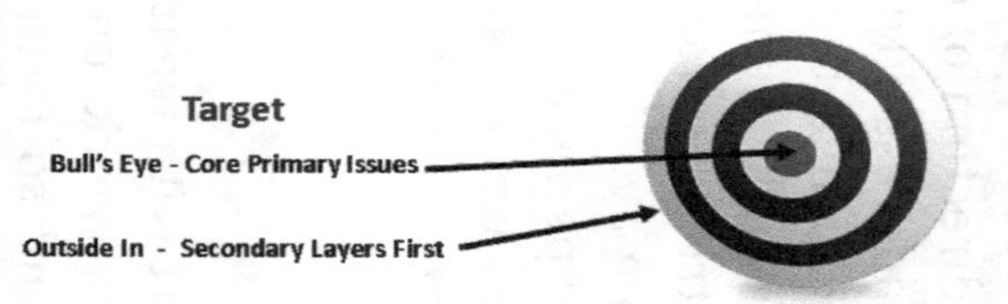

Target

Bull's eye —Core or primary issues (initial sensitizing events)

When the client begins their personal problem solving work from the outside in they are dealing with flight or flight, seek or avoid, and identify or alienate beliefs, habits, and maladaptive behaviors, first, known as secondary issues or layers. (symptom producing or symptom intensifying events)

As hypnotherapists we often think we want to deal with core or primary belief issues first (such as the thought, "I am not good enough", (amplified to 2,500 times) and hit the bull's eye, or the center of the target.

We understand and teach that it is better to use processes which allow the client to choose the direction of each session and what they are willing to address in each visit. To probe for primary, core belief system, behavior-causing thought processes before the client is ready to deal with them, can potentially release volcanic eruptions of strong emotional content and physical abreactions, which can be avoided by the client if they choose to work on more minor experiences first. There is no real problem with doing strong emotional release work if you are trained and know how to handle it, but it can be uncomfortable if you are not experienced.

Clients report on "onion-peeling" experiences

Client: I'm Cathy and I worked with Dennis some twenty years ago. At that time, I was a person who was very introverted, drawn into myself, very afraid to reach out and touch other people in any way whatsoever. I didn't know who I was. I didn't know that I really had value, and I struggled with this for years.

It's amazing to be reborn at forty. With Dennis' help, "peeling the onion" as he called it, we were able to go through and talk about every situation that blocked me in my life. We were then able to take that layer of the onion, pull it off, set it out in front of me, look at it, and decide, "Do you want to keep it, or do you want to let it go?" I usually found a way to let it go, and my way was flipping a domino, meaning I learned to bounce out and collapse inappropriate thoughts before they had any effect, by not allowing them to pass through my critical factor intentionally.

Along with that, Dennis suggested that I find a place to go mentally where I could be very comfortable. My place has always been in the water, so in my mind I would focus on a stream in the woods, a river, or the ocean, and that would bring peace and quiet to me. As we went through and peeled the onion and looked at things and decided about them, he also taught me how to give of myself, to reach out to people. It has been such a wonderful experience.

I am now able to reach out and talk to people. I can talk to anyone now. It's so amazing to be able to do that. It opens my mind to a whole new world. I find myself using this time and time again, and not just for me. I talk with my children; I talk with other people. I've been able to see them differently, love them differently, and say to them, "Maybe you want to let go of whatever is bothering that you're holding onto." It's been an incredible journey. I am so grateful for that, and Dennis is a friend I will have for the rest of my life. As well as the lessons has taught me.

Dennis and another client is Speaker 2.

Speaker 2: I'm sure you run into people who feel that sometimes it's not healthy to dig up the past.

Dennis: Yes, I do hear that sometimes. We all have our opinions and beliefs.

Speaker 2: I have a husband who would probably say those exact words.

Dennis: I get that, but we don't usually probe for any particular emotional content. What we tell people is that we're going to start with whatever your heart, mind, spirit, and Intelligence want to work with first, because your spirit knows. Okay?

So what happens is what is called layering. You might look at this as a target. As therapists, we all like to hit bull's-eyes, meaning we'd like to knock out some big issue and see a miraculous change in our client. Of course we'd like that, right?

But if you look at it as a target, what happens most often or a lot of the time, is that people have been to other places first seeking assistance. They've tried this and they've tried that; they've tried everything. So they think, well, okay, I'll try hypnotism and see what it can do.

What they don't understand is that you can sit and talk about your problems on the conscious side of the mind forever. So let's compare your behavior problem to a weed in the garden of your mind. Your conscious view of it, what you get to know of the weed, is everything you see above the ground.

You can whack away at all the leaves and all the branches above ground, but if you don't get to the other side of the mind, the subconscious mind, and pull the root out, that weed will keep growing back over time. When the client goes into trance, we're going to be pulling out roots, and we do it at a pretty rapid rate. We also teach clients how to pull out the roots of their own problems, so they can self-maintain.

Speaker 2: Okay. Then what about a person who has planted their garden and that's what they know? They don't want to pull out any roots, because then they might become very vulnerable. I mean, do you teach them how to replant?

Dennis: For sure. When people like that come in, we start out slower. We'll start on an outside layer and then we'll conquer one layer of personal problem-solving here and then another layer there. Every layer that we get done gives them greater mental and emotional energy, power to conquer the next layer. Does that make sense?

And so they'll work their way in and every layer that we get done they're picking up a greater emotional, mental, psychic strength. So when they finally hit the main root of their behavioral problem, it's not that big a deal because they have all this other energy freed up. They have all this other mental and spiritual ability that they didn't have before.

When they finally get to their core root beliefs, there is probably something here that has troubled them for their whole life, but they're now ready to take it on. They will go in and dump the whole thing. So some people like to go to the core and then work their way out. Others want to work their way in. It's just a matter of which way they want to do it. There's no wrong or right way to it, just different ways. It's just a question of what they're ready to do now.

Venting

Some of the most natural venting processes of the body and the mind are crying and laughing. Almost everyone cries as they start to vent in trance. This sometimes worries people who've never been trained in hypnotherapy, because all of a sudden someone will start crying and the untrained aren't sure how to handle it. Many hypnotherapists do what they can to avoid this, calling it an unwanted abreaction. Yet if they had experienced my own first personal episode with hypnotherapy they would know that there is a bottom to the box.

No one needs to be afraid of their accumulated emotional content. Allowing the client to vent accumulated "emotional content boxes," as we call them, is both relieving and cleansing. Hypnosis doesn't cause conditions; it reveals them. I believe one of the best things we do for people is put them in the position where they can vent off old, pent-up emotions. One of the greatest things about hypnotherapy is that it can help with this.

Sometimes people may want to scream and carry on. It is part of the process of freeing them and helping them to change.

After the venting, my job is to teach them how not to refill the box. We help people learn how to control and turn down their imagination—how to turn it down and then turn it off.

The Hollywood version of this phenomenon is shown in movies like *First Blood*, when John Rambo (Sylvester Stallone) finally exceeds his capacity to hold his emotions under control. His emotional box is full and pressurized, and he releases the pressure as he breaks down and cries, with the Major talking him through some thought processes that allow him to further empty the box. In this state of emotions an individual is already in trance or hypnotized naturally and thus suggestions made at that time may be readily accepted. Once the pressure was gone, released through crying, Rambo was once more back in emotional self-control.

Another example is Mel Gibson's balcony scene in *Ransom* where he, as Tom Mullen, vents the highly amplified sensations and emotions of his intense fears about losing his son who has been kidnapped and is in danger.

People who have not allowed themselves the opportunity to cry for long periods of time, because of some false sense of manhood like "big boys don't cry" and so forth, can be walking emotional time bombs to one degree or another. When such a person finally takes the lid off their emotional box to stuff more emotions into it one more time, and there is no more room or capacity, emotions comes spewing out all over, often in total disproportion to what the current stimulus is. We call this final event before the release "the straw that broke the camel's back!"

Some may call this state when a person's ability to hold all the emotional content in is exceeded a mental or emotional breakdown. Because trance accesses the subconscious functions of memories and imagination, we may release the pent-up emotional content that is driving inappropriate habits and behaviors when reviewing our life's experiences in trance.

In our school, we teach students several effective ways to achieve this release in the way most beneficial to the client in being able to desensitize in a safe environment and once again have excess emotional capacity. Again, as hypnotherapists we should teach them how not to refill the box.

You may also release pent-up emotional pressures by exercising or participation in sports—you'll feel better and your mind will be clearer. Should you feel like crying, do so, as crying is a healthy emotional release. Crying is a physical abreaction to thoughts. You may find real benefit in letting go and just having a good cry. But when the release is over, it is important to seek understanding of why you were crying in the first place if it is not immediately clear to you. Begin to resolve the thoughts that prompted it. You may want to seek some assistance, especially if you find yourself crying consistently or for long periods of time without being aware of the reason. It is one thing to empty the emotional box, but learning how not to keep refilling the box is essential.

Weeding the garden of our minds

The Bible says, "As a man thinketh in his heart, so is he." I personally like Brian Tracy's spin on this statement: "You are not what you think you are, but what you think, you are."

We have the agency to choose our thoughts and actions, and the natural ability to reason in making decisions and choices. The latter is what makes us accountable and responsible for our choices and actions. We want to learn the lessons to be gained from each of life's experiences, in ways that improve and refine us.

Natural rewards for correct and right choosing exist, as do natural consequences for incorrect and wrong choices. There are also blessings and penalties attached to keeping or breaking laws—natural laws, God's laws, or governmental laws.

The law of the harvest says, “As ye sow, so shall ye reap.” It doesn’t say that you might reap, or that you could reap. It says, “We shall reap what we sow.” You never can, or ever will be able to plant corn and harvest wheat. We will reap what we sow.

And so it is with the thoughts and beliefs that we currently have planted in the gardens of our minds. Some of these thoughts are simply weeds. They need to be pulled out and replaced with the flowers and vegetables of nutritious wholesome thoughts that can feed our minds and spirits in healthy, positive, and productive ways. We want to feed our "heart hungers" with wholesome mental and spiritual food, instead of attempting to satisfy them with physical food. Our CD recordings are an important part of this replanting of a positive, productive new crop of helpful and healthy thoughts.

There is no question left in someone's mind about when they have accomplished a change of predominant thoughts and beliefs. They find themselves automatically doing the new and desired behaviors. Old habit patterns vanish and new productive behaviors are put firmly in place. Many people continue to strengthen their changes by listening to these recordings on a regular basis.

CHAPTER ELEVEN

Sports Mind Management
By Dr. Debra Crews

Dennis and the author of this chapter, Dr. Debbie Crews, have joined to test and understand the effectiveness of the new hypnotherapy techniques taught in this book as Spiritual Mind Management. Earlier in 2013, they worked with several golfers at the professional and collegiate level. Dennis did hypnotherapy sessions with the golfers, clearing up old inhibitions and mental fixations that were inhibiting their sports performance, and Debbie did several before and after tests. We plan to do more in the future, but we wanted to share some initial findings here as well as a piece Debbie has written on the effectiveness of self-hypnosis and hypnotherapy on sports performance.

Earlier in this book we outlined the idea that our Intelligence moves from place to place in our minds. Dennis and Debbie worked with these golfers until they had full control of the movement of their Intelligence and could change the effect of being in their imagination, memories, or emotions at will. They could choose whether they wanted to identify with or alienate from, seek or avoid, fight for or flee from each image, thought, memory, or emotion in each compartment of their minds. They could also come back to full consciousness at will. Debbie brain-mapped these sessions, some of which are included here for your interest.

Golfer Consciousness

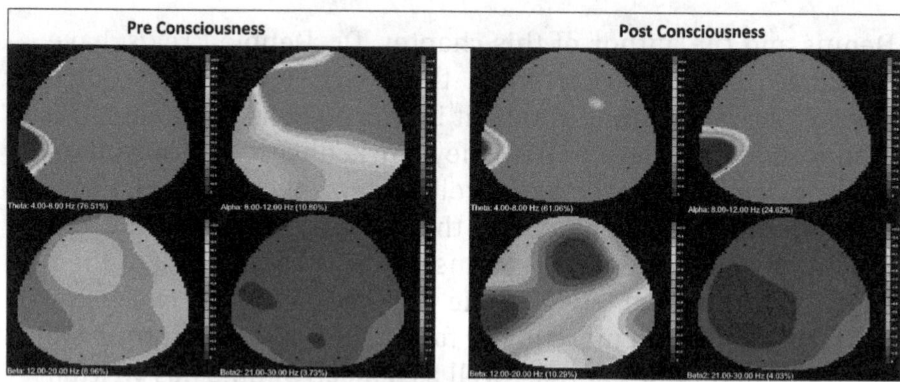

This female professional golfer (age 24 years) participated in four Golf Mind Management training sessions. Her state of mind was recorded using electroencephalography (EEG) from 14 locations on the right and left side of her brain. As previously discussed, theta (top left map), alpha (top right map), beta (lower left map) and beta2 (lower right map) indicate changes in activity at the conscious level of the brain. The changes at the subconscious level of the brain are not likely to be detected with EEG. So we are viewing the changes in the conscious brain that result from changes in the subconscious brain. Since we are only viewing one case study, and individuals respond differently relative to brain function, results will be described in general terms.

EEG patterns were collected for small periods of time (seconds) as the trainer determined the golfer was in a defined state of mind. The four states included consciousness, memory, imagination, and emotion. These were considered our "base" measures before and after the four training sessions. While different experiences may have been described by the golfer during those four states, they reflect the results of the training. For example, in the emotion, the "pre" map represents anger while the "post" map does not, since anger is no longer the emotion that surfaces.

During the "conscious" state it is clear that alpha and beta activity increased following four sessions of training. This recording indicates increased activation in the brain and is interpreted as being more "conscious." The state was achieved by simply asking the golfer to "look at my hand." Data was recorded in eyes open and eyes closed state (the golfer created the image). Eyes closed is displayed in all the maps, since most images in the pretest were created more effectively with eyes closed.

"Being in the present" refers to playing from a more conscious state of mind. The ability to recognize consciousness and increase this state in the brain allows athletes to play in the present and perform from a state of heightened awareness (the definition of "the zone").

Golfer Imagination

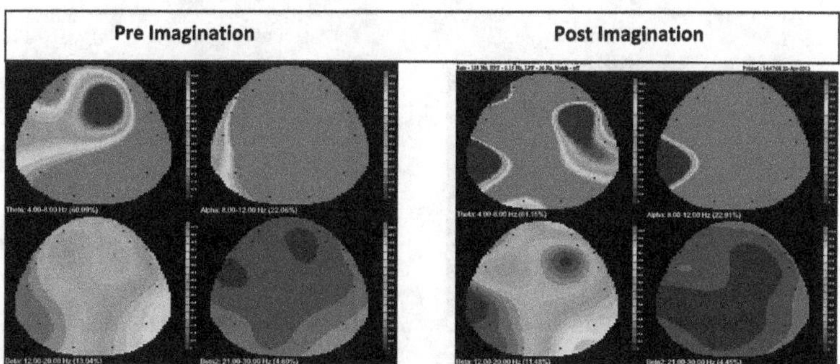

A simple example of imagining a rose was used to elicit imagination in the brain. During the pretest the rose was reported as red and pink and represented both comfort and anger to the golfer. In theta the activation appears to be more right-sided. In alpha and beta the activation is mostly central/right. At the posttest the golfer initially saw the red rose from the center forward portion of her brain as indicated by her pointing to the location of the rose. The brain maps show a change to more balance in theta and less left activation in alpha. At the posttest she was able to move the image of the rose freely around in her brain. As she moved the rose to the left it appeared black/brown and was dying. As the rose moved to the right it became yellow, bigger, brighter, and clearer. The ability of an athlete to be able to simply move an image to different areas of their brain and change the perception of the image allows them to easily change their perceptions. It is often necessary to change perceptions in order to change behavior. The golf swing is a behavior. Thus, simply moving a thought to a different location in the brain, in the short periods of time allotted, can potentially change the swing that is produced and the outcome of the performance.

Golfer Emotion

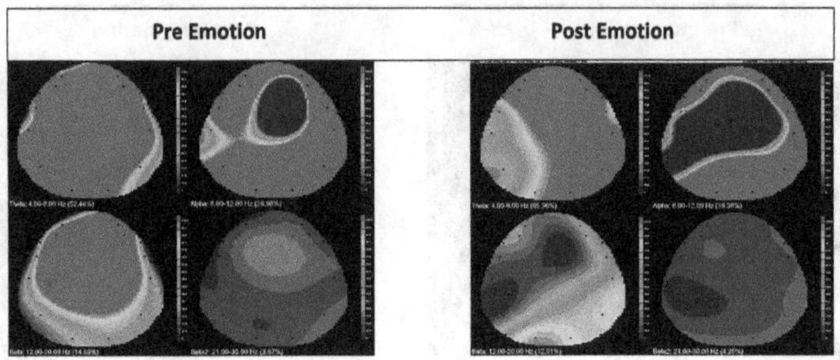

Anger was the emotion reported during the pretest. As indicated by theta, alpha, and beta; the anger elicits high activation and is quite balanced between the two hemispheres of the brain. The posttest emotion was pleasure from a meal this golfer had experienced earlier in the day. The base activation levels were much lower and more right sided in theta, alpha and beta. At the posttest the golfer was easily able to turn up and turn down any emotion at will. This is a remarkable skill for athletes during competition. Thus, they learn to use the emotion to their advantage instead of letting their emotions run them.

The Clinical Hypnotherapy Process with Athletes

As Dennis completes a session with the golfers it is apparent that there are changes in the brain corresponding to the directions and inquiry of the session. The three brain maps below show the average of four golfers going through the initial phase of the induction process. Focus on the hand activates the lower frequencies in the brain (theta and alpha) while the address/phone and rose activate all the frequencies of the brain.

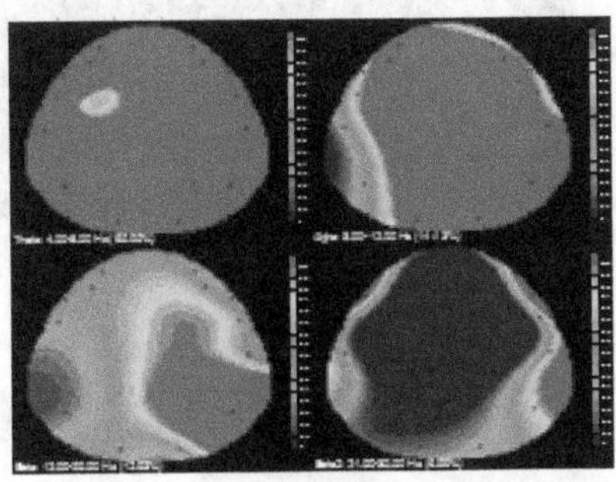

Hand

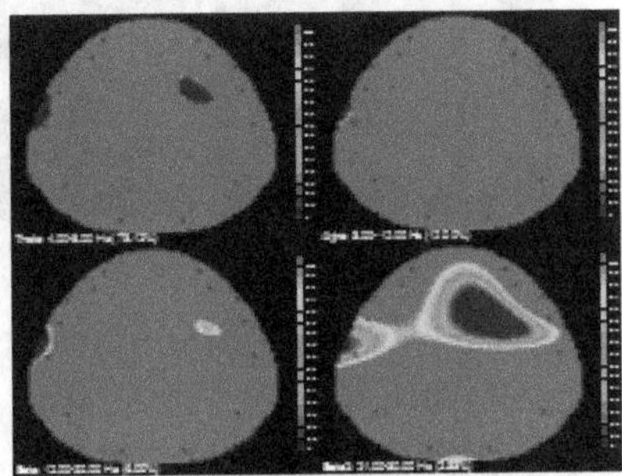

Address Phone

Average of 4 Golfers

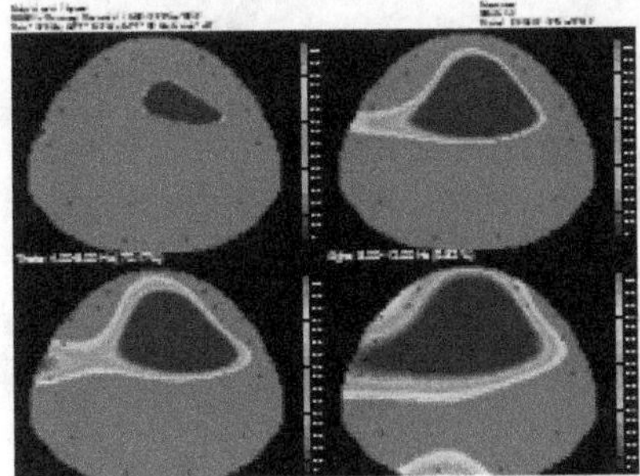

Rose

In each session, Dennis asked the golfers to magnify the emotion. Below is an example of how the brain responds. Activation clearly increases two times or more.

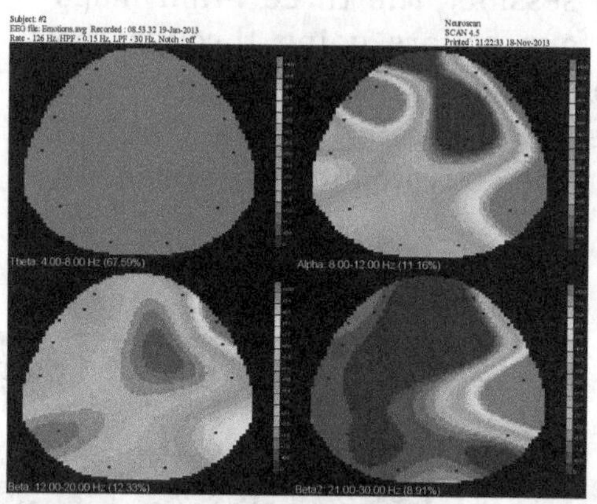

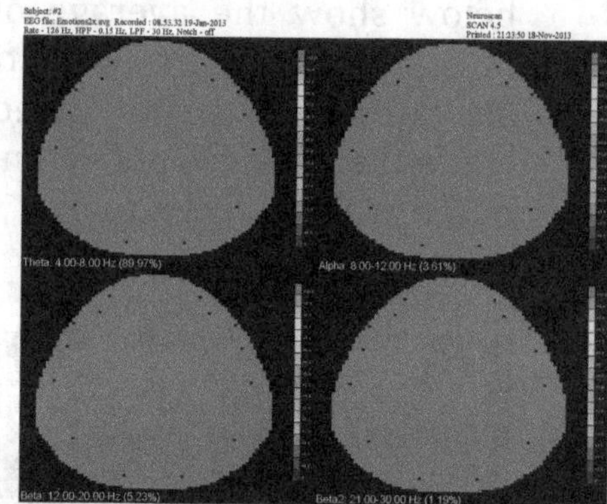

As Dennis asks the golfer to move the rose to different locations in the brain, the rose looks different, as does the processing in the brain.

Left – Black and White

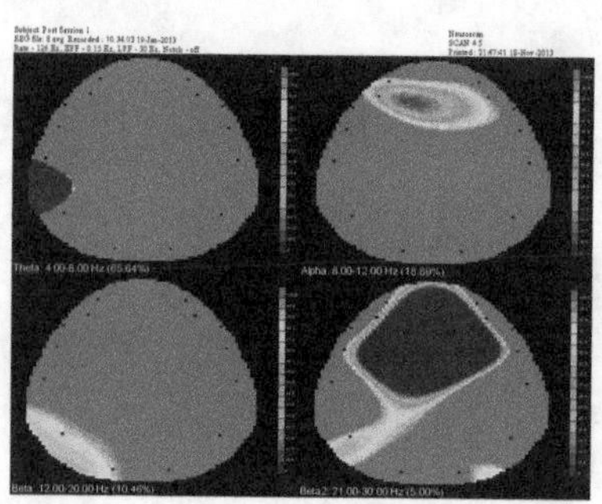

Top – Bright and Vibrant

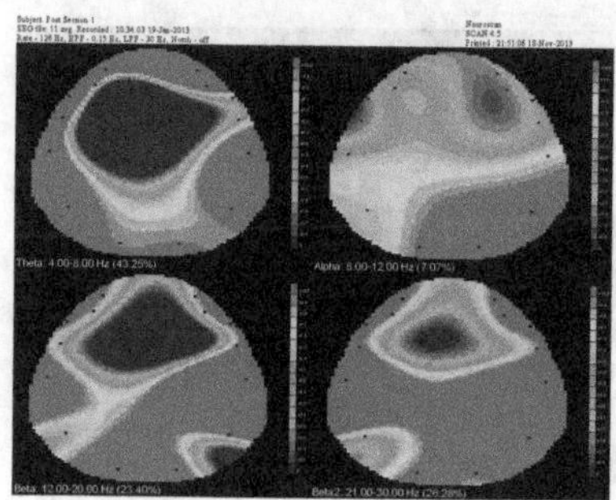

Right - Lighter

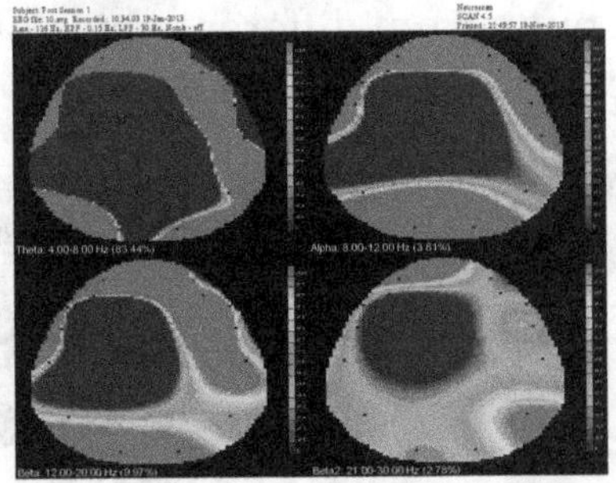

It appears that as we think of the same thoughts pre and post-hypnosis the activation in the brain is higher following hypnosis. Perhaps consciousness has increased as we focus on the task. Also, when the image is in the top center portion of the brain it appears more synchronized (balanced) than when it is in the back center of the brain following hypnosis. This is illustrated below.

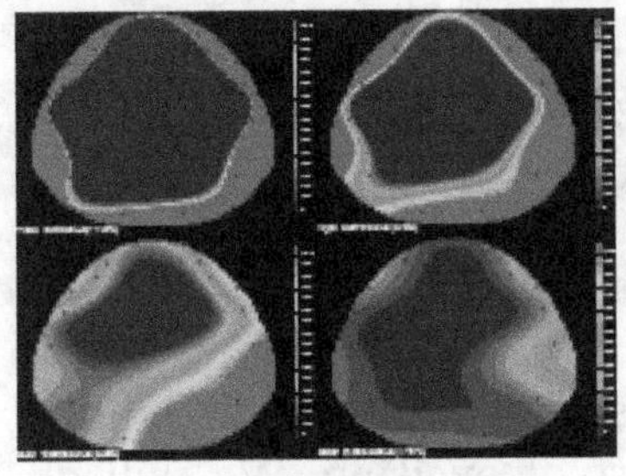

Pre Hypnosis

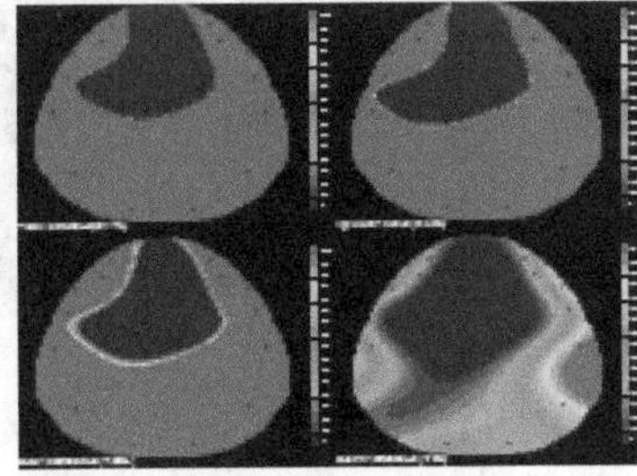

2 + 2 Back Center

2 + 2 Top Center

2 + 2 Back Center

2 + 2 Top Center

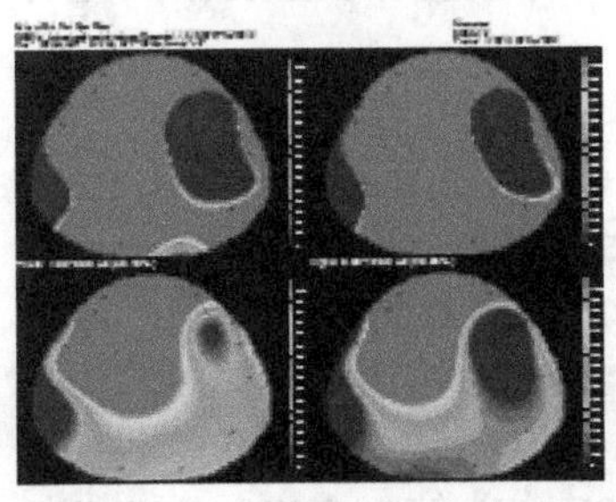

Post Hypnosis

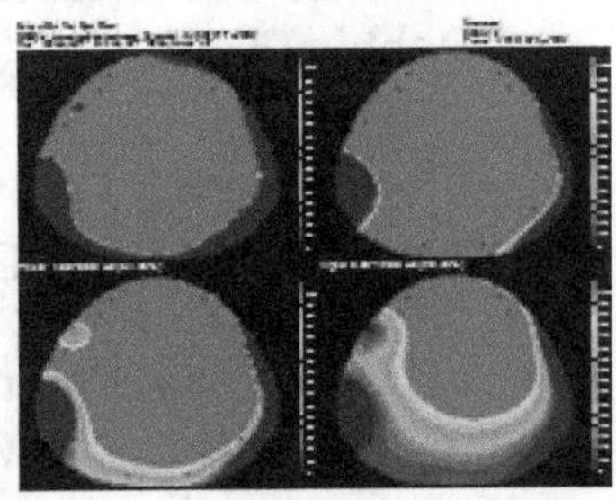

The maps on this page illustrates actual putting as the golfer focuses on putting twelve foot putts from different areas of the brain. This was done after three sessions of hypnosis.

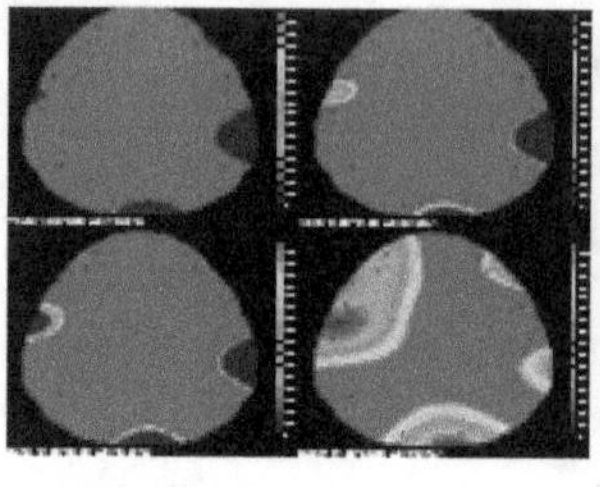

Base Putt
0/3 Putts Made

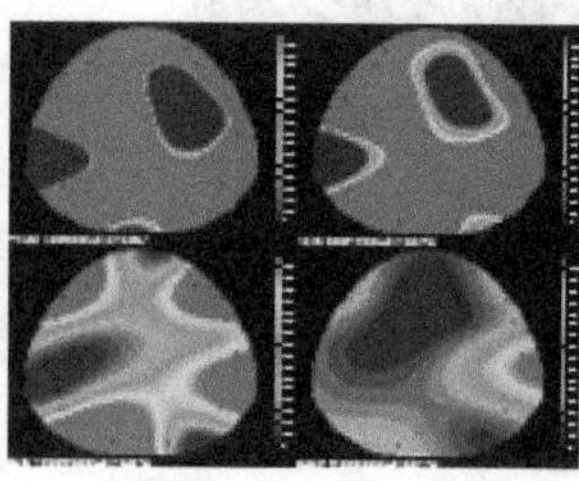

Center Back Putt
0/3 Putts Made

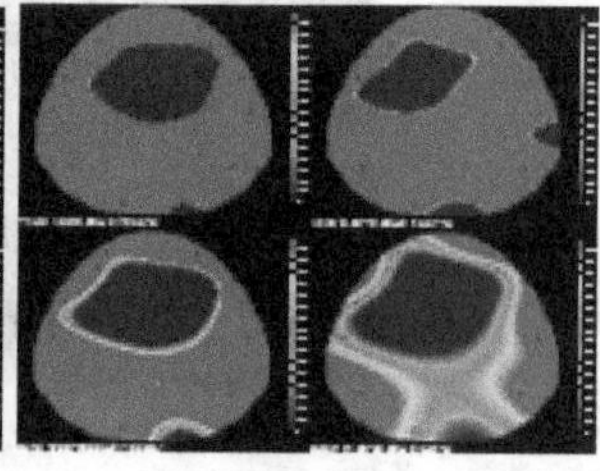

Back Right Emotion Putt
1/3 Putts Made

Post Hypnosis Putting from Different Areas of the Brain

Center Conscious Putt
2/3 Putts Made

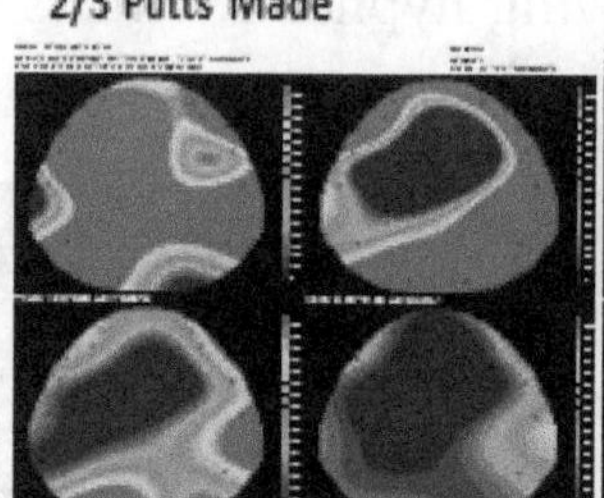

Memory Putt
1/3 Putts Made

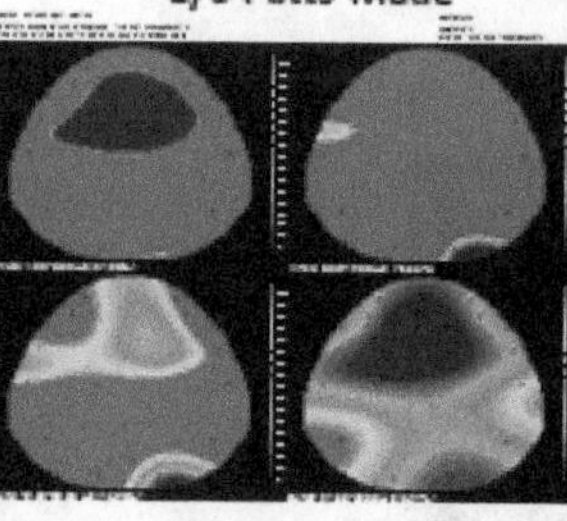

Right Putt
2/3 Putts Made

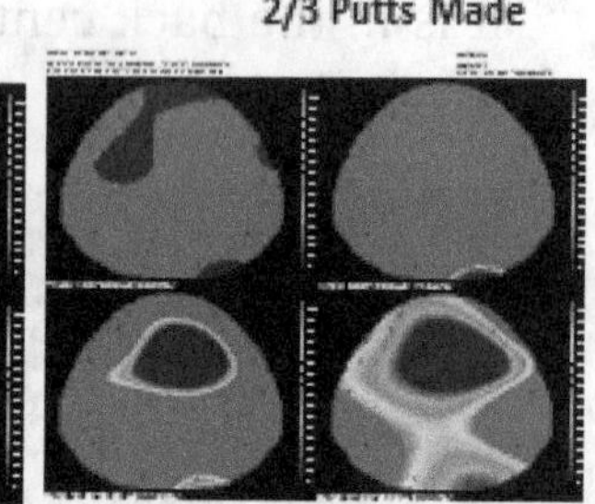

The effectiveness that these sports programs have demonstrated so far is nothing short of exciting. We will go into greater detail on this topic—share more of our findings and information in another book. However, an introduction to and overview of this subject follows. We are offering a glimpse of some of the fascinating research being accomplished by Dr. Debbie Crews.

After studying consciousness, specifically attention for the past 25+ years, it is apparent that athletes would benefit from an understanding of the subconscious mind. Consciousness is a very important part of learning and preparation for optimal performance. However, at elite levels (college and professional) the motion is performed by the subconscious mind. Furthermore, if there are beliefs, blocks, memories, etc., stored in the subconscious mind that inhibits performance, it would be beneficial to address them through hypnosis. This is the goal of sports Mind Management.

The ultimate state for sport performance is synchronization of the conscious and subconscious mind. If the conscious is on one page and the subconscious is on a different page, the chances of good performance are probably 50% or less. The two minds must work together. In sport, I refer to the conscious mind and our thoughts as the "Coach" and the subconscious mind and our feelings as the "Team." Now you see why they must work together. The Coach is in charge, but the Team performs.

Sports Mind Management teaches clinicians and athlete's techniques to self-regulate their conscious and subconscious minds. Questions of importance include: a.) What is the efficacy of using hypnosis in sport? And b.) What is the training program to be used by athletes for optimal performance? This chapter will address these questions and provide recommendations to clinicians and athletes.

Sport Research

There is a paucity of research using clinical hypnotherapy in sport. It is likely that there are numerous clinicians using clinical hypnotherapy with athletes; however, the research testing the effects is minimal. Pates has conducted several studies showing the effectiveness of clinical hypnotherapy for golfers (Pates & Maynard, 2000), badminton players (Pates & Palmi, 2002) and basketball players (Pates, Cummings, & Maynard, 2002; Pates, Maynard, & Westbury, 2001). Baker and Jones (2005, 2006, 2008) found positive effects with footballers, cricketers, and martial artists. Lindsay, Thomas and Maynard (2005) improved the performance of cyclists using hypnosis. *See references for complete names and titles.*

The four studies by Pates and colleagues used a hypnosis intervention consisting of a) Hypnotic induction for deep relaxation, b) Hypnotic regression designed to relive an earlier life experience of their optimal performance, and c) a trigger control to pair the hypnotic state with a stimulus. Thus, the stimulus would elicit the optimal performance state. Participants reported enhanced mental states and enhanced performance.

Golf Research Studies

We have conducted six pilot case studies on golfers of high skill level (n=5) and on a clinical hypnotherapist (n=1) using self-hypnosis for putting. One male participant played on the Nike Tour and was preparing to qualify for the PGA Tour. Two female golfers played on the Futures Tour, and two female golfers played collegiate golf. The players ranged from 20-30 years of age and had played golf since they were young. The hypnotherapy sessions consisted of a.) a relaxation induction phase, b.) a hypnotic regression phase relative to their life experience (not specifically golf), c.) a treatment phase, and d.) a connection to golf putting phase. Thus, the state of mind attained during the hypnosis was made relevant to the task of putting. Three of the golfers putted ten, 12ft putts before and after the hypnosis intervention. Quality of each putt (scale 1-10, 10 is high), centimeter error from the hole, and number of putts made were recorded.

EEG brain activity is a representation of conscious activity in the brain. It is not clear how deep the electrodes record the activity, so we can only make assumptions regarding consciousness. The brain activity was also recorded using standard research protocol (International 10/20 System, Jasper, 1958) from 10 or 12 locations on the right (5 or 6 locations) and left (5 or 6 locations) side of the brain. Brain maps were created (power spectrum analysis) for the baseline pretest putts and the post-hypnosis putts. The maps, similar to a graph, are an indication of the amount of activity at each electrode location (black dots). Higher activity is displayed as red and lower activity is blue. Each set of four maps represents the 1 second prior to the beginning of each putt. In each set of four maps, the top left maps are theta (4-7 Hz), top right maps are alpha (8-12 Hz), the bottom left maps are beta (13-20 Hz) and the bottom right maps are beta2 (21-30 Hz). The brain maps are oriented so we are looking at a top down view with the nose being at the top of the map and the back of the head being at the bottom of the map. The right side of each map is the right side of the brain and the same for the left side. Synchrony is present when the color and pattern in all 4 brain maps (theta, alpha, beta and beta2) look similar to each other. It doesn't matter if the activity is high (red) or low (blue), only that it is similar. This is important for athletes since adrenaline may kick in and cause high brain activation; however, if it is synchronized, the athlete will perform well.

The first brain maps (on the following page) represent a Future Tour player who had issues from her younger days. She accidently hit a family member with a golf club and sent him to the hospital when she was 4 years old. Hypnosis was used to clear the event and the resulting brain map (next page) is much more synchronized.

Pre-Hypnosis Putting **Post Hypnosis Putting**

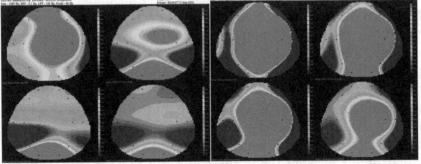

Futures Player during Putting

A clinical hypnotherapist who played golf and worked with many skilled golfers wanted to test the self-hypnosis techniques she used with herself and her golfers. Her brain maps (below) indicate a quieter and more synchronized brain following the self-hypnosis technique.

Pre- Hypnosis Putting

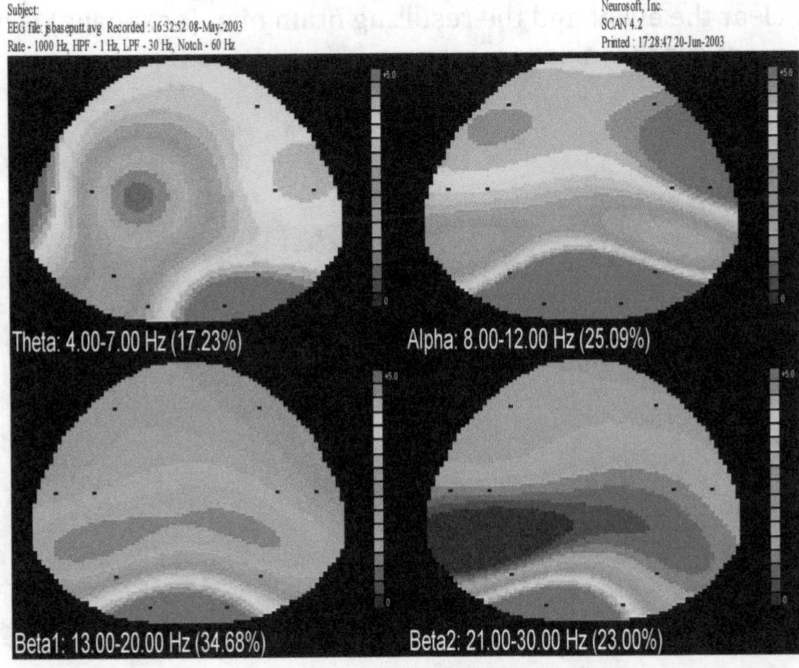

Post-Hypnosis Putting

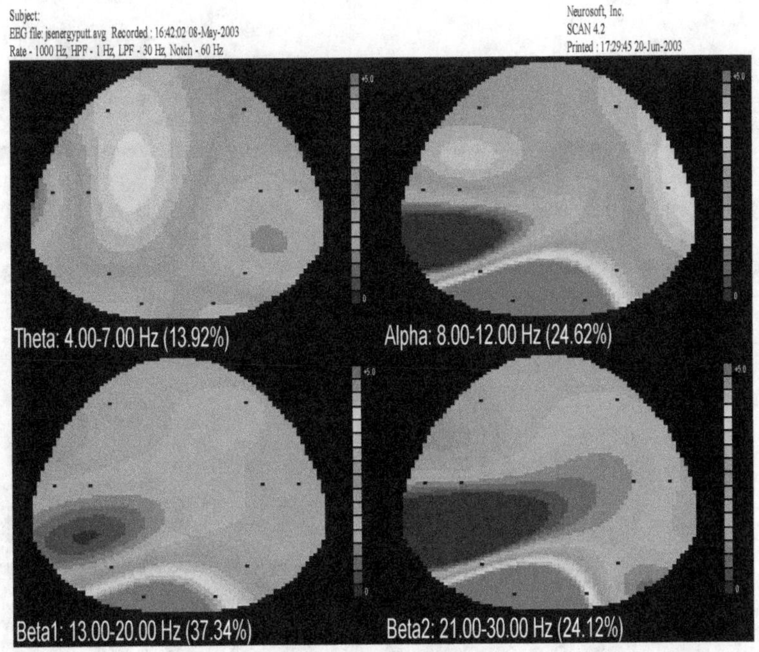

Golfer Clinical Hypnotherapist

A male tour player from the Nike Tour experienced clinical hypnotherapy in preparation for qualifying for the PGA Tour. He went through a traditional hypnotherapy protocol to remove blocks from golf and life. His pre and post resting brain maps were not clearly different; however, the brain maps from the hypnosis sessions were of interest. Fear and anger were displayed as synchronous high activity states. His feeling of a "halo" state, or always being taken care of in sport and his "golf is mine" state, or his own territory, are also quite synchronous.

Pre-Rest

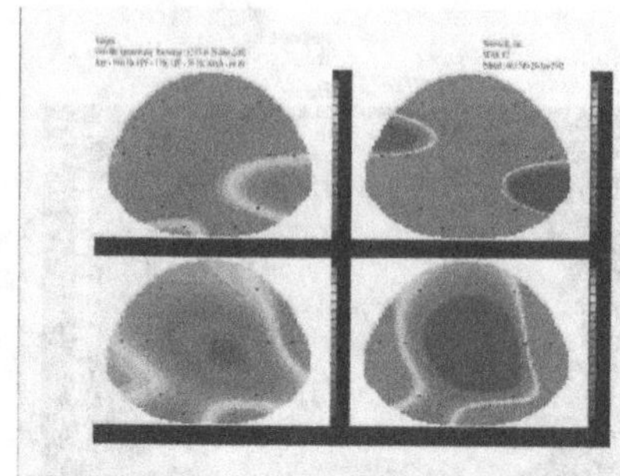

Post-Rest

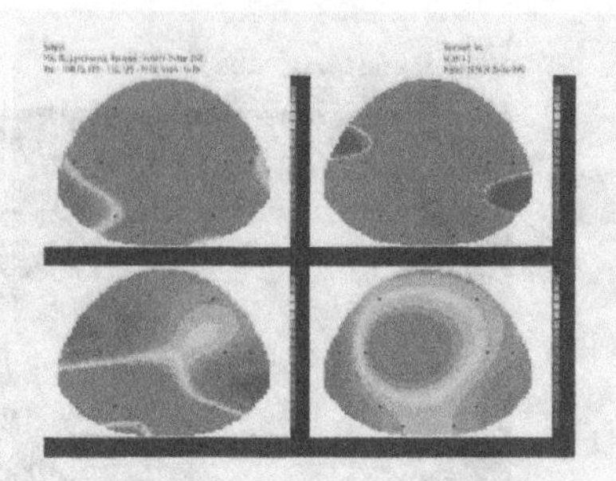

Fear (Tentative)

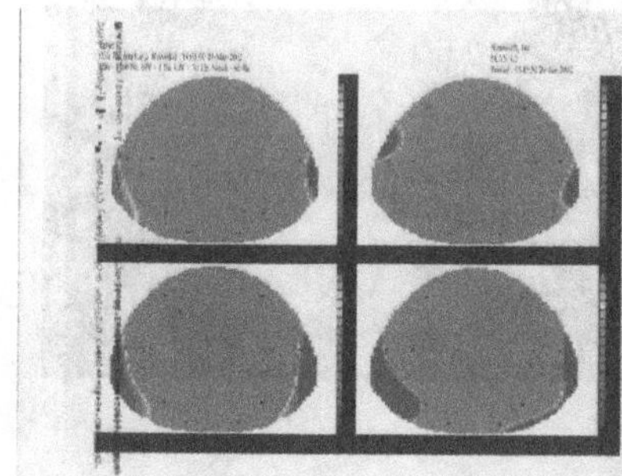

Anger

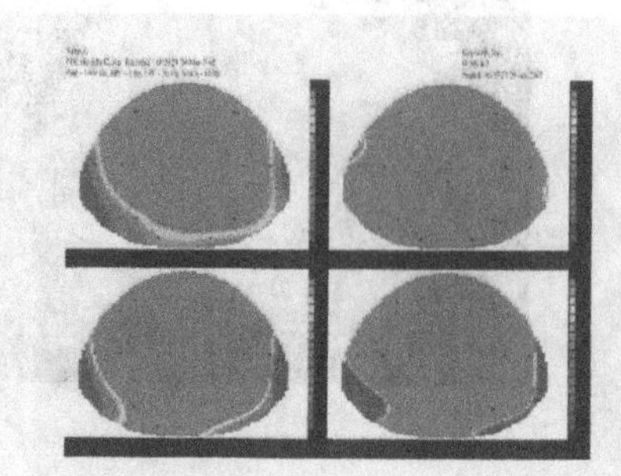

Halo State (Good)

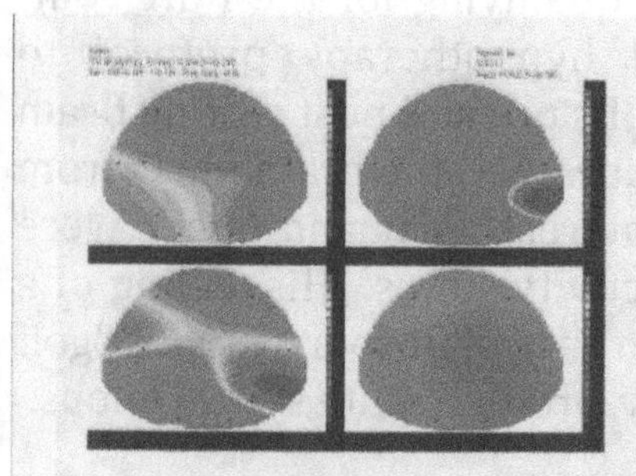

Golf is Mine (Good)

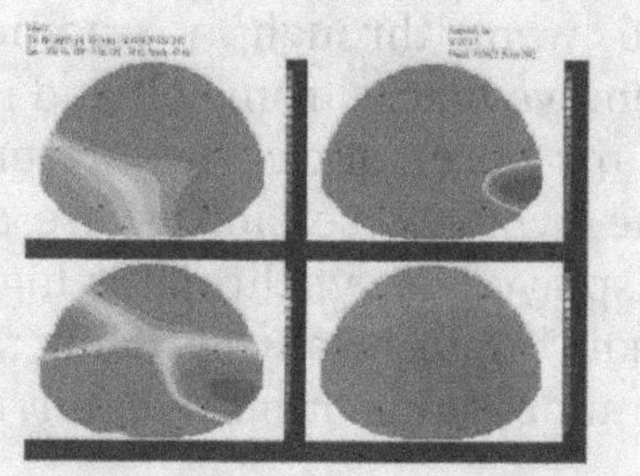

The final case study is a Future Tour player who was looking for a win. This particular golfer had experienced many wins as a junior golfer, so these were all stored in her subconscious mind. However, her beliefs about her current ability to perform were not as confident as in her younger years. In addition, she had experienced considerable negative feedback from the outside world in her years of development as a golfer. The hypnosis intervention addressed both her image of herself as a winner and extinguishing the negative feedback beliefs about her game.

It appears that the success of hypnosis in sport is issue specific. For example, when the hypnosis was directly related (stimulus) to the state of mind used to perform the putt (response), the putting performance improved. However, when the issue was to reduce migraine headaches, the migraines were eliminated, but putting performance did not directly improve. It is likely that the ability to practice and perform may improve in a longitudinal assessment, but not necessarily from an acute (60 min) intervention.

5-step Hypnotherapy for Sports Mind Management

Clinical hypnosis offers five important techniques beneficial to any athlete attempting to manage their mind. Since thought precedes motion, it is critical that the athlete be aware of the thought that they are using, and have the skill and ability to choose otherwise if so inclined. For example, with golfers the thought comes first, motion comes second, the ball is third, and the outcome is last. All of sport is a transfer of energy. What energy do you want to transfer to the ball from a conscious and subconscious level? We have the awareness, skill, and ability to choose!

The five-step program for training sport Mind Management includes:

1. Inside

2. Gatekeeper
3. Dial
4. Perception
5. Beings

Inside

"Go" inside is the induction technique of hypnosis that allows for access of the subconscious mind. A combination of breathing and focus bring a sense of calm to our mind and body. In sport, when we are in an optimal performance state we are breathing rhythmically, even with adrenaline. If fear is present we tend to hold our breath. The mind and body are not happy without oxygen, so it is critical that we keep breathing in a rhythmic manner. Breathing can take us deep inside our body. With each breath in we go deeper inside and with each exhalation we clear our self of any thought or feeling that doesn't serve us and our performance. It doesn't matter if the thought or feeling is real, only whether it will help us with our performance right now. Using the image of a thermometer from our lungs to our center navel, each inhalation takes us lower on the thermometer. This is where all great performances come from in sport!

Gatekeeper

The "Gatekeeper" is the sport label for the critical factor in hypnosis. The gate opens to let thoughts into our subconscious and closes to keep thoughts out of our subconscious. Likewise, the gate opens to let feelings into our conscious from our subconscious and closes to keep feelings from entering our conscious. We are the gatekeepers and it is up to us to guard our gate well for best performance.

Dial

The "Dial" refers to the intensity of our emotions and the level we "choose" to fuel our thoughts. Clinical hypnotherapy teaches us that we can amplify our thoughts by many times using our emotions. This is turning the dial to the maximum. If we can turn the dial up, we can also turn it down. Thoughts that don't serve us well are reduced with the dial by turning down the emotions. It sounds simple, although it is not always. Imagery can be used to help turn the dial up and down. Images of past experiences or a clear image of "how" we choose to "be" in sport can help. The important question: "Is this who you want to be?" If not, it is up to us to learn and practice adjusting the dial.

Perception

Perceptions are formed from our conscious and subconscious mind. Perceptions refer to how we see our world and they may be correct or incorrect and will certainly influence performance. Sport psychologists debate whether perceptions or reality are more important to create best performance. We may have the perception that we are a great performer even when our current results do not show that. This perception may be very valuable at this time. In contrast are athletes with the perception that everything they are doing is fine when, in fact, it is not helping them achieve their best performance.

For an athlete, it is often important to understand the difference between perception and reality. An example exists in golf putting. When testing golfers, we asked them to rate the subjective quality of a putt on a scale from 1-10 (10 is high) relative to their "best" feeling putt. The objective measure of their performance is total number of putts made and centimeter error from the hole (missed ball). It is often the case that the golfer's "10" rated putts do not go in the hole while their "8" rated putts go in the hole. Thus, the feeling (subconscious) that they are attempting to create on each putt is not the motion that actually puts more balls in the hole. The perception for the golfer is "when I create a '10' feel the ball will go in the hole" and this is not correct. So the golfer has a choice to make—create the feel I like or putt the ball in the hole.

Misperceptions can be corrected with clinical hypnotherapy. The conscious and the subconscious are not on the same page. When the two minds confront each other and make a clear decision, they will improve performance. When the conscious (Coach) is clear with their plan and instructions, the subconscious (Team) can perform and adapt accordingly.

Beings

It may seem strange to think of performing in sport as multiple versions of our self (beings); however, we wake up different every day and our goal is to perform. As individuals, we are slightly different on the outside when we go to school, play sports, attend church, etc. So in sport, whoever steps up to the plate from our Team today is first at bat. We can be whomever we choose to be to perform successfully. Whatever perception works today is the one we choose. Some days it may be Superman/woman, other days it may be the Genius or Curious George. There isn't one way we are "supposed" to be to perform well. There are many roads that will reach our destination; which one works today.

Self-hypnosis can easily train us to be the performer of choice. The clinical hypnotherapist that came to the lab put on several different states of mind to putt. The maps I presented were her baseline and her "energy" states. She also used relax stress to channel and program as identified states of mind. Energy worked the best for her on this day and this makes sense because synchronized energy (as seen in the maps) is an optimal state for performance. On a different day, another state may be optimal for performance. Athletes at the top know they can perform no matter what the day brings. They simply put on the "state" to "be" who they want to be for the day and win.

Performance

The ultimate goal for athletes is winning. We can certainly define winning in several ways (i.e., #1, did I do what I asked myself to do, Personal Best, etc.), but outcomes speak for themselves. The research alluded to in the Introduction of this chapter mentions improvements in a variety of sports following a hypnosis intervention. Sports Mind Management has also begun to track the outcomes of athletes. The first pilot data collected has been in golf putting. Golfers subjective quality rating of putts (1-10, 10 is high) is given below, followed by the percentage of putts made before and after a single hypnosis session. The performance data is provided for those athletes in whom performance was addressed in the hypnosis session. It seemed necessary to link the results of the hypnosis session to the "state" used for putting. This is called "transfer" in sport and is one of the most important variables used to facilitate performance in a real setting.

Golfer	Quality of Putt		Percent Putts Made	
	Pre	Post	Pre	Post
Male Tour	8.3	8.6	20%	36%
College Female 1	9.5	9.9	10%	30%
College Female 2	8.0	8.6	60%	80%
College Female 3	6.9	7.4	30%	40%

Summary

The two questions of interest addressed the efficacy of clinical hypnotherapy for sport performance and the nature of the training program to facilitate sport performance. It appears that evidence is building to support the efficacy of hypnosis with athletes. The hypnosis that is geared to sport performance (identifying the optimal state and practicing it) shows performance enhancement. Hypnosis that creates a state that can be transferred and used in sport performance also appears to influence outcomes. Clearly more research and longitudinal assessments are needed; however, these preliminary findings look promising.

The clinical hypnotherapy training programs that use sport performance directly or add a transfer technique to relate the hypnosis back to sport appear to be most effective. Since best sport performance is created at the level of the subconscious, it is logical that the conscious uses a stimulus to elicit the response from the subconscious for optimal performance.

It is exciting to think of where we can take the field of clinical therapy within the realm of sports. In both fields it is the subconscious that is tapped into and the conscious that learns the most appropriate techniques to make this happen. The Coach and the Team learn to work as one (won)!

References

Barker, J.B., & Jones, M.V. (2005). Using hypnosis to increase self-efficacy: A case study in elite judo. Sport and Exercise Psychology Review, 1, 36-42.

Barker, J. B., & Jones, M. V. (2006). Using hypnosis, technique refinement and self- modelling to enhance self-efficacy: A case study in cricket. The Sport Psychologist, 20, 94-110.

Barker, J. B., & Jones, M. V. (2008). The effects of hypnosis on self-efficacy, affect, and sport performance: A case study from professional English soccer. Journal of Clinical Sport Psychology, 2, 127-147.

Lindsay, P., Maynard, I.W., & Thomas, O. (2005). Effects of hypnosis on flow states and cycling performance. The Sport Psychologist, 19, 164-178.

Pates, J.K., Cummings, A., & Maynard, I. (2002). The effects of hypnosis on flow states and three-point shooting performance in basketball players. The Sport Psychologist, 16, 34-47.

Pates, J.K., & Maynard, I. (2000). Effects of hypnosis on flow states and golf performance. Perceptual and Motor Skills, 91, 1057-1075.

Pates, J.K., Maynard, I., & Westbury, A. (2001). The effects of hypnosis on basketball performance. Journal of Applied Sport Psychology, 13, 84-102.

Pates, J.K., Oliver, R., & Maynard, I. (2001). The effects of hypnosis on flow states and golf putting performance. Journal of Applied Sport Psychology, 13, 341-354.

Pates, J & Palmi, J (2002). The effect of hypnosis upon flow states and short serves badminton performance. Journal of Excellence, 6, 48-62.

CHAPTER TWELVE

Be Involved with Us in the Subjects of this Book

Three Options:

1) Come Join Us, Become a Certified Clinical Hypnotherapist

You may want to attend Certified Hypnotherapy Training School, either online in live virtual classroom settings, (we train individual's online nationwide), or in person in Farmington, Utah, to become an A.C.H.E Certified Hypnotherapist or Certified Clinical Hypnotherapist. Or you may want to become a non-certifying student in that you desire to have the clinical behavioral modification skills taught in the school to enhance your current career and skill sets, but you do not intend to set up a hypnotherapy practice. Parents and Grandparents take the courses, just to know how to work with their families, and loved ones.

Certified Hypnotherapy Training School is a Postsecondary Proprietary School of Hypnotherapy in the State of Utah, registered and bonded with the Department of Commerce. The School trains individuals in hypnosis, self-hypnosis, and hypnotherapy to be Certified Hypnotherapists and Certified Clinical Hypnotherapists through the American Council of Hypnotist Examiners.

There are about a dozen certifying organizations in the US that are considered to be leaders in the field of hypnotherapy which insurance companies recognize as offering sufficient training through their programs to warrant offering professional malpractice insurance coverage to their graduates. Should you be thinking of participating in hypnotherapist training, you may want to check with your insurance carrier to see if they would recognize a certificate from the school you are considering. A.C.H.E Hypnotherapist Certificates are re-cognized in all 50 states and 21 other countries.

W. Dennis Parker owns and operates Certified Hypnotherapy Training School. Dennis is a board-certified Hypnotherapy Examiner, Instructor, and Approved School Operator. He is a noted motivational and inspirational public speaker, Spiritual Mind Management self-hypnosis Trainer, and Certified Clinical Hypnotherapist. He does seminars, workshops, and individual training in a variety of subjects.

Dennis speaks, trains, and does seminars or workshops at sports training camps, business meetings, school gatherings, or other events. Dennis also speaks and trains at hypnotherapy conferences, executive and management retreats, sales events, and wherever people are interested in learning behavioral modification techniques through self-hypnosis, hypnotherapy, and our unique and proprietary Spiritual Mind Management systems and protocols.

His seminars and workshops are enhanced by his years of experience of working with people in their personal lives and developing their career performance. Assisting people to achieve their goals and being part of the success of others is a key motivator for him.

We invite you to visit the website as all of the school information is there. Please watch our free educational introductory videos and read up on the school offerings. We know that the closer you look at the package offering we give you as a student, the better we look, as we are very unique in the way we work with students, and the quality of the clinical hypnotherapy procedures taught. We are known for our clinical hypnotherapy techniques and protocols. Please call Dennis directly to answer questions about the school or courses offered. *W. Dennis Parker – (801) 628-0693*

Advanced Health Clinic - (801) 447-8680 is where Certified Hypnotherapy Training School is held. Dennis has his office there and is a contract hypnotherapist for the clinic. He does individual session of hypnotherapy, in person at the clinic, or on line through SKYPE or other means. We provide specialized group classes of "Spiritual Mind Management Course Trainings" with emphasis on various topics, where students and clients are taught simplified, easy to use, and the most effective Self-Hypnosis and Hypnotherapy techniques, for personal change in overcoming self-limiting beliefs, eliminating inappropriate habits, and conquering maladaptive behaviors. We teach personal problem solving skills where clients learn to be clear and free minded learning new mental and emotional self-reliance skills. Then we teach them to maintain their clear and free mind through utilization of "Spiritual Mind Management" techniques and protocols.

Kevin was a student in the school. He is now a Certified Clinical Hypnotherapist. He explains:

"I worked with Dennis during 2012 and I was 37 years old at the time. Initially, my goal was to improve my self-confidence and self-esteem. What I didn't realize at the time is how far reaching this work would be.

Prior to working with Dennis, I felt disconnected from my emotions and found it difficult to speak with others. As I worked with him, I was able to feel more connected to my emotions (not to mention feeling free to express them) as well as being more confident in myself to speak to others.

Learning the Spiritual Mind Management principles have enabled me to maintain the changes that I have experienced. This has been invaluable to me because there are always opportunities in life to think that I don't deserve good things or that I am not good enough. These principles have helped me make better conscious decisions and avoid the garbage thinking that was so easy to fall into previously.

What I learned inspired me to be trained with Dennis and it has been the catalyst for me to help many other people overcome their inner problems. The Mind Management principles have also helped them maintain their changes as well.

I would encourage everyone who is struggling with their personal challenges (whatever they may be) to give hypnotherapy a try. It has been the tool that allowed me to change what I needed to change personally. "

Here is what some of our students and others are saying:

Deanne

My name is Deanne and I'm a hypnotherapy student. During the day, I also work as a school psychologist where one of my duties is to work with students to help them change their behavior, to bring about behavior modification. Most of the problems I have to deal with involve courses of treatment that are maybe 10 or 16 sessions long, so it takes a good deal of time. I was amazed my first night of class when I came here and watched Dennis do in one or two sessions what takes me weeks to accomplish.

On a personal level, I was able to overcome some of my own self-limiting doubts and beliefs that I had since childhood and learn how to manage my mind so that I can take care of those same problems in the future if they come back. Even if I never use these skills in a career, it has been worth it to know that I can help my friends, family, and myself.

I would recommend this school to anyone who wants to learn more about themselves or wants to learn how to help people to change their behavior.

Wendy

After they worked with Dennis, the change in my parents was amazing. My mom was very shy and introverted before she started, and now you can't get her to stop talking to people. But she truly cares about them; she's very sweet. My dad was afraid of success, very afraid to move forward, and he's so much better now, eager to move forward in his work.

Daryl

I worked with Dennis more than twenty years ago. I was terminated at my job then, and had problems in my relationships with other people. What Dennis gave me was a way to block out the negative and incorporate the positive into my life. He gave me the opportunity to move on, especially in my employment. I was able to get over any termination issues and go to a place that was much more to my liking, and yet still doing what I know best how to do. Actually, my income increased threefold after that, and I attribute all of this to what Dennis did for me.

Paige

This school has changed my life in every way you can imagine. Hypnotherapy truly allows you to be free, happy, calm, and relaxed. I am now a non-smoker, better mother, and I love who I am, all because of my training and personal hypnotherapy experiences in this school. Thank you for assisting me to change my life and for teaching me to know how to assist others to do the same.

Robyn

I am happy to share my opinions of Dennis Parker and the Certified Hypnotherapy Training School.

My initial involvement was twofold, I was in the midst of a career change due to health reasons and I also had interest in many holistic aspects of wellness and found Hypnotherapy as a viable tool to incorporate wellness into my life.

I can tell you it was nothing I had expected and turned out to be so much more for me personally, as well as for the individuals I work with. I considered myself a well-balanced, responsible individual with not a terrible amount of trauma that had affected my life prior to taking this course. What I discovered was although I had not had significant earth shattering events occur in my life, I did have many self-defeating thoughts that were really holding me back from being who I really wanted to be.

Through Hypnotherapy, I have learned how to find the origination of the thoughts and see how they have manifested themselves throughout my life---either good or bad and how to correct my incorrect thinking. Even greater was learning the ability to manage my mind so as to watch my current thoughts and what I will allow or not allow so as keeping a better balanced life. It is continual "homework" everyday (the good kind) and always will be and now I have the tools to maintain a balanced life and self-correct if needed. In addition, I learn more about myself, each time I help someone else through Hypnotherapy and it is a win/win all around.

Dennis has been a great mentor and never ending resource. I knew right up front that he wanted good things (i.e. peace, balance and freedom) for those he works with both on a student level and through individual therapy. He is insightful and his years of experience working with people both in the therapy environment as well as the Corporate arena has provided him with some incredible skills that he has been able to share with others to master.

I have to say, getting involved with Hypnotherapy has been the best decision I have made in my life as I have seen such dramatic changes in myself and others in such a short period of time. The beauty of it is I have a sense of freedom and peace that I know is never ending as long as I use the tools I have gained to maintain this lovely space and I know myself and anyone else is capable of doing it.

Bianca

I have discovered that with exercising the power of our minds and love, you can accomplish anything. Hypnotherapy needs to be part of education, so that youth can learn how to recognize what is going on in their minds and the effect of those thoughts on their behaviors.

2) Attend one of our Unique Spiritual Mind Management Hypnotherapy Group Trainings Online Nation Wide, or in Person in Farmington, Utah at the School

These courses are generally sixteen to thirty-two hours of specific Spiritual Mind Management Hypnotherapy trainings in the areas of application you are interested, such as weight loss, sports, sales, pain control, unwanted habits, and so forth. To be successful you must do the work, which includes watching the introductory training videos and understand these processes, attend the course trainings you have signed up for in Farmington, Utah or online in a virtual classroom setting nationwide, do the homework, study the course book, listen to the CDs we recommend, and journal your experiences of change. (Recording your original negative beliefs and the new personal truths that have replaced them reinforces the positive changes.) Group hypnotherapy allows for the economy of scale and gives you the best value for the time and money being spent.

Some of the hypnotherapy techniques you will be utilizing will include:

Part 1 - The Pre-Talk: This is a full explanation of hypnosis and hypnotherapy, including why it works when it does, and why and when it may not. It facilitates the work because people then know what to do and expect as they go in and out of trance and how to work with the processes. This in-depth orientation for clients speeds up the process and increases our success rates as we do the work.

Part 2 - Age Regression Therapies: These therapies generally address primary core issues. They give each client the time, chance, and the opportunity to understand and know those experiences they have had in life that are still binding them down, holding them back, and keeping them from being all they want to be. This therapy allows clients to achieve goals they have only wished for before. We teach clients how to challenge and change the negative, non-constructive predominant behavior-producing thoughts and beliefs that were generated by the primary experience. When these original thoughts and beliefs are challenged and changed, behaviors change automatically and easily.

Part 3 - Gestalt Therapies: Gestalt therapy, as explained earlier, addresses secondary defense mechanisms and secondary payoffs, which are learned responses to primary core experiences. Both need to be dealt with to accomplish complete change and have it be permanent.

Part 4 - Spiritual Mind Management: Explains the importance of free agency and conscious choice, and that our God-given natural trance abilities are personal empowerment that will give people greater control of themselves than ever before. You will learn here where consciousness, imagination, memories, and emotions are in the mind and how to control your inner Intelligence in order to be present in the current moment of time rather than locked into some negative memory or emotion of the past that is continuing to ruin the present and the future.

You will not reveal anything you do not want to in this setting, as we utilize a code word "Myself" during group sessions, meaning that you want to work on a particular issue yourself. Then no one in the group will know what you are working on. You can schedule individual hypnotherapy sessions for those issues you wish to deal with privately.

Weight Loss Mind Management

Consciously, we know we ought to be healthy and physically fit. The problem is in the subconscious mind, where we often hold opposing thoughts and beliefs. These subconscious negative beliefs create opposing forces within us, which require hypnosis at deep levels to access, challenge, and change our inner thoughts by bringing the conscious and subconscious minds into alignment. When the minds are aligned, we move forward without hesitations, inhibitions, and procrastinations. We move forward comfortably and confidently towards our goals.

This Weight Mind Management course will teach you a system of impulse control that really work to consistently overcome urges to eat inappropriate things, such as junk food, soda pop, candy, and other refined sugary and starchy substances. You will lose all desire for these so-called foods that are high in calories and low in nutritional value. They are really non-foods, being not merely non-nutritious, but actually injurious to your body. Achieving impulse control will be a major part of your program to achieve your goal of reaching your ideal weight.

What are your reasons for overeating? This program will enable you to identify them, trace them down, and find better ways to satisfy them.

This program will also focus on helping you create new subconscious habits so that the things you desire to do will happen easier and faster. When you make new choices at this deeper level, things like exercise, eating the right foods, and taking care of yourself become easier than ever before.

You will also learn to break unhealthy food associations. There are certain foods with which we have developed emotional associations and attachments. These associations have been developed from our life's experiences, which included these foods. We have traditions of having birthday cake and ice cream, for instance, which we may continue to eat regularly on non-birth days (every day) to stimulate the feelings of our favorite birthday party enjoyments and the love and caring of family and special friends. You will learn here how to enjoy these wonderful feelings in your life without having to stimulate them through eating the negative foods associated with those feelings. We will assist you to undo the association. You get to keep the positive feelings and eliminate the negative foods associated with them comfortably from your diet!

For more information on this program including dates and times, please visit: http://www.weightmindmanagement.com

Executive Mind Management

Our executive training model has had some pretty amazing results because it can be universally applied to every part of a business enterprise. We consider our training to be "The training before job specific training is done." Anyone who is familiar at all with painting on a personal or commercial level knows that the surface has to be prepared properly in order to have the paint adhere properly and leave the lasting impression that was intended. The application principles of identifying the *barriers in belief* are the basis on how we work with the executive level management. By starting at the top of the hierarchical pyramid instead at the bottom, we enact change at the level that most of the time requires it from others but may not even realize that they are the biggest obstacle to increased corporate performance.

Throughout this book, we have talked about the critical need to attack any problem at the foundational level in order to have a long lasting measured effect. If the executive staff are looked to as the true leaders of the organization but yet have foundational beliefs that are compromising the structure at the foundational level, problems mushroom. Overlay those inappropriate beliefs with a high probability that they will remain unknown and undiscovered; the organization now has a structural flaw that will continue to undermine its stability until it implodes on its self or can no longer stay up with the competition.

Let me give you a real life example of what I am saying:

In a training where we had every member of the management team present, we turned to the general manager and asked him what his belief was for the team and the enterprise as a whole. It was very predictable that of course they wanted to be number one in the market in every category. How could anyone refute that claim or belief? However, as we pealed back the onion as we referred to in a previous chapter, we discovered something completely different. In fact, the opposite belief was unveiled, *"We can't be number one"*. This was not easily identified because no one wants to admit to themselves let alone to the other members of the team what the real belief is. As the group started to identify the "non" number one things that were going on within the organization, one of the managers piped up and said "We can't be number one, look what we are doing."

We had to essentially deconstruct the old beliefs and their commensurate behaviors and rebuild the structure with true and correct thoughts and actions that will drive the enterprise forward. Although the team had many important and effective items in place and was successful, the correct core belief had to be identified and established for any meaningful shift in performance to have greater than average gains. Remember from an earlier discussion, geometric gains are what we expect not just average performance, after all who wants to be average? This enterprise has since seen record profits month after month.

Certainly, this enterprise did not achieve records by just thinking their way there, they are talented professionals who understand how to operate and manage but were constrained by an incorrect belief that drove their behavior. Once the barriers in belief were eliminated, the structure came into plumb and the surface was now right for the proper "job specific" training to have a lasting impression. They simply and methodically put into practice the principles that being truly number one would dictate. We have many examples of how once barriers are removed, people and businesses can now freely move towards the predominate goals they want instead of wishing in vain for them and never understanding why they don't happen. With over 200 executive team members having been trained in the past year, everyone has been able to identify at least one limiting belief that has negatively impacted their job performance. In most of the cases, they were very surprised what their old beliefs were and that those beliefs were in reality keeping them from what they most wanted. A very interesting paradox!

Sales Mind Management

Imagine the improvements in your sales revenues, gross profit incomes, and bottom line profits when your sales team is 5–25 percent more effective because they are better prepared to deal with customers and the increased stresses of being in sales today! Our Sales Mind Management seminars and workshops teach salespeople the new mental and emotional skills they need to compete and win in today's sales environments.

We teach salespeople the same techniques of mental focus and concentration as well as the emotional techniques and skills we teach athletes to enhance their sports performance. We teach sales people how to overcome cold call prospecting reluctance, immediately conquer daily disappointments and discouragements, and stay in positive go-forward mental states. These skills are the same ones they need to be comfortable with public speaking and demonstrating.

Salespeople don't necessarily need to be physically tough, but they do need to be tough as nails mentally and emotionally. They need the mental ability to dissociate from the negative comments and disappointing experiences most salespeople encounter every day. These negative experiences accumulate in the subconscious mind as emotional stress.

This stress compounds over time, increasing negative energies. Sales people need to be trained and understand how to release and desensitize these negative non-productive energies on a regular basis. Otherwise, they become crippling to one's motivational drive, performance, and health. Some naturally identify these negative mental states, calling them a sales slump or a sales drought.

The mental and emotional skills taught in this Sales Mind Management training course strengthen the sales person in every area of sales and life, producing winning results. Give yourself and your sales team the time, chance, and opportunity to learn and experience the winning advantages that utilizing Sales Mind Management techniques and protocols provide!

We will also teach them advanced intrapersonal and public communication techniques necessary for professional closing skills, and the latest in relationship building. Acquiring instant rapport and trust is the foundation of successful customer relationships.

The bottom line in sales is whether your customers feel you have their best interests at heart. We assist you to achieve these mental states that can't be faked, as people discern and know if you are real and genuine. It is a decision and choice, and we teach you how to make it, again and again, with each winning sales call.

For more information about this program including dates and times, please visit*: http://www.salesmindmanagement.com*

Pornography Mind Management

This is a Christian-principled hypnotherapy in which you will learn to utilize self- hypnosis for impulse control, to have impulse control over the promptings and urges to engage in inappropriate pornographic activities. You will learn new mental Spiritual Mind Management techniques and skills to overcome those things that you know are damaging to you and your relationships, and are inhibiting you from achieving your righteous goals.

Consciously we all know we ought to be disciplined, worthy, and loyal to our spouses or significant others. The problem is in the subconscious mind, where we hold opposing predominant thoughts, images, and behavior-producing beliefs. These subconscious negative beliefs create opposing forces within us requiring hypnosis access in order to challenge and change them. By bringing our conscious and subconscious minds into alignment, we put an end to troublesome double-mindedness in this area of life.

You will have the opportunity to learn a system of overcoming temptations that really works to consistently overcome inappropriate urges of lust. You will have control over desires for activities and behaviors that are self-demeaning and personally destructive to yourself and your relationships. The Spiritual Mind Management self-discipline and self-control techniques are state of the art behavioral modification.

You will also learn here how to break unhealthy mental and emotional triggering associations—the sexual stimuli with which we have developed undesirable emotional associations and attachments. We have methods and protocols of self-hypnosis and hypnotherapy that will address and undo these inappropriate emotional triggers and associations. You get to eliminate negative, inappropriate stimulations and still keep the positive desired feelings in your marriage or relationship.

You will be thrilled with the personal discipline, self-control, and self-mastery you will achieve with these processes. Achievement of your righteous goals, dreams, and desires will be edifying with your personal integrity intact. You will enjoy your new and permanent lifestyle changes.

For more information about program dates and times, please visit*: http://www.pornographymindmanagement.com*

Parent Mind Management

We teach parents and grandparents in the various trance levels and how to use them for positive personal programming and goal achievement. You will learn how to teach your children to understand the Spiritual Mind Management principles which will help them stay focused in school or on their homework, take tests in a more relaxed manner and having better recall, be more harmonious with family members and others, help them sleep and relax having a peaceful and quiet mind free from imaginary fears and mind chatter. You will gain some understanding and skills to assist yourself and your child with enhanced peace of mind.

Parents will also learn a way to influence the behavior of their children based on principles of what we call "self-talk." These principles will make it so that parents can help their children accomplish their goals and dreams, overcome their negative behaviors, and achieve more than they previously thought possible.

For more information about this program, please visit: *http://www.parentmindmanagement.com*

Sports & Golf Mind Management Hypnotherapy – Seminars & Workshops, Training & Coaching

"I have been testing the effects of clinical hypnotherapy for several years with Dennis. The brain changes have become more coherent, synchronous and clear. The role of the subconscious in sport is tremendous. Having tested and worked with the conscious mind for 30 years, I am grateful to have these techniques (Spiritual Mind Management) to work with the subconscious mind and unite the conscious and subconscious minds!" **Dr. Debbie Crews**

These courses teach the mental skills of concentration and focus, and the emotional techniques and skills that will enhance your sports performance.

The improvements in personal performance that these processes and skills make are well known and documented in the world of professional sports. Many of the winning athletes of our time utilize these self-hypnosis concepts daily.

Dr. Debbie Crews and W. Dennis Parker, CHT, join to bring you this innovative Sports Mind Management Hypnotherapy to assist athletes to enhance their individual and team performance. Debbie is well known internationally in the golf and sports world as a scientist, sports psychologist, trainer, and coach. See more information on her website: *http://performancemindmanagement.com/* and *http://optiherence.com/*

Golf Mind Management

Our Golf Mind Management seminars and workshops, available as group and personal hypnotherapy training sessions, give you the information and skills you need to stay focused, concentrate, and "keep your head in the game." The techniques you learn here will improve your golf performance, lowering your scores!

Golf challenges us in hundreds of ways, and research scientists never seem to tire of exploring new ways and angles to improve performance through equipment and individual conditioning, both physical and mental. Golf requires us to think of a multitude of things at once, and challenges our athletic, mental, and emotional abilities continuously.

Golf Mind Management is a series of powerful and beneficial presentations about the way we think and how to maintain a positive mental state, both consciously and subconsciously. This provides greater emotional stability, as well as the focus and concentration abilities and skills required to play great golf.

The Golf Mind Management seminars and workshops teach new mental and emotional skills. You will learn self-hypnosis techniques that unify the conscious and subconscious minds, eliminating distracting double-mindedness. You will learn how to be mentally tough, so that you have the ability to dissociate from negative comments and experiences that can affect performance and even health and stamina.

For more information about this program, please visit: *http://sportsmindmanagement.com/*

Pain Mind Management

The mind can detach from any sensory perceptions such as smell, noise, allergens, or pain. This course will teach you how to do so and give you skills and abilities to control sensory perceptions at the levels you choose. You will be amazed at how much power of self-control you can learn to exercise in your own behalf.

We will teach you several advanced methods of pain management and/or elimination that we use at Advanced Health Clinic on a routine basis. We also include complete trainings in what we teach in Certified Hypnotherapy Training School. You will be glad you learned these advanced mental skills, to enjoy painless child birthing, eliminate migraine pain for which the Doctors cannot find a reason to have them, be free of long-term chronic pains in the many forms we identify it. These skills require practice as they are new mental skills. The more you learn and practice them the better you will become at living pain free. Get started now and enjoy the life you want!

For more information about this program, please visit:
http://painmindmanagement.com

Anger Mind Management

As you read my personal story, you learned that anger was the major behavioral problem for me and the reason I ended up in hypnotherapy. Once again, the reason why hypnotherapy and what we do is so effective is that it gives us access to those buried and repressed subconscious imaginations, memories, and emotions which are bothering us and holding us back the most.

We can know what our personal problem triggering events are and learn how to desensitize from them. Learning these desensitizing processes are life-changing as we can continually use them as new coping skills for the rest of our life. We can learn to live anger free, and enjoy life more than you ever thought possible.

The one thing that I tell our students of hypnotherapy and clients who come in for Anger Mind Management is that, I know there is a bottom to our emotional boxes. Most people who struggle with anger as a behavioral driver do not understand that their emotional box of anger needs to be systematically emptied and desensitized. We then teach them how not to refill the box.

Please join us in a group of Anger Mind Management or schedule individual sessions of hypnotherapy and we will be happy to assist you in living a happier, anger free life!

For more information: *http://angermindmanagement.com/*

Our guarantee is another opportunity free.

When you participate in Mind Management group training and coaching and self-hypnosis for personal behavioral modification, if you've had to miss a class or for any reason you are not satisfied by where you are in your personal understanding and progress at the end of the class schedule, you may participate in another group of the same subject as the one you attended for free. Or, if you would just like to continue your personal behavior modification work with assisted practice and improving your self-hypnosis skills, you may do the same.

This offer gives you sixteen hours in the next available scheduled group of your chosen subject for free—plenty of time and opportunity to gain further understanding and practice of your self-hypnosis skills. We want to assist you in your goal achievement and have you be your own best behavioral therapist. You can schedule your personal attendance (attendance can be live or online nationwide) in a Mind Management group in Farmington, Utah or individual sessions with Dennis at Advanced Health Clinic in Farmington, Utah. Phone: (401) 447-8680. To schedule online attendance in a Spiritual Mind Management group or individual sessions of hypnotherapy online with Dennis Parker, utilizing Skype, or call (801) 628-0693, or email Dennis at:
parker@certifiedhypnotherapytrainingschool.com.
Or visit our web site at:
http://certifiedhypnotherapytrainingschool.com/

3) Individual Sessions of Spiritual Mind Management Hypnotherapy

W. Dennis Parker offers private sessions of hypnotherapy in most areas of hypnotherapy. Please call him for a free phone consultation and discuss your goals and desires. You can then make an educated decision as to what is right for you! These sessions can be accomplished on SKYPE or other such means, or in person in Farmington, Utah at the Advanced Health Clinic.

To contact Dennis Parker, call (801) 628-0693, or email Dennis at: *parker@certifiedhypnotherapytrainingschool.com*.

Key Note Speakers, Conference Seminars and Workshops

Dennis, Craig and Debbie, are all noted public speakers. They each do seminars and workshops on Self-Hypnosis, Hypnotherapy, and a variety of Spiritual Mind Management subjects at conventions and conferences. Please contact them about availability and pricing to participate in your next event. You will be glad you did, as the information is fresh, exciting, extremely helpful, and useful in increasing self-confidence, personal self-esteem, and enhancing performance and productivity.

You can purchase Hypnotherapy Books, CD's, and Videos, at the school's online store at the Certified Hypnotherapy Training School website:

http://certifiedhypnotherapytrainingschool.com/

About the Authors

W. Dennis Parker

A noted Certified Clinical Hypnotherapist, W. Dennis Parker is a Board Certified Hypnotherapist Examiner, Instructor, and Approved School Operator with the American Council of Hypnotist Examiners (ACHE). He and his wife, Susie own and operate the Certified Hypnotherapy Training School (CHTS) in Farmington, Utah where students are trained in hypnosis, self-hypnosis, hypnotherapy, and the unique proprietary Mind Management protocols described in this book.

Dennis is also a contract clinical hypnotherapist with Advanced Health Clinic in Farmington, Utah where he does individual hypnotherapy sessions as well as Mind Management group training. A seasoned motivational speaker and sales trainer, he provides seminars and workshops on Mind Management for a variety of applications, including pain management and stress management.

Dennis believes that what is called "trance" in hypnosis and hypnotherapy is the same state referred to as pondering or meditation in the Bible. "From a spiritual viewpoint," he explains, "when we seek to obtain inspiration from the Lord, we use these processes."

Accordingly, he points to Proverbs 4:26-27: "Ponder the path of thy feet, and let all thy ways be established. Turn not to the right hand, nor to the left: remove thy foot from evil." He notes, "If we are to 'ponder the path of [our] feet,' then it is a worthy goal to meditate upon our life experiences—one layer at a time, one experience after another—and learn the lessons to be gained from each of them. We then can apply what we learn to our future experiences and begin to conduct ourselves in a way that will receive our Creator's support and blessings.

"Pondering and meditation take us to a higher state of insight, beyond our normal reasoning capabilities or our creative imaginations. Often this spiritual state is achieved when we ask our Creator for wisdom, understanding, and healing—both physically and spiritually. And we naturally experience this state when we hear a heart-touching sermon that we feel was meant for us or when we read sacred writings that speak to our hearts, opening our minds to a state of deep reflection."

On his sixtieth birthday, Dennis wrote a new life mission statement, part of which he shares here:

"I will accomplish more good things in the last twenty years of my life than I have in the previous sixty years combined. I will assist more people to better their lives and fulfill their desires, dreams, and goals by teaching and coaching them in self-hypnosis and hypnotherapy . . . I will assist others to overcome self-limiting beliefs, eliminate self-defeating habits, and conquer maladaptive behaviors, and do so myself as well. I will teach these personal problem-solving skills that have changed and improved my life in numerous ways to as many as have interest in and want to learn them."

So he started the Certified Hypnotherapy Training School, where he has the opportunity to achieve such goals. The course trainings in the school are a positive influence in the lives of others, and create a ripple effect of good through the students, as they in turn assist their clients in positive personal improvements and goal achievements.

Craig A. Bickmore

Craig A. Bickmore is a Board Member of the Hypnotist Examining Council of Utah and an active guest presenter and lecturer at the Certified Hypnotherapy Training School in Farmington, Utah.

A native of Cedar City, Utah, he served an LDS mission to California and attended what is now Southern Utah University. There he met and married Lori, the love of his life, and began raising a family that now includes six children. He worked part time in several businesses "to pay for life and school" and later received an MBA in business administration from Utah State University.

For the past twenty-five years, Craig has been employed by one of Utah's finest trade associations, giving him the opportunity to work with various members of the Utah State legislature as well as with regulatory agencies, state and federal. He participates on several boards and currently serves as the past-chair of the American Cancer Society Advisory Board of Utah.

With many others in the state, Craig is actively engaged in the fight to eliminate cancer.

The development and practice of hypnosis, hypnotherapy, and behavioral modification training has become one of his greatest passions. He is dedicated to helping people understand that hypnosis, once understood and applied, can be an effective and powerful tool in overcoming life's challenges and concerns.

Craig believes that "the heart of most self-improvement processes is removing *barriers of belief* by focusing and re-focusing on what you want and eliminating the obstacles that impede personal progress, regardless of whether those obstacles are self-caused or arise from other circumstances." He believes, "If you want to make significant gains in your life—geometric gains—then take the time to learn and practice the principles of hypnosis and self-hypnosis. This will get you where you want to go faster than anything else."

Dr. Debra Crews

Dr. Debra Crews Ketterling is a Research Analyst with Kinesiology at Arizona State University (ASU) and is a Sport Psychology Consultant for the ASU Men's and Women's Golf Team. She is also a Master Professional in the Ladies Professional Golf Association (LPGA), Teaching and Club Professional (T&CP), and serves on the LPGA National Education and Research Board. An LPGA National Education Program (NEP) Instructor since 1997, Debbie has assisted with the development and research for LPGA teacher education programs. As an applied sport psychology consultant, she has also assisted many LPGA and PGA professionals as well as elite amateur golfers.

Debbie has conducted research in golf for over 25 years, studying the behavioral, cognitive, and psychophysiological variables that lead to optimal performance. Specifically, she has studied attention in golf by examining brain and heart activity— the only measures that accurately assess whether the performer is in an "automatic" state for optimal performance during the final seconds prior to performing the motion. She has both defined this successful state and produced it, using biofeedback training to facilitate learning.

Her golf research has been published in research journals (Medicine and Science in Sport and Exercise), proceedings (Science and Golf II, III, and IV), applied journals (Scholastic Coach), and the popular press (Golf Magazine, Golf Digest, Newsweek, and The Wall Street Journal). She was recently selected as #8 among America's Top 50 Women Golf Instructors by Golf Digest.

NBC Dateline and Scientific American Frontier have also covered Debbie's research. She received the first Science in Golf Award from Golf Magazine (2001) for her research on "choking." Collaborative ventures include several studies on the "yips" in golf with the Mayo Clinic, an imagery study using fMRI measures with the University of Chicago, and a vision/EEG study in conjunction with the University of Calgary. Her research has led to the design and patenting of a golf putter that aids in alignment, balance, and performance.

In addition, Debbie has developed a golf research program at ASU called GREAT (Golf Research, Education, and Training) where golf serves as a medium to teach learning and performance skills that can be transferred to life. In the late 1990s, Debbie founded the Alternative Intervention Research Clinic at ASU. This clinic offers nondrug alternatives for special populations. The most successful program, following 6 years of research, was the Equine Therapy Intervention that now services about 350 youth per week.

http://performancemindmanagement.com/
and *http://optiherence.com/*

EPILOGUE

By now you know that all hypnosis is self-hypnosis. This means that if you desire to have success with this wonderful, life-changing process, you must follow the suggested prompts and hypnotize yourself. So make the decision now to allow yourself to do so, and follow the suggestions that are right for you.

May God bless you as you learn the lessons of this life that are designed for your learning and growth from each of your many life experiences. One day, every experience of our lives can turn for our good, as we learn to do good from the lessons we have learned from those experiences. Marilyn Humphries, the hypnotherapist I worked with originally, said it best, "We make all of our life experiences good as we learn to do good from the lessons learned from those experiences."

When you learn and practice the techniques taught in this book, you will become your own best therapist. You will come to know the predominant thoughts that you have been acting out in your behaviors, and you will have ways to challenge and change them. You will also have the opportunity to review former learned beliefs and judgments and to change them as well—all by using Spiritual Mind Management.

A person with a free-functioning Intelligence enjoys the power and freedom of agency and choice. They can accept responsibility and accountability for their actions. This means no more excuses—they can live in truth, which not only sets them free, but keeps them free!